BASIC Programming
for the Apple® Computer

BASIC Programming
for the Apple Computer

Robert M. Bateson
Anoka-Ramsey Community College

Robin D. Raygor
Anoka-Ramsey Community College

Gregory Bitz
Illustrator

West Publishing Company

St. Paul   New York   Los Angeles   San Francisco

COPYRIGHT © 1985 by WEST PUBLISHING CO.
50 West Kellogg Boulevard
P. O. Box 43526
St. Paul, Minnesota 55164

Library of Congress Cataloging in Publication Data

Bateson, Robert.
  BASIC Programming for the Apple Computer

  Includes index.
  1. Apple computer—Programming.   2. Basic (Computer program language) I. Raygor,
Robin D.   II. Title.   III. Title: B.A.S.I.C. Programming for the Apple Computer
QA76.8A66B37   1985   001.64'2   84-17332
ISBN 0-314-85290-5

Copy editing: William N. Olson
Text design: Lucy Lesiak Design
Composition: Rolin Graphics
Technical artwork: Century Design

For Betty and Sharon

CONTENTS

CHAPTER **5**

Going Around Again Looping with a FOR/NEXT

Statement 61

CHAPTER **6**

Where Do We Go From Here? Branching with IF

Statements 79

CHAPTER **7**

Getting Artistic Printing Patterns with Subroutines 103

CHAPTER **8**

Functioning Using Functions Properly 115

CHAPTER **11**

Flying Saucers Using Sound and Graphics

PREFACE

SOME WORDS ABOUT THIS TEXT

This book is intended as an introduction to programming in BASIC for people with little or no background in computers. It may be used in a class in programming, or as a self-instruction manual. The information in the book is oriented to Apple® or Apple-compatible microcomputers although much of it applies to the many other microcomputers, which are programmable in BASIC.*

No knowledge of computer science or advanced mathematics is assumed of the student using this book. Even if you have never seen a computer before, you should be able to write moderately sophisticated programs (or modify existing programs) by the time you finish this text. We have tried to make this process as painless as possible and sincerely hope you enjoy your first encounter with small computers.

THE APPENDICES

APPENDIX A The Mini–Manual

The Mini–Manual is a compact reference manual for the Applesoft language. Some people prefer to work their way through the text, referring to the Mini–Manual only when necessary. Others like to read the Mini–Manual before going on to Chapter 0. Whichever method you choose, it is certainly a good idea to familiarize yourself with the Mini–Manual now so that you will be able to make efficient use of it when you need it.

APPENDIX B Error Messages

This is a list of the error messages you might see on the screen, with explanations of what they mean and how they usually occur. If you are ever confused about an error message, by all means consult this appendix. Note whether the error message you see on the screen has a question mark at the beginning; this will help you find it in the appendix.

*Apple is a registered trademark of Apple Computer, Inc.

APPENDIX C Reserved Words

This is a list of words which may not be used as variable names or parts of variable names. For example POINT would not be a legal variable name because it has the reserved word INT in it. When listed, a line like the one below

```
10 LET POINT = 10
```

would be listed as follows:

```
10 LET PO INT = 10
```

and this would cause an error.

APPENDIX D Initializing A Diskette

This appendix describes how to initialize a new, blank diskette.

APPENDIX E Flowcharts

This appendix contains information about flowchart symbols and program design.

THE EXERCISES

At the end of each chapter there is a series of exercises designed to test your knowledge of the concepts taught in that chapter. In the early chapters, you are advised to do all of the exercises, since each tests a different concept. In the later chapters, where you are asked to do just one of the exercises provided, we have tried to order the exercises according to their difficulty so that you can choose one that will challenge you without frustrating you. The easier exercises are presented first, the later ones are more difficult, with the last one or two being very difficult.

ACKNOWLEDGEMENTS

Many people have been involved in the production of this book. Curt Austin, Jeff Cole, Sharon Raygor, Amelia Gast, Jonathan Borden Sisson, Lora P. Conrad at Northwest Alabama University, James W. Cox at Lane Community College in Oregon, Joseph W. Frasca at Sonoma State University in California, Bill Haga at Oakland University in Michigan, and Kathleen B. Leitzell at Central Dauphin East High School in Pennsylvania reviewed and tested early versions of the text and made many valuable suggestions. Peter Marshall, Jane Gregg, Bill Olson, Lucy Lesiak, and numerous others at West Publishing worked tirelessly to support the authors and contribute to the design and production of the book.

The authors would especially like to thank the friends and family members who put up with us during the difficult phases of manuscript preparation.

Robert M. Bateson

Robin D. Raygor

Gregory W. Bitz

INTRODUCTION
Computers in Society

COMPUTERS OF THE FUTURE

Computers and computer components are becoming more powerful and at the same time less expensive every day. Economic and social forces are causing all of us to consider computers a part of our daily lives. Many of us have small computers on our wrists that tell the time, day, and date (many also play

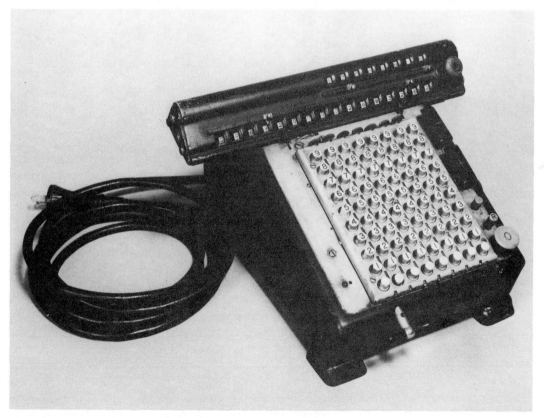

Not so long ago, this was considered to be a very modern calculator.

a different tune for each day and remember holidays and important events; some are also calculators or games). Not so long ago, these wrist "computers" would have cost hundreds of thousands of dollars. A little before that they could not have been built at all. Not that long ago, a large business machine company produced a desk calculator that was considered to represent the state of the art at that time. It was about the size of a very large typewriter and had a huge carriage that moved from left to right. The numbers were on little drums which rotated to display each number in a small window. If you divided a fraction that was a repeating decimal, the machine would run until you unplugged it. The machine was extremely expensive and could only add, subtract, multiply, and divide. It couldn't even do square roots. One of the authors' fathers had such a machine, and quite often friends and neighbors would come by to admire it. It was considered to be a scientific wonder.

You don't have to be an expert in computer science to see how far the computer industry has come since then. This trend is clearly continuing, and soon the computers of today will seem like that dinosaur that was so admired in the past. Before long, computers will be designing, building, programming, and repairing other computers (it's already happening) and it's hard to imaging where all this will lead.

The computer room of a large company.

WHY LEARN PROGRAMMING?

Some have suggested that if the computers of the future will be so powerful, they'll probably speak English and be able to figure out what we want, thus making the learning of programming a waste of time.

There are several good replies to this argument. First, the kind of computers and programming necessary to fulfill this fantasy are some way off. Second, someone is going to have to program those computers to be so smart. And third and probably most important, we have found that people cannot learn to use computers and computer programs comfortably and efficiently unless they truly understand the structure and operating system of computers in general. There is no better way to come to understand how computers work than by learning to program.

THE BASIC LANGUAGE

Every computer language was designed with a specific function in mind. Some languages are designed primarily for accounting, others like COBOL

The owners of this bicycle shop use a microcomputer to help run their business.

for general business applications, and still others like FORTRAN (and its cousin RATFOR) for scientific and mathematical applications.

BASIC was originally designed as a teaching language. The "words" of the language were chosen because they were easy to understand. Terms like PRINT, LOAD, SAVE, READ, and WRITE are easy for beginners to understand and use. Because of the tremendously widespread use of BASIC, however, it has expanded into a more sophisticated language which is used widely in personal computers and increasingly in business applications.

Because of the original purpose and limitations of early versions of BASIC, some programmers consider BASIC to be a toy language and don't take it seriously. They accuse BASIC of being an unstructured language. The authors would like to argue that although BASIC does not *force* programmers to use structured techniques, it certainly does not prevent them. We believe that well structured or poorly structured programs can be written in any language. We also believe that the techniques of structured, modular programming are best taught using a language that is easy to understand and that uses a "nonthreatening" vocabulary and syntax. Faster and more powerful versions of BASIC are becoming available all the time, some with all the structured programming capabilities of any other language. In this text we have tried to introduce the BASIC language in a way that is easy and painless without sacrificing the learning of programming standards and structured programming techniques.

CHAPTER 0

GETTING STARTED
Basic Computer Skills

NEW CONCEPTS TAUGHT

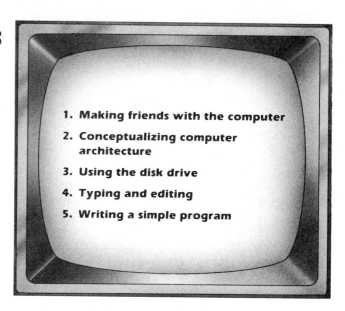

1. Making friends with the computer
2. Conceptualizing computer architecture
3. Using the disk drive
4. Typing and editing
5. Writing a simple program

OVERVIEW

We know that it's not common for books to have a chapter 0. We've done it here for two reasons. First, many computer operations do start their numbering at zero; it saves memory and sometimes makes things easier to understand. Second, this chapter is a little different than the other chapters of the book (though just as important). The purpose of this chapter is to make sure that you have the skills and knowledge necessary to carry you smoothly through the rest of the book. You may find that you can skip parts of this chapter. If you already know how to type, for example, the section on typing won't be much help to you. We warn you, however, not to neglect this chapter. Some of the material in here can save hours of your time; other parts of the chapter can save you from disaster.

We advise you to read this chapter while sitting at the computer. In this way, you can play with the computer as you read. This will give you a much fuller understanding of the concepts being taught. (It will also be more fun.)

MAKING FRIENDS

Many people have an initial fear of the computer that makes it harder for them to learn how to program it. Some of this fear is due to unfamiliarity. Much of it is really a fear that they might break the computer or damage it accidentally. Unlike the computers in TV comedy shows which go up in smoke at the drop of a hat, the modern microcomputer is actually a pretty tough little machine. Unless you are using a hammer or blowtorch in your programming efforts, it is very unlikely that you will damage the computer. Like a pocket calculator, the computer is designed so that there is no way you can cause damage by pressing the wrong button. If you really knew what you were doing, you could enter commands that would alter the computer's memory in such a way that it wouldn't work properly, but 1 the chances of doing this by accident are very slim and 2 the memory could be restored to normal simply by turning the machine off and turning it on again (don't try this while writing a program though, since it erases the program from memory). So you can rest assured that no matter how serious an error might seem to you, it won't hurt the computer.

PLAYING AROUND

For your first experience with the computer we recommend the following. First, you should have a diskette which has been initialized (no this doesn't mean putting you initials on it). Diskettes, as they come from the manufacturer, are not initialized; they are like blank keys which do not yet fit any lock. If you are using this book as part of a course in programming, the instructor will help you initialize your diskette. If not, see appendix D.

Diskettes should be treated very delicately. If you need to write on the label of a diskette, use a felt pen or, better yet, write on the label before putting it on the diskette. The gray or brown magnetic surface of the diskette is exposed at the read/write opening and hub-ring (see figure 0.1). Be careful not to touch these areas and try to protect them from dirt and dust. In addi-

FIGURE 0.1

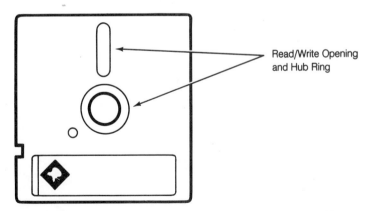

Read/Write Opening
and Hub Ring

Be careful not to touch the magnetic surface of the diskette where it is exposed at the Read/Write opening and the Hub Ring.

tion, keep diskettes away from magnets and magnetic fields. The magnetic code on the diskette is very weak and can be easily damaged. A paperclip from a magnetic clip holder can make a diskette unusable.

With the computer turned off, gently slide the initialized diskette into the disk drive in the manner shown in figures 0.2A and 0.2B. Put your right thumb on the label as you insert it. This will make sure it is going in correctly. Next, close the disk drive door and turn the computer on. Always put the disk in before turning on the computer. This is done because the computer needs to read information off the diskette in order to get ready to work. This process is called *booting* or *boot-up*, and if it is not done, you may be able to write a program, but you won't be able to save it. Needless to say, this is somewhat unpleasant as it means you must type the entire program over again.

When you turn on the computer's power switch, you will see the light on the disk drive go on and hear some noises from the drive. If the diskette is initialized properly and the disk drive door is closed, these noises will stop in a few moments and the light will go out. You should be able to see something now on the monitor (TV screen). If not, turn it on. **Caution:** don't turn the monitor on or off during boot-up as this can interfere with the booting

FIGURE 0.2A

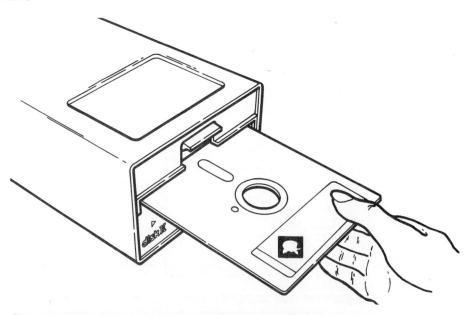

Correct Disk Insertion — Apple External Drive.

process and can sometimes wreck the diskette (called "blowing the disk"); this is to be avoided if possible. What you see on the screen at this point will depend on how the diskette was initialized. You should be able to see the cursor, a little square of light on the screen. You will be seeing quite a lot of the cursor. The cursor is a signal that the computer is ready to accept information.

> **CURSOR** The cursor is a light square on the TV screen that marks the current location on the screen. When a key is pressed, the character of the key appears on the screen where the cursor was, and the cursor is moved one position to the right.

When you type characters from the keyboard, they will appear at the cursor location. Any information coming into the computer (from the keyboard, for example) is called *input*.

FIGURE 0.2B

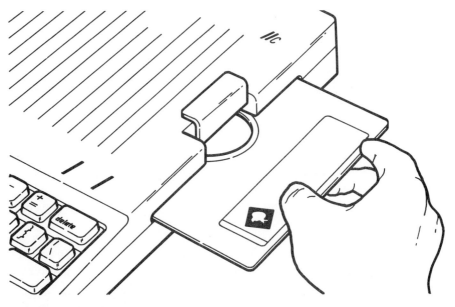

Correct Disk Insertion — Apple IIc Internal Drive.

APPLE IIe/IIc NOTE: We recommend leaving the CAPS LOCK, at the lower left of the keyboard, locked in the down position any time you are working on programs or exercises in this book. On the IIc we recommend leaving the "40-/80" switch at the upper left of the keyboard in the down position and the keyboard "switch" right next to it in the up position. If the keyboard switch is locked in the down position, the keyboard is switched to a Dvorak Simplified Keyboard. This arrangement is easier on the fingers, but all the symbols on the keycaps are wrong for this so it is not very useful.

Try typing some characters on the keyboard. If things are going properly, they should appear on the screen. The computer will not respond to any input until you press the key marked ⟨RETURN⟩ at the right side of the keyboard. This is your way of letting the computer know that you are done typing and want to be taken seriously. It is not really like the return key on a typewriter even though it often has the same effect (moving the cursor to the left side of the screen on the next line). On some computers this key is more appropriately marked ENTER.

RETURN KEY You press the return key at the end of each line in your program and after typing a command such as RUN or LIST. The return key initiates the computer's response to the line you just finished typing.

Try typing some characters and then ⟨RETURN⟩. Unless you are very lucky or know something about computers, the computer probably responded with ?SYNTAX ERROR. This is because what you typed was not a legitimate command. Don't let this bother you; just keep typing. If you like, you can try to guess words which the computer can understand (PRINT is one of them). Notice that you can use the right and left arrow keys at the right side of the keyboard to correct mistakes in typing. We will discuss editing and the correction of errors more fully later, for now just play with the keys until you are comfortable with the keyboard.

Now let's try some legal commands. Try typing INVERSE and pressing ⟨RETURN⟩. As you continue to type, things should look a little different. To get rid of this effect, type NORMAL and press ⟨RETURN⟩. Remember, all commands must be followed by ⟨RETURN⟩.

INVERSE and NORMAL If you type INVERSE and press the return key, messages on the screen will have black letters on a white background. You can reverse this effect by typing NORMAL and pressing the return key. If you type NORMAL and press the return key, the screen will return to a display with white letters on a black background.

Now try FLASH (from now on we won't remind you to press ⟨RETURN⟩). Once again things look quite different and can be made normal again by typing NORMAL.

FLASH If you type FLASH and press the return key, messages printed on the screen will alternate between white on black and black on white to produce a flashing appearance. You can turn the FLASH off by typing NORMAL and pressing the return key.

Now try typing PRINT "ABCDEF" (enter quotation marks as shown). Notice that when you press ⟨RETURN⟩, the computer does exactly what it's told. This is what computers do best. Try putting some other things inside the quotes and see what happens. If you like you can go back to INVERSE or FLASH and see what happens. By the way, the characters being printed on the screen in response to your print commands are called *output*. If the screen gets too full of output for your taste, you can clear it by typing HOME.

HOME If you type HOME and press the return key, the screen will be cleared of all text, and the cursor will be in the upper left corner of the screen.

Let's try something fancier. Leave out the quotes and type PRINT A. The computer probably responded by printing a "0." This is because you told it to print the value of the variable named A. Since A has no value yet, it prints 0. Now try typing LET A = 35 (⟨RETURN⟩). Then type PRINT A. Now A has a value. If you give B a value by typing LET B = 12, you can get even fancier by typing PRINT A + B or PRINT A / B, etc. Something a little fancier yet would be to type IF A = 35 THEN PRINT "YES A DOES EQUAL 35" or IF A ⟩ B THEN PRINT "A IS GREATER THAN B".

If you don't completely understand what's going on here, don't worry; it will be explained in more detail later. Just continue to play with the keyboard until you feel comfortable with it.

A SIMPLE IMAGE

To many people the computer is a strange territory. Their attitude is like that of a person waking up in the dark in a strange house. The sense of confusion this causes can interfere with learning. To help with this we would like to offer the following simple image of a computer to give you a kind of mental map and hopefully make you feel more at home in this strange territory.

A Simple Image of a Computer

The Image

Our image begins with a desk. On the desk are three things: a keyboard, an electronic calculator, and a printer. The keyboard is used to put messages into a box marked INPUT. The printer prints copies of messages from a box marked OUTPUT. The calculator and the printer are each operated by the brain of the computer (called the central processing unit or CPU) under the direction of a set of internal instructions. Some of these instructions are etched in the circuits of the computer (hardware) and some are in the computer's memory only when it is turned on (software).

These instructions allow you to communicate with the computer and tell it what you want it to do. When you tell the computer to PRINT "HELLO", hundreds of operations take place inside the computer. In the old days, programmers had to program each of these operations individually. Now, because we have higher-level languages like BASIC, we can give relatively simple commands and let the computer take care of the details. The set of commands we give the computer is called a program and making up the set of commands that will do what we want is called programming.

Beginning students often don't realize that the computer understands only a relatively small set of commands, and takes them literally. The operations inside the computer take place at high speed, but the computer can't think for itself. It has to be told exactly what to do and it follows its orders blindly. If you tell it to wipe out a program that you spent six years working on, it will do it in an instant.

Now, back to our image. Behind the desk is a very large number of boxes, similar to the mail boxes in a post office. Each box has a place for a name card. A box can hold only one number or one group of letters; when a new number or group of letters is placed in the box, the previous contents are destroyed. We will call these boxes memory cells. We call the name placed on the box a variable name. While you were playing with your computer, you placed the number 35 in the memory cell named "A". It may still be there. "A" is the variable name. It is called that because its value may vary. If you type LET A = 23 or LET A = 48, the value of A (or the number stored in the memory cell named "A") will change. Instead of a number, a memory cell might contain a group of letters such as "BOB," "ABCDEF," or "HOLD THE ONIONS." The computer has to handle these letters differently than numbers, but it can't always tell numbers from letters; to help out, we place a "$" at the end of the names on the boxes that contain groups of letters.

You can make use of this by typing LET C$ = "HOLD THE ONIONS" ⟨RETURN⟩. Then type PRINT C$. If you don't put a dollar sign after the name of a variable containing letters, the computer will complain. Try typing LET A = "BOB" for a demonstration.

VARIABLE NAMES Variable names are used to identify memory cells that each contain a single number or a string of characters. Variable names that refer to a string of characters must be followed by a dollar sign and are called *string variables*. A variable name must begin with a letter of the alphabet and may be followed by a second letter of the alphabet or a digit from 0 through 9. Applesoft allows up to 236 additional alphanumeric characters, but only the first two characters are used to distinguish one name from another.

Examples of variable names:

    A   **B$**   **C2**   **BOX$**   **SUM**   **PRODUCT**

NOTE: The variable names SUM and SUMMATION would identify the same memory cell because the first two letters are the same.

In creating a program, we put our directions for the computer in the input box by typing the program on the keyboard. When we want the computer to carry out our instructions, we type the word RUN on the keyboard and press ⟨RETURN⟩. The computer takes the program from the input box and then rushes around carrying numbers and messages between the INPUT box, the memory cells, the calculator, and the OUTPUT box as directed by the program. The calculator and the printer also do their thing as directed.

If you have ever seen a BASIC program, you may have noticed that there are a series of numbers in order at the left side of the page. These are the line numbers and they tell the computer in what order to perform the tasks specified in the program. These instructions can be typed in any order and the computer will put them in order by line number. Usually we number the lines by tens in case we're not perfect and have to insert some more lines into the program later on.

A SIMPLE PROGRAM

Now that you have some idea what goes on inside the computer, let's look at how a program completes a simple task. In this program we'll put the ages of three students in memory cells, calculate the sum of the three ages, place the sum in a fourth memory cell, and print the sum of the ages of the three students.

Let's assume that the three ages are 18, 24, and 32. Our first instruction will direct the computer to put the first age in a memory cell. We must give the computer a name to put on this memory cell. We will use A1 as the name of the memory cell that contains the first age. Since this is our first instruction, we will give it the line number of 10 and give the other lines higher numbers. Here is the first line of our program:

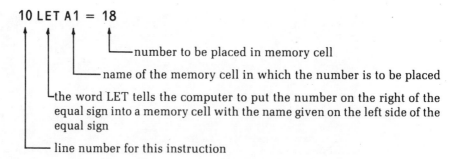

```
10 LET A1 = 18
```
number to be placed in memory cell

name of the memory cell in which the number is to be placed

the word LET tells the computer to put the number on the right of the equal sign into a memory cell with the name given on the left side of the equal sign

line number for this instruction

The next two instructions direct the computer to put the remaining two ages in the memory cells A2 and A3:

```
20 LET A2 = 24
30 LET A3 = 32
```

The fourth instruction directs the computer to send copies of the numbers in memory cells A1, A2, and A3 to the calculator with directions to add the three numbers and put the sum in memory cell S:

```
40 LET S = A1 + A2 + A3
```
expression to be calculated

name of the memory cell in which the sum is to be placed

The last instruction directs the computer to take a copy of the number in memory cell S and place it in the OUTPUT box:

50 PRINT S

Our completed program looks like this:

```
10 LET A1 = 18
20 LET A2 = 24
30 LET A3 = 32
40 LET S = A1 + A2 + A3
50 PRINT S
```

When the above program is carried out (if you would like to try it, just type NEW, and the program as it appears here, then type RUN) the number 74 should be printed.

> **NEW** If you type NEW and press the return key, the program in your computer's memory will be removed. It cannot be recovered.

Although this image oversimplifies the interior of the computer, we hope it is useful and accurate enough to remove some of the mental blocks that have hindered students in the past.

THE DISK DRIVE

When you turn off the computer, your program and the value of all variables are wiped out of the computer's memory. It would be very tedious if we had to type in the whole program every time we wanted to run it. Luckily, programs can be stored on the diskette and loaded easily into the computer's memory. When you type a program on the keyboard, it is stored in a special part of the machine's memory. To store that program on a diskette, you simply type SAVE followed by the name you have given the program; you can use any name shorter than thirty characters. Most people like to use names long enough to remind them what the program is, but short enough that they can be typed easily. Every program must have a name. If you type SAVE and just press ⟨RETURN⟩, the disk-drive light will come on but nothing will be saved.

SAVE If you type SAVE followed by a name for your program and press the return key, the program in computer memory will be saved on your disk with the given name.

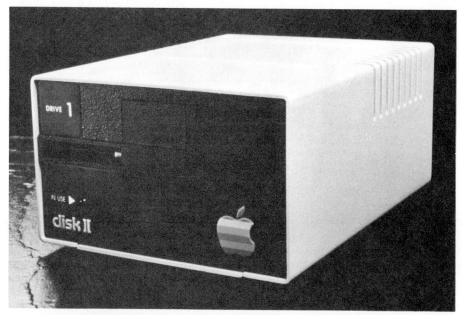

Apple external disk drive.

If you type SAVE PROGRAM ONE and there is already a PROGRAM ONE on your diskette, the old version will be erased and replaced with the version currently in memory. If you type DELETE PROGRAM ONE, PROGRAM ONE will be erased and replaced with nothing. It is always a good idea to stop and think before typing SAVE or DELETE.

DELETE If you type DELETE followed by the name of a program on the disk in the disk drive and press the return key, the named program will be removed from the disk.

RUN If you type RUN followed by the name of a program on the disk in the disk drive and then press the return key, the named program will be copied from the disk into computer memory and a RUN will be executed. Typing RUN by itself will cause the program in memory (if any) to be executed.

Programs on the diskette may be run by simply typing RUN and the name, or they may be loaded into the machine's memory by typing LOAD and the name. Then you may look at the program lines by typing LIST, or run the program by simply typing RUN.

LIST If you type LIST and then press the return key, your entire program will be listed on the screen. Other possibilities are illustrated below (any numbers may be substituted for 60 and 120 in the examples below as long as the second number is larger than the first).

EXAMPLE 1	**LIST 60**	will list only line 60 of your program.
EXAMPLE 2	**LIST 60,120** or **LIST 60-120**	will list all lines in your program from line 60 to line 120 inclusive.
EXAMPLE 3	**LIST 60,** or **LIST 60-**	will list all lines in your program from line 60 to the end of the program
EXAMPLE 4	**LIST ,60** or **LIST -60**	will list all lines in your program from the beginning to line 60 inclusive.

To make changes in a program called "BOB" you would type LOAD BOB, then make the changes; type RUN to see if the changed version works right; and type SAVE BOB to replace the old version with the new one. Alternately, you might type SAVE BOB2. Then you would have both the old and new versions.

LOAD If you type LOAD followed by the name of a program on the disk in the disk drive and then press the return key, the named program will be copied from the disk into the computer memory.

After you run or save a program to the diskette, it is still in the memory of the computer and may be run or listed as many times as you like. The program will stay in memory until the machine is turned off, you type NEW, or you load or run another program which replaces it.

The NEW command erases all programs and variables in memory, as does turning off the machine. Be sure you have saved your program before typing NEW or turning off the machine.

When you type LOAD or RUN followed by the name of a program on your diskette, any program in memory is wiped out and replaced with the named program, so be sure as well that the current program is saved before loading or running another program. Even experienced programmers sometimes lose programs that took them hours to type because of this oversight.

RUN, LOAD, NEW, and turning the computer's power off affect only the computer's memory; they have no effect on programs stored on the diskette.

Another important thing to remember is that if you or someone else has had a program in memory, it is still there unless the computer has been turned off or NEW has been typed. So if you finish working on one program and begin typing in a new program without clearing memory, you will end up with some combination of the two in memory, a condition which can lead to some very interesting effects when you try to run it.

CATALOG If there is a disk in the disk drive and you type CATALOG and press the return key, a list of the programs stored on the disk will be displayed on the screen.

Typing CATALOG will show you a list of the programs on the diskette in the disk drive. It has no effect on memory, so if you want to save a program called "BOB VERSION 4" you can check to make sure you don't already have a version 4 before saving it. When writing a program, especially a long program, it is often a good practice to save successive versions of it so that if the one you are working on gets accidentally erased or stops working you can fall back on a previous version.

RENAME Files may be renamed by typing RENAME followed by the old name, a comma, and the new name.

TYPING AND EDITING

Now it's time to try writing a real program and at the same time learn some editing and typing techniques that can save you many hours in the future.

Typing

First, a few words about typing (if you have some typing experience you can skip this paragraph). In the course of using this book you will have to do a great deal of typing. If you have never typed before, or have never been taught how to type properly, we have a few suggestions that will seem uncomfortable at first but that will save you a lot of time in typing the programs

The Apple II+ keyboard.

The Apple IIc keyboard, pictured, is based on the design of the Apple IIe keyboard.

necessary to complete the book. These may seem simple-minded, but a surprising number of people ignore them.

1. Use both hands.

2. Put your left index finger on the ⟨F⟩ key.

3. Put your right index finger on the ⟨J⟩ key.

4. Try to leave them there.

5. Use the little finger of your left hand for the control and shift keys on the left side.

6. Use the little finger of your right hand for the ⟨RETURN⟩ and shift keys on the right side.

7. Rest your thumbs on the ⟨SPACE BAR⟩ and use them to press it.

8. Try to use all ten of your fingers.

APPLE IIe/IIc NOTE: Remember that the IIe and IIc have repeating keys. Don't hold them down too long.

These techniques may seem awkward at first, but we assure you that this will not last long and that your typing speed will rapidly increase to a point where you can easily type circles around a one- or two-finger typist.

APPLE IIe/IIc NOTE: Although the IIe and IIc have more keys than the II or II+, the tips presented here apply equally to all four and to other similar computers as well.

Editing

Another thing you will have to do a lot of in the course of this book is to change the lines of programs to try and make them run properly. To eliminate an unwanted program line, carefully type the line number followed by ⟨RETURN⟩. The line will be removed from memory. There is no way to get it back without retyping it.

One way of changing a program line is to simply retype it from the beginning, starting with the line number. The new line will replace the old line in memory, with the old line being lost forever. If the line is very long, however, this can be tedious and inefficient (also unnecessary). The computer has a built-in editing system which is well worth the time and trouble it takes to learn to use it.

You have probably already noticed that the right and left arrows can be used to move the cursor back and forth over a line. When the ⟨RIGHT ARROW⟩ is used to move the cursor over characters on the screen, it is as if the characters are being typed; using the ⟨LEFT ARROW⟩ is sort of like "untyping" them. Try typing the following line exactly as it appears (including the mistake) and press ⟨RETURN⟩.

```
10 PRILT "THIS MAY TAKE A WHILE"
```

Now think about how to correct this line without retyping it. What we need is a way to get the cursor back to the beginning of the line; this may be done by using what is called the "escape mode." To enter the escape mode, press the ⟨ESCAPE⟩ key (the key marked ESC at the upper left of the keyboard) once. Now you may use the ⟨J⟩, ⟨I⟩, ⟨M⟩, and ⟨K⟩ keys to move the cursor anywhere on the screen. Notice that the keys form a sort of a diamond pattern. They move the cursor in the directions you might guess they would. While in the escape mode:

⟨I⟩ — moves the cursor up

⟨J⟩ — moves the cursor to the left

⟨K⟩ — moves the cursor to the right

⟨M⟩ — moves the cursor down

While in the escape mode, all characters that the cursor passes over are ignored. You can remember these keys by noticing that they spell "Jim K." Jim K. is a real person and is, in fact, the inventor of the adhesive horseshoe.

Use the ⟨ESCAPE⟩ key to move the cursor to the beginning of line 10. To edit a line, the cursor must always be placed over the first digit of the line number. Press the ⟨ESCAPE⟩ key once, then use ⟨I⟩, ⟨J⟩, ⟨K⟩, and ⟨M⟩ to move the cursor until it is on top of the "1" at the beginning of line 10. Now, in order to make the correction, we need to get out of the escape mode. This is best accomplished by pressing the ⟨ESCAPE⟩ key again (just once — twice will put us back in the escape mode). Now use the ⟨RIGHT ARROW⟩ to copy the line until the cursor is over the L in PRILT. Type the correct letter (N) and then use the ⟨RIGHT ARROW⟩ to copy the rest of the line. When the cursor is past the end of the line, press ⟨RETURN⟩. Now type "LIST 10" to make sure that the line has been changed. If not, try this procedure again until you get the hang of it.

APPLE IIe/IIc NOTE: On the Apple IIe and IIc, you may use the four arrow keys as the equivalent of ⟨I⟩, ⟨J⟩, ⟨K⟩, and ⟨M⟩ while you are in the escape mode, but you *must* follow the instructions here carefully and remember to press the ⟨ESCAPE⟩ key again to get out of the escape mode.

If you remember that while in the escape mode all characters the cursor passes over are ignored, we can do some more fancy editing. Type the following line just as it appears.

    10 PRINT "THE QUICK FOX JUMPS"

Now we need to add the word BROWN between QUICK and FOX. Press the ⟨ESCAPE⟩ key once to enter the escape mode, then use ⟨I⟩, ⟨J⟩, ⟨K⟩, and ⟨M⟩ to move the cursor over the "1" at the beginning of the line and press the ⟨ESCAPE⟩ key again to get out of the escape mode. Now use the ⟨RIGHT ARROW⟩ to copy the line until the cursor is over the space between QUICK and FOX. The character under the cursor has not been copied yet so we have copied QUICK but we have not copied the space. Now press ⟨ESCAPE⟩ and ⟨I⟩ to get into the escape mode and move the cursor above the line. Now press the ⟨ESCAPE⟩ key once to get out of the escape mode and then type one space and the word "BROWN." Now we have to go back and copy the rest of the line, so press ⟨ESCAPE⟩ once to get back into the escape mode and use ⟨I⟩, ⟨J⟩, ⟨K⟩, and ⟨M⟩ to put the cursor back over the space between QUICK and FOX (the exact route you take doesn't matter); type ⟨ESCAPE⟩ again to exit the escape mode and then use the ⟨RIGHT ARROW⟩ to copy the rest of the line. When the cursor is past the end of the line, press the ⟨RETURN⟩ key. Now cross your fingers and type LIST 10. If everything went well the line should now look like this:

    10 PRINT "THE QUICK BROWN FOX JUMPS"

Don't feel bad if this doesn't work for you right away; it takes a little while to get good at it.

Now that you know how to insert extra material in the middle of a line, let's try deleting extra characters in a line. Type the following equation:

    10 LET X = 23 * 253 / 100 + 6

Now suppose you discover that the first part should be divided by 10 instead of 100. Rather than retype the whole line let's use our editing skill to fix it. First, list the line and press the ⟨ESCAPE⟩ key to enter the escape mode. Now use ⟨I⟩, ⟨J⟩, ⟨K⟩, and ⟨M⟩ to move the cursor over the 1 in the line number and press the ⟨ESCAPE⟩ key again to get out of the escape mode. Use the ⟨RIGHT ARROW⟩ key to copy the line until you get to the 100. Now you have two choices. One is to use ⟨ESCAPE⟩ ⟨K⟩ to skip over one of the zeroes, then to press ⟨ESCAPE⟩ again to get out of the escape mode and to use the ⟨RIGHT ARROW⟩ to copy the rest of the line. If this part of the line were in quotes this would be necessary (we'll explain why in a moment), but since there are no quotes in this line you have another option. You can just use the ⟨SPACE BAR⟩ to blank out one of the zeroes. Surprisingly, it doesn't matter which one. If you blank out the middle one the computer will push the remaining one and zero together to make a "10" (try it). You will find that the computer has very definite ideas about what individual program lines should look like. For a demonstration of this, type the following line exactly as it appears:

```
20FORI = 1 000TO10 000
```

Now list it to see how the computer thinks it should look.

The rules that the computer uses in adjusting program lines do not apply to anything inside of quotation marks. This is why we said above that another technique would have to be used for material inside quotes. To the computer, material inside quotation marks is sacred and will not be adjusted at all. To see this try typing the following line:

```
20PRINT"FORI = 1 000TO10 000"
```

Now when you list the line you may notice that the word PRINT has been adjusted slightly but the material inside the quotes is unchanged. This can create a particular problem when you need to make a change in a line with a long quotation. For example, type the following line:

```
10 PRINT "THIS LINE IS A LONGER LINE"
```

Now list the line and you will see that it does not look the same as when you typed it. When you list a program, the computer shrinks the screen width to 33 characters. This means that lines longer than 33 characters (like the one you just typed) "wrap around" to the next line. Notice that when you type RUN, the screen width is the normal 40 characters (you may want to delete line 20 by typing just the line number and pressing ⟨RETURN⟩).

Suppose that we want to change the quote to read "THIS IS A LONG LINE." List the line and use the escape mode to change the line as described above. When using the ⟨RIGHT ARROW⟩ to copy the end of the line, be sure to go all the way around to get to the end of the line *before* pressing ⟨RETURN⟩.

Now list and run the program. If you have been following directions carefully, something strange has happened. A bunch of blanks have been added to the line. This is because when you used the ⟨RIGHT ARROW⟩ to get the cursor to wrap around to the end of the line, you were copying the blanks on the right side of the screen. If the right side of the screen were not inside of the quotes this would make no difference since the computer would remove the spaces. Since the blanks are inside the quotation marks, however, they are considered sacred and are left in the line. There are two ways to avoid this problem, but only one is safe for beginners to use. You may already have thought of it. It is to copy the first part of the line in the usual way and then re-enter the escape mode and skip over the blanks (using the ⟨K⟩ key). After skipping the blanks, press ⟨ESCAPE⟩ again to exit the escape mode and copy the rest of the line. Remember that this technique is only necessary when the right side of the program line is inside of quotation marks. If it is not inside quotes then it's OK to just use the ⟨RIGHT ARROW⟩ to move the cursor past the very end of the line and press ⟨RETURN⟩. This is usually done by holding the ⟨RIGHT ARROW⟩ and the ⟨REPEAT⟩ key down together.

APPLE IIe/IIc NOTE: On the IIe and IIc there is no ⟨REPEAT⟩ key, but because all the keys will repeat if held down, this can be accomplished simply by holding down the ⟨RIGHT ARROW⟩.

A REAL PROGRAM

Now that you have developed some typing and editing skills it's time for you to do some actual programming. The following program won't exactly calculate the Gross National Product of Bolivia, but at least it's a real program. For the first step, type NEW and then type the program exactly as it appears in figure 0.3. Be sure to include all the line numbers, dollar signs, and quotation marks. When you are finished entering the program, type RUN and compare your run with the one in figure 0.3. If it does not run properly, type LIST and carefully compare your listing with the one in figure 0.3. Correct any differences and make sure the program runs correctly. Remember that you can type HOME at any time to clear the screen. This will have no effect on the program in memory.

When your program produces the run pictured in figure 0.3, use the escape mode and editing functions to replace the values for NA\$, AD\$, and ST\$ with your actual name and address. Remember that to change the program, you must edit the actual program lines. To do this you must type LIST to get the lines on the screen. Editing the output of the program (changing the messages the program prints on the screen when it runs) will change what's on the screen, but will have no permanent effect on the program in memory.

When you get the new version to run properly, save the program to the diskette by typing:

SAVE FIRST PROGRAM

Now type CATALOG to make sure it is there. It should have an "A" and a number to the left of it. The "A" indicates that it was written in Applesoft BASIC (the language this book is about). The number is the size of the file on the disk; it should be greater than 1. If it is only 1, this means you typed SAVE when no program was in memory (maybe you typed NEW at the wrong time). If the number is greater than 1, everything should be going fine. Now work up your nerve and type NEW. This wipes your program out of memory

FIGURE 0.3

```
]LIST
10 REM MY FIRST PROGRAM
20 LET NA$ = "YOUR NAME"
30 LET AD$ = "YOUR STREET ADDRESS"
40 LET ST$ = "YOUR CITY, STATE, ZIP"
50 HOME
60 PRINT NA$
70 PRINT AD$
80 PRINT ST$
90 END
```

RUN

```
YOUR NAME
YOUR STREET ADDRESS
YOUR CITY, STATE, ZIP
```

(but has no effect on the disk). Now type LIST and RUN to assure yourself that the program is really gone. Then type:

LOAD FIRST PROGRAM

If you get a FILE NOT FOUND message it means that you are typing the name incorrectly. It must be exactly the same as when you saved it including all spaces (if you continue to have trouble, check the catalog again). If you don't get an error message, the program has loaded properly and you may run or list it to your heart's content. If you like, you can now print the variables in immediate mode by running the program and then typing PRINT NA$ (or any of the other variables). This is extremely useful when trying to find and fix mistakes in a program (called "debugging" the program), and also for reminding you of the program name when it's time to save the program.

At this time you may also save the program under another name, in which case you will have two identical versions of it on the diskette. You may also erase one or both programs by typing DELETE and the program name. Keep at least one copy of the program; when you become a famous programmer it will be a valuable collector's item.

CHAPTER 1

COUNTING EGGS
Using the LET statement

NEW CONCEPTS TAUGHT

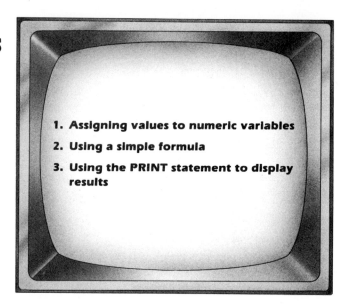

1. **Assigning values to numeric variables**

2. **Using a simple formula**

3. **Using the PRINT statement to display results**

HOW MANY EGGS?

Program 1A (see figure 1.1) is not very fancy or impressive, but it gets the job done and is easy to understand. It has only two variables, GUESTS and EGGS. We could use just G and E, but using longer names makes the program easier to understand. Both variables are numeric variables; that is, the value they represent is a number.

In line 10 we set the value of GUESTS to 12. This places the number 12 in memory cell called GUESTS. In line 20 we set the value of EGGS to two times the value of GUESTS. The computer, when it gets to line 20, looks to see what value is currently stored in the memory cell labelled GUESTS; it then multiplies that value (which happens to be 12) times two and puts the result in the memory cell labelled EGGS.

In line 30 we instruct the computer to print the number currently stored in the memory cell labelled EGGS, and then in line 40 we tell the computer to relax.

Although this program is very simple, it can be useful; imagine that you are having a major banquet and serving many different kinds of food. With a little extension, this program could calculate the necessary amounts of the various foods. Best of all, when it was finished you could get results for various-sized parties simply by changing the value of GUESTS in line 10.

EXAMPLE 1A   How Many Eggs?

Problem   You are having a breakfast party where you will serve scrambled eggs. You estimate that you will need two eggs per guest and are expecting 12 guests. Write a program that will calculate the total number of eggs needed and print that value on the screen.

FIGURE 1.1

```
]LIST
10 LET GUESTS = 12
20 LET EGGS = GUESTS * 2
30 PRINT EGGS
40 END
```

```
]RUN
24
```

Program 1A

Assign
Number
of Guests

Calculate
Number
of Eggs

Print
Number
of Eggs

End

FLOWCHARTS

The flowchart, or flow diagram, is one of the methods used by programmers to assist in writing a program. Flowcharts are most useful in keeping track of details in complex programs with decision points and multiple branches. The flowchart introduced in figure 1.1 (program 1A) presents some of the flowchart symbols used in this book. (Refer to appendix E for a complete list of flowchart symbols.) However, you should understand that the usefulness of a flowchart may not become apparent until you have to deal with more complex programming problems.

In the flowchart for program 1A, the oval-shaped symbol is used to designate the beginning and the end of a program. The name "program 1A" is written in the beginning symbol, and the word "end" is written in the ending symbol. The parallelogram-shaped symbol is used for input operations, and the message ASSIGN NUMBER OF GUESTS identifies the input variable. The rectangle-shaped symbol is used for processing of data or any time none of the other symbols apply. The processing step CALCULATE NUMBER OF EGGS is written inside the processing box. The torn-page symbol is used for output operations. The message PRINT NUMBER OF EGGS describes the output operation.

The arrows in a flow diagram indicate the direction of flow and, hence, the order in which operations are performed. The order of operations is of paramount importance, and the flowchart is one method the programmer uses to keep the operations in the proper order. Obviously, we would not calculate the number of eggs before the input of the number of guests, or print the number of eggs before calculating that value. However, a common error in beginning programs is incorrect order in the sequence of operations. Careful attention to a flow diagram would eliminate most, if not all, errors in the sequence of operations.

PRINT The PRINT statement is used to display the number stored in the memory cell named EGGS. The statement

> **30 PRINT EGGS**

tells the computer to display the value of the variable named EGGS at the left side of the screen or paper.

LET The LET statement is used to assign a name to a memory cell and put a number or message into the named memory cell. The general form of the LET statement is as follows:

> *(line number) LET (variable name) = (number or arithmetic expression whose value will be placed in memory)*
> or
> *(line number) LET (string variable) = ("message")*

The equal sign in the LET statement has a different meaning than it does in a mathematical equation. The LET statement instructs the computer to replace the contents of the memory cell named on the left side of the equal sign by the value of the expression on the right side. For this reason the equal sign in the LET statement is sometimes referred to as the "replaced by" symbol. Computer scientists would have preferred to use a left arrow rather than an equal sign to express this operation but it wasn't available on the keyboard.

The statement LET X = X + 1 means replace the contents of the memory cell named X with the old contents of X plus one. If the memory cell named X contains the number three, the statement LET X = X + 1 will replace that three with a four.

Example LET statements:

> **10 LET A = 2**
> **20 LET X = 2 * A + 4.324**
> **30 LET B$ = " JOHN JOHNSON "**

The use of the word LET is optional; the statements 10 LET A = 2 and 10 A = 2 are equivalent.

SELF-TESTING QUESTIONS

Select the word from the list below that best matches each question.

A. Arrow keys	B. CATALOG	C. DEL
D. DELETE	E. ESC I, J, K, M	F. HOME
G. LET	H. LIST	I. LOAD
J. NEW	K. PRINT	L. RETURN
M. RUN	N. RUN (name)	O. SAVE
P. SYNTAX ERROR		

1.1   Used to remove the program from the computer's memory and leave a clear workspace.

1.2   Used to clear the screen.

1.3   Used to enter (or conclude) a line or command.

1.4   Used to see the program in the computer's memory.

1.5   Used in a program to calculate the value of a variable.

1.6   Used in a program to show the results produced by the program.

1.7   Used to execute the program in the computer's memory.

1.8   A message the computer prints when something is wrong.

1.9   Used to move the cursor left or right.

1.10   Used to edit a line in a program.

1.11   Used to remove lines from a program.

1.12   Used to store a program on a disk.

1.13   Used to list the names of the programs on a disk.

1.14   Used to copy a program from a disk into the computer's memory.

1.15   A single command used to copy a program from a disk into the computer's memory and execute the program.

1.16   Used to remove a program from a disk.

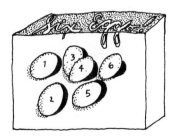

EXERCISES

1.1   Follow the nine steps listed below.

1. Type the program exactly as it appears in example 1A.

2. Run the program to make sure it gives you the run you see in figure 1.1.

3. When the program runs properly, save it by typing SAVE PROGRAM 1A.

4. Using the escape mode, change line 10 and try various values of GUESTS.

5. When you are satisfied with this, add shrimp to the menu and label this program 1B.

6. Assume that you will need three shrimp per guest.

7. When this new version runs properly, save it by typing SAVE PROGRAM 1B.

8. Turn on the output to the printer (PR#1) then type RUN and LIST.

9. Turn off the output to the printer (PR#0).

TIPS

1. Remember to type NEW before starting.
2. Note that you will need two new lines, one to calculate the number of shrimp and one to print this value.
3. Be sure to have the program calculate the number of shrimp before you have it print this value.

CHAPTER 2

DOING IT RIGHT
Programming Standards

NEW CONCEPTS TAUGHT

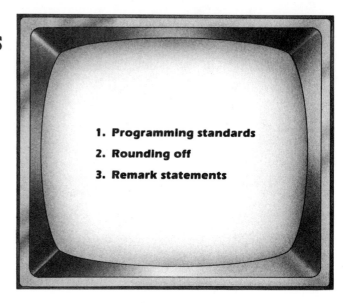

1. **Programming standards**
2. **Rounding off**
3. **Remark statements**

PROGRAMMING STANDARDS

In this chapter, we are introducing several new concepts. One of them is the idea of programming standards. Most programmers have certain rules they follow in writing programs. Although these rules may seem restrictive to you at first, they are almost always to the advantage of the programmer. They make programs more reliable, easier to read, easier to modify, and in the long run, easier to write.

One of our rules (a very common one) is that every program should contain the program name, the name of the programmer, and the date. To make this information easy to find, we put it at the beginning, in lines 1, 2, and 3.

Another rule is that there should be standard sections of the program reserved for various purposes. In the program shown in figure 2.1, we have set aside lines 10 to 39 for the description of variables used in the program and lines 40 to 49 for defined functions (more about these later). The main program (the part of the program that does the real work) always starts at line 100.

The colon symbol ":" between statements allows us to make multiple program statements in a single line. In line 101, for example, we have three program statements separated by colons. It is legal to have many more as long as the entire line (including the line number) does not contain more than 256 characters.

In line 101, the first statement uses the HOME command to clear the screen. Then we use the HTAB statement and the PRINT PN$ statement to position and print the name of the program on the screen (PN$ is assigned in line 1). The HTAB command moves the cursor to the column specified by the number following the HTAB. In this case we have used a formula so that this line will center the program name regardless of its length. The formula uses LEN(PN$), which is the length of the program name, divides it by two, and tabs to 20 minus that number. Since HTAB 20 would be the center of the screen, this automatically centers the name on the screen.

If you don't understand this completely, don't worry; just copy the line exactly and everything will be fine.

The standards and rules we have talked about here will apply to all the programs in this book. All programs in this book will have the form of program 2A. They will have the program name, the programmer's name, and the date assigned to the variables PN$, NA$, and DA$ in lines 1, 2, and 3 of the program. They will also maintain the same sections for variables, defined functions, and the main programs as follows:

Variables — lines 10 through 39
Defined Functions — lines 40 through 49
Main Program — lines 100 through 199

Since many programs will be using the rounding functions, we will include these as a standard part of the section for defined functions.

Because you will be using this same form for all the programs you will write for this book, it will be very convenient to write and save a kind of skeleton program like the one in figure 2.1. Call this program STARTER and save it under that name. That way you can start all future programs by typing NEW and then typing LOAD STARTER. This will save you a lot of typing and will make it easy to stick to the programming rules discussed above. The biggest advantage of this method is that once you have the rounding functions correct, you won't have to type them again.

REMARK STATEMENTS

We usually use REM statements to designate parts of a program (as in lines 10, 40, and 100 of figure 2.1). REM statements are completely ignored by the computer; they have no effect on the execution of the program. We use them to make the program easier to understand and to make comments about the program to remind us how it works.

REM The REM statement allows us to insert any message we wish in a program. REM statements are ignored by the program.

EXAMPLE

```
5 REM    THIS IS AN EXAMPLE OF A REMARK.
6 REM    ALL CHARACTERS ON THE KEYBOARD
7 REM    CAN BE INCLUDED IN A REMARK.
8 REM    THE COMPUTER IGNORES ALL REM
9 REM    STATEMENTS WHEN IT RUNS A PROGRAM.
```

ROUNDING OFF

Often when the computer divides one number by another, or does a square root, the answer is an awkward number with many decimal places. Many times we don't need such accuracy and would like to have the number rounded off before printing it. Some versions of the BASIC language have a built-in command for rounding off numbers. Unfortunately, Applesoft is not one of them. Applesoft has the INT command, but all it does is shorten the number rather than round it off; for example, INT(1.9) becomes 1. To get true rounding, we have to use either a somewhat complicated formula which varies depending on the number of decimal places we want, or use the defined functions you see in lines 41 through 48 of figure 2.1. Those of you with weak math backgrounds, please don't panic; it's not necessary for you to understand the mathematical details of these functions. We will talk more about functions in chapter 8; for now you only need to copy these functions as they appear here, and learn a simple method for using them to round off numbers.

DEF The DEF statement allows us to define the operations that will round a number to the nearest whole number or to a given number of decimal places. We will use FN A to round numbers to the nearest whole number, FN B to round to one decimal place, FN C to round to two decimal places, and FN D to round to three decimal places.

EXAMPLE
 The following statement defines FN B to round numbers to one decimal place.

    44 DEF FN B (X) = INT (10 * X + .5) / 10

The following statements use FN B to round the values of the variables X and SUM to one decimal place.

    140 LET X = FN B (X)
    160 LET SUM = FN B (SUM)

EXAMPLE 2A   The Starter Program

Problem   Write a program that will serve as a starting point for future programs. Reserve space at the beginning for the name of the program, the programmer, and the date. Include a line that will print the name of the program (centered on the screen) when it is run. Have designated sections for functions, variable descriptions, and the main program. Put the standard functions for rounding off in the function section with remarks indicating how many decimal places each function will round to. Figure 2.1 shows the list for example 2A.

FIGURE 2.1

```
]LIST
1 PN$ = "PROGRAM NAME"
2 NA$ = "YOUR NAME"
3 DA$ = "00/00/00"
10 REM ===== VARIABLES =====
40 REM ===== FUNCTIONS =====
41 REM ROUND TO WHOLE NUMBER WITH FN A(X)
42 DEF FN A (X) = INT (1 * X + .5) / 1
43 REM ROUND TO ONE DECIMAL PLACE WITH FN B(X)
44 DEF FN B (X) = INT (10 * X +.5) / 10
45 REM ROUND TO TWO DECIMAL PLACES WITH FN C(X)
46 DEF FN C (X) = INT (100 * X + .5) / 100
47 REM ROUND TO THREE DECIMAL PLACES WITH FN D(X)
48 DEF FN D (X) = INT (1000 * X + .5) / 1000
100 REM ===== MAIN PROGRAM =====
101 HOME : HTAB 20 - (LEN (PN$) / 2): PRINT PN$
```

Using the Rounding Functions

Notice that the four rounding functions are labelled A, B, C, and D. A rounds to whole numbers (no decimal places), B rounds to one decimal place, C to two, and D to three. Suppose you have a variable called A which has a current value of 3.6789 and would like to round it off. If you have the defined functions entered in lines 41 to 48 you may use them to do this. As the program goes past lines 41 to 48, the computer makes a note of the functions so it will know what to do if you mention them later in the program. If you want to round your variable to two decimal places, you will use function C (notice that the remark statement in line 45 tells you this). All you need to do is put the following in the program: LET A = FN C(A). The computer first looks to the right of the equal sign. This part tells it to take whatever is in memory cell A and apply function C to it; it remembers function C from line 46. The computer does its work and then notes that the left side of the statement tells it to put this result back in the memory cell named A. When it is finished, if we add the command PRINT A we will find that A is now 3.68. If this is a bit confusing, remember that all you really need to know is the following:

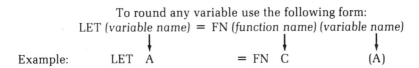

To round any variable use the following form:
LET *(variable name)* = FN *(function name)* *(variable name)*

Example: LET   A   = FN   C   (A)

(Variable name) is the name of the variable you want to round off, and *(function name)* is the name of the rounding function (in this case A, B, C, or D).

PRINT The PRINT statement is used to display the contents of memory cells or the value of an expression.

Examples of PRINT statements:

Statement	Result
70 PRINT	Leaves a blank line on the screen or paper.
80 PRINT X	Displays the value of X at the left side of the screen or paper.
100 PRINT "X = "; X	Displays the message followed immediately by the value of X.

COMPUTING MILEAGE

One of the things a microcomputer is best at is arithmetic. Our example of this is a simple program for computing mileage. If you go a certain distance in your car and use a certain number of gallons of fuel getting there, you can easily figure out your miles per gallon by dividing the number of miles by the number of gallons. This procedure is the basis for program 2B.

One problem we must solve is how to tell the computer how many miles we traveled and how many gallons of fuel we used. There are several ways to do this. In lines 110 and 120 of this program, we will enter the values right into the program. In chapter 3 we will see two other ways to do this. In line 110 of figure 2.2 the variable DIST, which stands for distance traveled, is set equal to 200 (miles); in line 120, the variable GAL, which stands for gallons of fuel used, is set equal to 33; and then in line 130, MPG (miles per gallon) is computed. In line 140 we round off the value of MPG; in line 150 we print the value of MPG and the phrase "MILES PER GALLON" to make it clear what the result in line 140 stands for.

EXAMPLE 2B   Miles Per Gallon (LET)

Problem   Using the program from example 2A as a starting point, write a program that will calculate the miles per gallon for your car on a single trip. Use LET statements to assign values to the variables for distance travelled and gallons used. In the variable section, describe the variables used with REM statements.

FIGURE 2.2

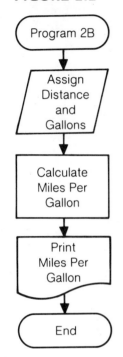

```
]LIST
1 PN$ = "PROGRAM 2B - MPG"
2 NA$ = "YOUR NAME"
3 DA$ = "00/00/00"
10 REM ===== VARIABLES =====
11 REM DIST = DISTANCE TRAVELLED
12 REM GAL = GALLONS USED
13 REM MPG = MILES PER GALLON
40 REM ===== FUNCTIONS =====
41 REM ROUND TO WHOLE NUMBER WITH FN A(X)
42 DEF FN A (X) = INT (1 * X +.5) / 1
43 REM ROUND TO ONE DECIMAL PLACE WITH FN B(X)
44 DEF FN B (X) = INT (10 * X + .5) / 10
45 REM ROUND TO TWO DECIMAL PLACES WITH FN C(X)
46 DEF FN C (X) = INT (100 * X + .5) / 100
47 REM ROUND TO THREE DECIMAL PLACES WITH FN D(X)
48 DEF FN D (X) = INT (1000 * X + .5) / 1000
100 REM ===== MAIN PROGRAM =====
101 HOME : HTAB 20 - (LEN (PN$) / 2): PRINT PN$
110 LET DIST = 200
120 LET GAL = 33
130 LET MPG = DIST / GAL
140 LET MPG = FN A(MPG)
150 PRINT MPG;" MILES PER GALLON"
160 END
```

RUN

```
        PROGRAM 2B - MPG
   6
```

SELF-TESTING QUESTIONS

Step through the program in each question and write the output produced when the program runs. Assume that all programs include lines 40 through 48 as found in program 2B–MPG in figure 2.2.

2.1   ```
110 LET DIST = 500
120 LET GAL = 20
130 LET MPG = DIST / GAL
140 LET MPG = FN A(MPG)
150 PRINT MPG;" MILES PER GALLON"
```

2.2   ```
110 LET DIST = 350
120 LET GAL = 13.3
130 LET MPG = DIST / GAL
140 LET MPG = FN A(MPG)
150 PRINT MPG;" MILES PER GALLON"
```

2.3   Same as question 2.2 except change line 140 to the following:

```
140 LET MPG = FN B(MPG)
```

2.4   Same as question 2.2 except change line 140 to the following:

```
140 LET MPG = FN C(MPG)
```

2.5   Same as question 2.2 except change line 140 to the following:

```
140 LET MPG = FN D(MPG)
```

EXERCISES

Do Both Exercises

2.1 Type the starter program exactly as it appears in figure 2.1, then run the program. If you get the SYNTAX ERROR message, you probably have made one or more typing errors. If you have typed the program correctly, nothing should happen when you type RUN except that the words PROGRAM NAME should be printed in the center of the line at the top of the screen.

   When you are satisfied that the program is typed correctly, save it by typing SAVE STARTER. You can then use this program as a beginning for all future programs.

TIPS

1. Remember to type NEW before starting.
2. Type carefully.

2.2 Write a program that will calculate the miles per gallon for your car on a single trip. Use LET statements to put the values for miles traveled and gallons of fuel used into the program. Start by typing LOAD STARTER. Then use the Edit Mode to change the program name in line 1 to "PROGRAM 2–MPG", then change line 3 to indicate the date. Use the program from figure 2.2 as a model for your program. Use 200 as the number of miles traveled and 33 as the number of gallons of fuel used.

Try versions of the program using all four rounding functions by changing line 140. For each of the four versions, get a printout of the LIST and RUN by typing

    PR#1
    LIST
    RUN
    PR#0

Do this four times, once for each rounding function. This will help you find any mistakes you may have in your STARTER program. When the program runs properly, save it by typing SAVE PROGRAM 2B–MPG.

TIPS

1. Follow these directions *very* carefully.
2. For a neater look to your run, be sure to put the space between the first quotation mark and the M in MILES in line 150.
3. If you find out there was an error in your starter program, be sure to go back and correct it *after* you finish this assignment.

CHAPTER 3

GETTING DATA IN
Two More Methods of Input

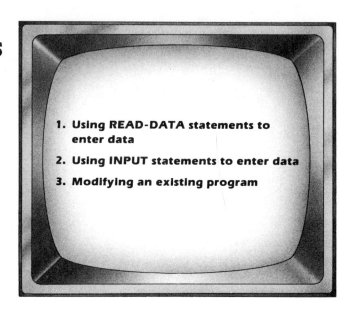

NEW CONCEPTS TAUGHT

1. **Using READ-DATA statements to enter data**
2. **Using INPUT statements to enter data**
3. **Modifying an existing program**

METHODS OF INPUT

In chapter 2 we used the computer to calculate our miles per gallon on a trip. We used LET statements to tell the computer how far we traveled and how much fuel we used on our trip. In this chapter we will see two other methods of giving a computer the information it needs to do its work.

READ/DATA Statements

READ statements and DATA statements are really two different things, but since each is useless without the other, they always go together; thus we usually refer to them as READ/DATA statements. You have probably seen the word data used in other contexts to refer to information; that's exactly what it means here. The DATA statement contains information the computer needs to do its job. The READ statement tells the computer that there is a DATA statement around somewhere that it should be aware of. Confused?

The concept of READ/DATA statements will be much more clear (hopefully) if we look at program 3A in figure 3.1. In line 170 there are two data values separated by a comma. This line could actually be placed anywhere in the program, even after the END statement, and it would still work. In any program that has a DATA statement, there is a kind of imaginary pointer, pointing to the first DATA value in the program, wherever it is. In this case it points to the 400 in line 170.

When the computer encounters the READ statement in line 110, it knows this means it should put the value that the DATA pointer is pointing ·at (400) in the memory cell labeled DIST, and move the DATA pointer ahead

EXAMPLE 3A   *Miles Per Gallon (READ/DATA)*

Problem Write a program that will calculate and print your miles per gallon for a single trip. Use READ/DATA statements to enter the values of distance traveled and gallons of gas used.

FIGURE 3.1

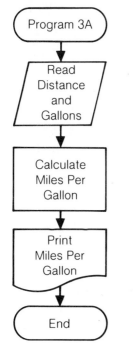

```
]LIST
1 PN$ = "PROGRAM 3A: MPG"
2 NA$ = "YOUR NAME"
3 DA$ = "00/00/00"
10 REM ===== VARIABLES =====
11 REM DIST = DISTANCE TRAVELLED
12 REM GAL = GALLONS USED
13 REM MPG = MILES PER GALLON
40 REM ===== FUNCTIONS =====
41 REM ROUND TO WHOLE NUMBER WITH FN A(X)
42 DEF FN A(X) = INT (1 * X +.5) / 1
43 REM ROUND TO ONE DECIMAL PLACE WITH FN B(X)
44 DEF FN B(X) = INT (10 * X + .5) / 10
45 REM ROUND TO TWO DECIMAL PLACES WITH FN C(X)
46 DEF FN C(X) = INT (100 * X + .5) / 100
47 REM ROUND TO THREE DECIMAL PLACES WITH FN D(X)
48 DEF FN D(X) = INT (1000 * X + .5) / 1000
100 REM ===== MAIN PROGRAM =====
101 HOME : HTAB 20 - (LEN (PN$) / 2): PRINT PN$
110 READ DIST
120 READ GAL
130 LET MPG = DIST / GAL
140 LET MPG = FN A(MPG)
150 PRINT MPG;" MILES PER GALLON"
170 DATA 400,19
180 END
```

RUN

one notch (which leaves it pointing at the 19 in line 170). When the computer gets to the second READ statement (in line 120) it puts the second data value (19) in the memory cell labelled GAL. It then calculates MPG, rounds it off, and prints the result as before. The DATA statement in line 170 is ignored. In fact, DATA statements are always ignored except when being referred to specifically by a READ statement. While the DATA statements may be placed anywhere, the placement and order of the READ statements is extremely important.

Some programs have many data values taking up many lines of the program. Here we only needed two, so we put them on a single line. We could have put them on two lines if we wanted to, like so:

```
170 DATA 400
175 DATA 19
```

INPUT STATEMENTS

The INPUT statement is a way of getting the computer to pay attention to the person sitting at the keyboard during the execution of the program. When an INPUT statement is encountered, the program stops and waits for something to be entered at the keyboard (followed by ⟨RETURN⟩ of course). So that the person at the keyboard knows what he or she is supposed to be entering, we usually have the program print a message on the screen. This message is called a "prompt" and is often in the form of a question.

In program 3B (see figure 3.2), we use INPUT statements to set the values of DIST and GAL. In line 110 the message "HOW MANY MILES" is printed on the screen. The semicolon (;) following the prompt is not necessary, but it lets the user enter the number of miles on the same line just to the right of the prompt. Without the semicolon, the number of miles would be entered at the left side of the screen on the line below the prompt. (You might say that the semicolon suppresses the carriage return that would normally follow this kind of statement.) In line 120 the computer puts whatever value the user types at the keyboard into the memory cell labelled DIST.

In line 130 the program prints another prompt on the screen and in line 140 puts the value typed at the keyboard into the memory cell labelled GAL. In lines 150 through 170 the miles per gallon for the trip are calculated, rounded off, and printed as before (notice the use of the semicolon in line 170 to keep the value of MPG and the label "MILES PER GALLON" on the same line). Notice also that with the printer turned on, the prompts appear on the paper as well as on the screen.

In chapter 4 we will use an alternate form of the INPUT statement that allows the prompt to be included in the INPUT statement itself.

EXAMPLE 3B   Miles Per Gallon (INPUT)

Problem   Write a program that calculates and prints your miles per gallon for a single trip. Use INPUT statements to enter the number of miles traveled and gallons of gas used.

FIGURE 3.2

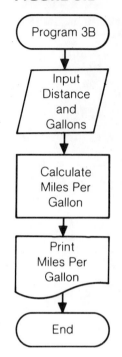

```
]LIST
1 PN$ = "PROGRAM 3B: - MPG"
2 NA$ = "YOUR NAME"
3 DA$ = "00/00/00"
10 REM ===== VARIABLES =====
11 REM DIST = DISTANCE TRAVELLED
12 REM GAL = GALLONS USED
13 REM MPG = MILEAGE
40 REM ===== FUNCTIONS =====
41 REM ROUND TO WHOLE NUMBER WITH FN A(X)
42 DEF FN A (X) = INT (1 * X +.5) / 1
43 REM ROUND TO ONE DECIMAL PLACE WITH FN B(X)
44 DEF FN B (X) = INT (10 * X + .5) / 10
45 REM ROUND TO TWO DECIMAL PLACES WITH FN C(X)
46 DEF FN C (X) = INT (100 * X + .5) / 100
47 REM ROUND TO THREE DECIMAL PLACES WITH FN D(X)
48 DEF FN D (X) = INT (1000 * X + .5) / 1000
100 REM ===== MAIN PROGRAM =====
101 HOME : HTAB 20 - (LEN (PN$) / 2): PRINT PN$
110 PRINT "HOW MANY MILES";
120 INPUT DIST
130 PRINT "HOW MANY GALLONS";
140 INPUT GAL
150 LET MPG = DIST / GAL
160 LET MPG = FN B(MPG)
170 PRINT MPG; " MILES PER GALLON"
180 END
```

RUN

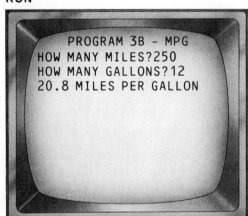

READ/DATA The READ and DATA statements are used together to assign names and put numbers or messages in memory cells. The READ statement gives the names for the memory cells. The DATA statement gives the numbers (or messages) that go into the named memory cells. The names and numbers, or messages, must be in exactly the same order in the READ and DATA statements. When the program run begins, the computer sets a DATA pointer above the first number (or message) in the first data statement in the program. Each time the computer encounters a variable name in a READ statement, it puts that number under the data pointer in a memory cell with the variable name just encountered in the READ statement. Then the computer moves the DATA pointer over the next number (or message) in the DATA statement.

EXAMPLE

The following statements will put the number 5 in A2, the number 8 in A1, and the number 6 in A3.

```
110 READ A2
120 READ A1,A3
200 DATA 5,8
210 DATA 6
```

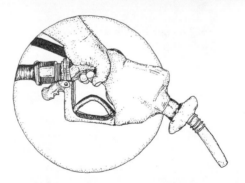

INPUT The INPUT statement is used to assign names to memory cells. When the program runs and the INPUT statement is executed, the computer waits for the user to type the data to be put into the memory cell named in the INPUT statement.

Examples of INPUT statements:

```
10 INPUT X
20 INPUT SUM
30 INPUT A$
40 INPUT TITLE$
50 INPUT N$
60 INPUT "TYPE YOUR NAME"; NAME$
```

SELF-TESTING QUESTIONS

Step through the program in each problem and write the output produced
when the program runs. Assume that all programs include lines 40
through 48 as found in program 3A–MPG, from figure 3.1.

3.1
```
110 READ DIST
120 READ GAL
130 LET MPG = DIST / GAL
140 LET MPG = FN A(MPG)
150 PRINT MPG;" MILES PER GALLON"
160 DATA 425, 15.2
```

3.2   Same as question 3.1 except change lines 140 and 160 to the following:

```
140 LET MPG = FN B(MPG)
160 DATA 285, 9.3
```

3.3   The first two lines of two runs of PROGRAM 3B–MPG are
shown below. Write the output produced when each run is
completed.

a. **HOW MANY MILES? 315**
    HOW MANY GALLONS? 8.6
b. **HOW MANY MILES? 405**
    HOW MANY GALLONS? 11.2

3.4
```
110 READ A
120 READ B
130 READ C
140 READ D
150 PRINT "THE LAST NUMBER IS ";D
160 DATA 4, 1, 8, 7, 3
```

EXERCISES

Do Both Exercises

3.1 Load the STARTER program you wrote in chapter 2 and change the name of the program in line 1 to read PROGRAM 3A–READ/DATA. Now, starting at line 110, type in the program you wrote (program 1A) to calculate the number of eggs and shrimp for the party (see figure 1.1). Be careful not to use the original line numbers since they conflict with those of the STARTER program. Change the program so that it uses a READ/DATA statement instead of a LET statement to set the number of guests. Assume that you will need 1.25 eggs and 1.33 shrimp per person. After calculating the necessary amounts of eggs and shrimp, round off to the nearest whole egg or shrimp. When the program runs properly, get a list and run on paper as described in chapter 1, and save program 3.A by typing SAVE PROGRAM 3A–READ/DATA.

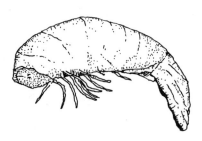

TIPS

1. Be sure to change line 1 as soon as you load the program.
2. If things get too messed up you can type NEW, reload the starter program, and start over; if you do this be sure you change line 1 again.
3. Look at the changes we made in example 2B to make it into example 3A.

3.2 After you have program 3A working and safely saved and you have a successful LIST and RUN, change the name of the program in line 1 to PROGRAM 3B–INPUT. Then modify the program so that it uses an INPUT statement to enter the value of guests. Have the program ask you "HOW MANY GUESTS" before inputting the number. When the program runs properly, get a list and run in the usual way and save this program by typing SAVE PROGRAM 3B–INPUT.

TIPS

1. Follow these directions *very* carefully.
2. This is a minor change from program 3A so don't expect to make a lot of changes.
3. Remember that when the program gets to the INPUT statement, it will stop and wait for you to type something.
4. Be sure to have the program print a prompt so that you will know things are working right.

CHAPTER 4

LET'S DO THAT AGAIN
Looping with GOTO and IF Statements

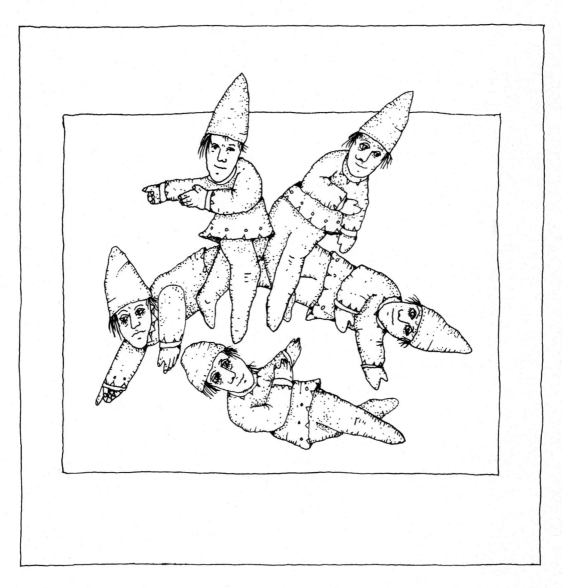

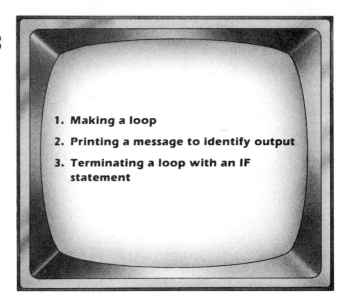

1. Making a loop
2. Printing a message to identify output
3. Terminating a loop with an IF statement

LOOPING

All of the programs we have seen so far have done a single task by proceeding directly from beginning to end. This method is simple and effective if you want to do a task only once. The real treat of having a computer, however, is in getting it to do boring, repetitive tasks while we are out reclining in the sun. Repetition in computer jargon is called *looping* and can be accomplished in several ways. One of these ways is to form a loop with a simple GOTO statement.

A Primitive Loop

In program 4A, the loop includes lines 110 through 160. As soon as the program gets to line 160, it is sent back to line 110. The END statement in line 210 is about as effective as sunglasses on an owl; the program will never reach line 210.

EXAMPLE 4A   Miles Per Gallon (READ/DATA and GOTO Loop)

Problem   Write a program that uses a GOTO loop to print your miles per gallon for a series of trips. Use READ/DATA statements to enter the values of distance traveled and gallons of gas used.

FIGURE 4.1

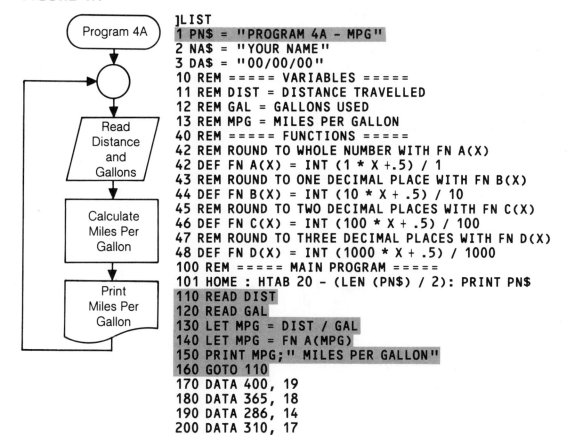

```
]LIST
1 PN$ = "PROGRAM 4A - MPG"
2 NA$ = "YOUR NAME"
3 DA$ = "00/00/00"
10 REM ===== VARIABLES =====
11 REM DIST = DISTANCE TRAVELLED
12 REM GAL = GALLONS USED
13 REM MPG = MILES PER GALLON
40 REM ===== FUNCTIONS =====
42 REM ROUND TO WHOLE NUMBER WITH FN A(X)
42 DEF FN A(X) = INT (1 * X +.5) / 1
43 REM ROUND TO ONE DECIMAL PLACE WITH FN B(X)
44 DEF FN B(X) = INT (10 * X + .5) / 10
45 REM ROUND TO TWO DECIMAL PLACES WITH FN C(X)
46 DEF FN C(X) = INT (100 * X + .5) / 100
47 REM ROUND TO THREE DECIMAL PLACES WITH FN D(X)
48 DEF FN D(X) = INT (1000 * X + .5) / 1000
100 REM ===== MAIN PROGRAM =====
101 HOME : HTAB 20 - (LEN (PN$) / 2): PRINT PN$
110 READ DIST
120 READ GAL
130 LET MPG = DIST / GAL
140 LET MPG = FN A(MPG)
150 PRINT MPG;" MILES PER GALLON"
160 GOTO 110
170 DATA 400, 19
180 DATA 365, 18
190 DATA 286, 14
200 DATA 310, 17
210 END
```

RUN

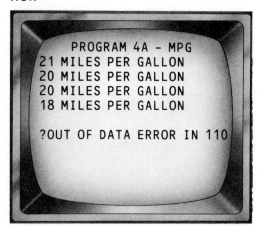

```
        PROGRAM 4A - MPG
21 MILES PER GALLON
20 MILES PER GALLON
20 MILES PER GALLON
18 MILES PER GALLON

?OUT OF DATA ERROR IN 110
```

The DATA statements in lines 170 through 200 are all right, however, since DATA statements can be anywhere in a program. When the program encounters the READ statement in line 110 it searches the whole program, disregarding all commands, looking faithfully for the first DATA statement and finding it in line 170. As we explained before, after the DATA value is read, the DATA pointer is pointed at the next DATA value in the program (also on line 170). Line 120 reads this DATA value and then leaves the pointer aimed at the first DATA value in line 180. The mileage is calculated and printed and when the loop executes again the DATA in line 180 are read.

We have put two DATA values on each line since two values are read each time through the loop. This makes the program easier to understand but is not strictly necessary. Actually we could have put all the DATA values on one line, provided they were in the right order.

After the loop has executed four times, the DATA pointer is left pointing past the end of the DATA. When the loop sends the program back to line 110 for the fifth time, the DATA pointer is not pointing to any DATA (you might think of it as pointing off into space) so the READ statement in line 110 causes the program to crash and produces the ?OUT OF DATA ERROR you see at the end of the run. Needless to say, this is not what we would call elegant programming. One of your tasks for this chapter is to learn how to terminate a loop more gracefully than this.

The Small Circle

A new symbol, the small circle, is introduced in the flowchart for program 4A. The circle is used as a connector symbol to join two branches at the beginning of the loop. One branch comes from the beginning of the program; the other branch is the return from the end of the program to start another pass through the input-processing-output operations. The term *loop* comes from the closed path formed in the flow diagram by the return branch.

A Better Loop

A more graceful method of terminating a loop can be seen in program 4B (figure 4.2). The loop in this program includes lines 140 through 210. Notice how the IF statement in line 210 determines whether the program loops or ends. The variable C in lines 200 and 210 is called the loop counter. Every time the loop is completed, the variable C is increased by one. That is, the first time through the loop, line 200 raises C from zero to 1; the second time through, it is raised from 1 to 2. Since in this example we entered 2 as the number of trips (N), when C reaches 2, line 210 does not send the program back to line 140; rather, it "falls through" to the END statement in line 220.

EXAMPLE 4B   Miles Per Gallon (INPUT and GOTO Loop)

Problem   Write a program that uses a GOTO loop to print a list of your miles per gallon for a series of trips. Use INPUT statements to enter the number of trips, miles traveled, and gallons of gas used. Use a loop counter to stop the looping after the specified number of trips.

FIGURE 4.2

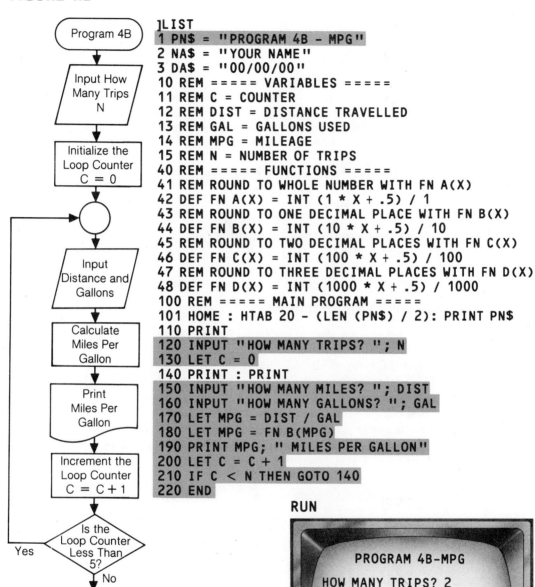

```
]LIST
1 PN$ = "PROGRAM 4B - MPG"
2 NA$ = "YOUR NAME"
3 DA$ = "00/00/00"
10 REM ===== VARIABLES =====
11 REM C = COUNTER
12 REM DIST = DISTANCE TRAVELLED
13 REM GAL = GALLONS USED
14 REM MPG = MILEAGE
15 REM N = NUMBER OF TRIPS
40 REM ===== FUNCTIONS =====
41 REM ROUND TO WHOLE NUMBER WITH FN A(X)
42 DEF FN A(X) = INT (1 * X + .5) / 1
43 REM ROUND TO ONE DECIMAL PLACE WITH FN B(X)
44 DEF FN B(X) = INT (10 * X + .5) / 10
45 REM ROUND TO TWO DECIMAL PLACES WITH FN C(X)
46 DEF FN C(X) = INT (100 * X + .5) / 100
47 REM ROUND TO THREE DECIMAL PLACES WITH FN D(X)
48 DEF FN D(X) = INT (1000 * X + .5) / 1000
100 REM ===== MAIN PROGRAM =====
101 HOME : HTAB 20 - (LEN (PN$) / 2): PRINT PN$
110 PRINT
120 INPUT "HOW MANY TRIPS? "; N
130 LET C = 0
140 PRINT : PRINT
150 INPUT "HOW MANY MILES? "; DIST
160 INPUT "HOW MANY GALLONS? "; GAL
170 LET MPG = DIST / GAL
180 LET MPG = FN B(MPG)
190 PRINT MPG; " MILES PER GALLON"
200 LET C = C + 1
210 IF C < N THEN GOTO 140
220 END
```

RUN

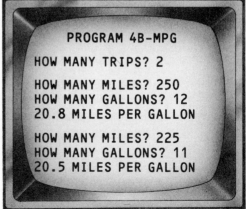

```
PROGRAM 4B-MPG

HOW MANY TRIPS? 2

HOW MANY MILES? 250
HOW MANY GALLONS? 12
20.8 MILES PER GALLON

HOW MANY MILES? 225
HOW MANY GALLONS? 11
20.5 MILES PER GALLON
```

Flowchart:

- Program 4B
- Input How Many Trips N
- Initialize the Loop Counter C = 0
- Input Distance and Gallons
- Calculate Miles Per Gallon
- Print Miles Per Gallon
- Increment the Loop Counter C = C + 1
- Is the Loop Counter Less Than 5? — Yes / No
- End

The first part of line 210 "IF C < N" we call a conditional. In any IF/ THEN statement, if the conditional (the statement between the IF and the THEN) is false, everything else on the line is ignored and the program goes on to the next line. Terminating a loop is only one use of this concept, as we'll see later. In this example, when C is no longer less than N, the program goes on to line 220. Notice that this technique could be used to avoid the crash that occurred in program 4A.

In some programs, you might not want to have to enter N. (For example, you might not know exactly how many entries there will be.) Another way to handle this loop would be to delete lines, 120, 130, and 200; change lines 150 and 210; and add a line 155 as follows:

```
150 INPUT "HOW MANY MILES (ENTER 9999 TO QUIT): ";DIST
155 IF DIST = 9999 THEN GOTO 220
210 GOTO 140
```

With the program changed like this, you can enter as many numbers as you wish and quit at any time by entering 9999 when prompted. This is one of many ways that programs can be made more convenient to use.

A New Form of the Input Statement

Notice the new version of the INPUT statement we have used in lines 120, 150, and 160 of program 4B. Compare this version with the combined PRINT and INPUT statements we have used previously. This new form of the INPUT statement provides a more concise way of printing a prompt and getting input from the user. It also avoids the question mark that is always printed with the other form of the INPUT statement; with this form you may use a question mark, colon, or other symbol at the end of your prompt. It is usually a good idea to put a space before the final quotation mark of this new form of INPUT statement to improve readability.

The Decision Symbol

The flowchart for program 4B introduces an important flowchart symbol, the diamond-shaped decision symbol. An expression called the conditional is written inside the decision symbol. In program 4B, the conditional is the expression C < N. Two branches leave the decision symbol, one marked "yes", the other marked "no". If the conditional is true, the branch marked yes is taken; if the conditional is false, the branch marked no is taken. In program 4B, the conditional is used to decide whether to loop back and calculate the miles per gallon for another trip, or to stop looping. In the BASIC program, the decision symbol is implemented by the following statement:

```
240 IF C < N THEN GOTO 150.
```

GOTO The GOTO statement tells the computer to jump to the line number that is written after the word GOTO and continue the run of the program.

IF/THEN The IF/THEN statement tells the computer to either execute or ignore the instruction following the word THEN, depending on the conditional (the statement written between the word IF and the word THEN). If the conditional is true, the computer will execute the instruction that follows the word THEN. If the conditional is false, the computer will ignore the instruction after the word THEN and go on to the next line.

EXAMPLE

```
180 IF X < 5 THEN GOTO 120
```

The above instruction tells the computer to check the value of X to see if it is less than 5. If the value of X is less than 5, the computer goes to line 120 for the next instruction. If X is not less than 5, then the computer ignores the GOTO 120 instruction and goes on to the next line after line 180.

SELF-TESTING QUESTIONS

Step through the program in each problem and write the output produced when the program runs. Assume that all programs include the lines 40 through 48 as shown in figure 4.2.

4.1
```
110 READ A
120 READ B
130 PRINT B
140 GOTO 110
150 DATA 4, 7, 3, 8, 9
```

4.2   Write everything that is printed when PROGRAM 4B–MPG is run with the following three trips as input.

> Trip 1: 412 miles and 11.8 gallons
> Trip 2: 360 miles and 21.2 gallons
> Trip 3: 385 miles and 14.5 gallons

4.3   An alternate version of PROGRAM 4B is given below. Write everything that is printed when this program is run using the input from the following two trips:

> Trip 1: 250 miles and 12 gallons
> Trip 2: 225 miles and 11 gallons

```
110 PRINT "ENTER A DISTANCE OR 9999"
120 PRINT "TO TERMINATE THE PROGRAM."
130 PRINT
140 INPUT "HOW MANY MILES? ";DIST
150 IF DIST = 9999 GOTO 210
160 INPUT "HOW MANY GALLONS?";GAL
170 LET MPG = DIST / GAL
180 LET MPG = FN B(MPG)
190 PRINT MPG;" MILES PER GALLON"
200 GOTO 130
210 END
```

4.4   The termination of the program in question 4.3 is quite abrupt. The
following version has a more graceful termination. Write everything that is printed when this program is run with the same input
as question 4.3.

```
110 PRINT "ENTER A DISTANCE OR 9999"
120 PRINT "TO TERMINATE THE PROGRAM"
130 LET C = 0
140 PRINT
150 INPUT "HOW MANY MILES? ";DIST
160 IF DIST = 9999 GOTO 230
170 INPUT "HOW MANY GALLONS? ";GAL
180 LET MPG = DIST / GAL
190 LET MPG = FN B(MPG)
200 PRINT MPG;" MILES PER GALLON"
210 LET C = C + 1
220 GOTO 140
230 PRINT
240 PRINT "PROGRAM TERMINATED AFTER"
250 PRINT C; " TRIPS. GOODBYE."
260 END
```

EXERCISES

Do Both Exercises

4.1 Load the program you wrote for exercise 3.1 and change the name of the program in line 1 to PROGRAM 4A–READ/DATA LOOP. Now change the program so that it prints out the number of eggs and shrimp needed for various values of GUESTS. Use READ/DATA statements to enter the different values of guests (use at least four values). Use a GOTO loop and a loop counter to terminate the program after the desired number of loops. Put a print statement inside the loop so that the printout looks like this:

```
2 GUESTS - 3 EGGS 3 SHRIMP
3 GUESTS - 4 EGGS 4 SHRIMP
5 GUESTS - 6 EGGS 7 SHRIMP
9 GUESTS - 11 EGGS 12 SHRIMP
```

As before, use 1.25 eggs and 1.33 shrimp per person and round off to the nearest whole egg or shrimp. When the program runs properly, save it and get the usual list and run on paper.

TIPS

1. Be sure to set the loop counter to zero before entering the loop.
2. Be sure you have one DATA value for each time the loop will be executed.
3. If the program runs endlessly and the cursor does not reappear, it means your loop counter is not working. Use CONTROL-C to stop the program. (Remember the ⟨Ctrl⟩ key and the ⟨C⟩ key must be held down at the same time.)

4.2 Load program 4.1 and change the name of the program in line 1 to PROGRAM 4B–INPUT LOOP. Then modify the program so that it has a loop and a loop counter and uses INPUT statements to let you enter various values of GUESTS. The program should print a prompt before getting the INPUT and print out the value of EGGS and SHRIMP each time through the loop. As before, use 1.25 eggs and 1.33 shrimp per person and round to the nearest whole egg or shrimp. Your run should look like the following:

```
HOW MANY GUESTS?2
3 EGGS 3 SHRIMP
HOW MANY GUESTS?3
4 EGGS 4 SHRIMP
     .
     .
     .
etc.
```

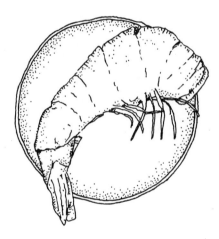

TIPS

1. Remember that during the run, the program is expecting input from the keyboard. At this time commands such as LIST, RUN, LOAD, etc., will not be executed.
2. If the program loops endlessly, the loop counter is not working and you must use CONTROL-C to stop things.
3. Look at program 3B to help remind you of what changes will be necessary.

GOING AROUND AGAIN
Looping With a FOR/NEXT Statement

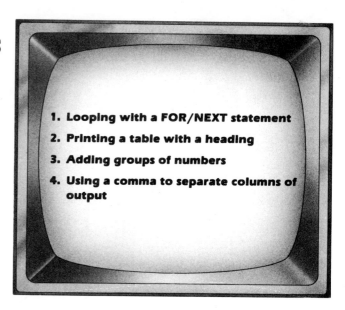

FOR/NEXT LOOPS

A FOR/NEXT loop is more sophisticated than a GOTO loop; it runs faster and has a built-in loop counter. Whenever the computer sees a FOR statement, it knows that this marks the beginning of a FOR/NEXT loop. It does whatever it's directed to do and when it reaches the NEXT statement it goes back to the beginning of the loop (if the loop counter has not passed its limit) and starts again. If the loop counter is above the limit, the program skips the loop and goes to the line following the NEXT statement.

Celsius to Fahrenheit

In program 5A in figure 5.1, we see a simple FOR/NEXT loop with only two variables used in the whole program. F stands for degrees Fahrenheit and C does double duty since it stands for both degrees Celsius and the loop counter. The program begins by printing the program name, two blank lines, and then, in line 120, the headings for each column. (Notice the comma between the two headings — we'll explain this later in this section.)

The loop begins at line 140 with the FOR/NEXT statement:

```
FOR C = 0 TO 100 STEP 10
```

The C in this line is the loop counter; the first part of the line tells the computer to set C to 0. The STEP 10 command tells the computer to increase C by 10 each time through the loop. (The STEP command is optional; if it is left out the loop steps by one.) Within the loop, F is calculated by using a formula to convert from Celsius to Fahrenheit (line 150) and then C and F are printed (line 160).

FOR and NEXT The FOR and NEXT statements are always used together to form a loop that counts the number of times the instructions inside the loop are repeated. The general form of a FOR/NEXT loop is:

(line number) FOR (variable name) = a to b STEP c

. . . .
. . . . } Instructions inside loop

(line number) NEXT (same variable name as in FOR statement)

1. STEP c is optional; if omitted, the step defaults to 1.
2. The variable named on the right of the FOR statement is called the loop counter (or control variable) of the FOR/NEXT loop.
3. The letters a, b, and c in the FOR statement represent numbers, variable names, or arithmetic expressions. During the first pass through the loop, the loop counter has the value of the number, variable, or expression represented by the letter a. At the end of each pass through the loop, the value of the number, variable, or expression represented by the letter c is added to the loop counter. If the number in the loop counter is not greater than the number represented by the letter b, then the loop is repeated again. If the loop counter exceeds the value represented by b, then the computer goes on to the instruction after the NEXT statement.

EXAMPLE

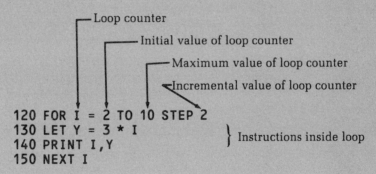

```
            Loop counter
            Initial value of loop counter
            Maximum value of loop counter
            Incremental value of loop counter

120 FOR I = 2 TO 10 STEP 2
130 LET Y = 3 * I
140 PRINT I,Y          } Instructions inside loop
150 NEXT I
```

The comma in line 160, like the one in line 120, splits the output into two columns. In Applesoft BASIC, the screen is divided into three sections, or columns (this program uses only the first two). A comma in a PRINT statement tells the computer to print whatever follows the comma in the next screen column.

When the computer sees the NEXT statement in line 170 for the first time it changes C from 0 to 10 and then checks to see if C is greater than 100 (the limit set in line 140). Since C is not greater than 100, the program loops back to the FOR statement in line 140 and executes the loop again. The program repeats the loop until C is greater than 100. In this example, C will have the value of 110 when the looping stops.

When C is greater than 100, the program skips to the line after the NEXT statement (line 180 in this example), and the program ends.

A Modified Decision Symbol

One type of conditional, the IF/THEN statement, was introduced in program 4B. Program 5A in figure 5.1 introduces a second type of conditional, the FOR/NEXT statement. FOR/NEXT statements are a convenient method for creating a loop when a definite number of passes through the loop are required. A modified decision symbol is used in this text to indicate the beginning of a FOR/NEXT loop, and the circle is used to indicate the end of the loop, as shown in the flowchart for program 5A.

EXAMPLE 5A   Celsius to Fahrenheit (FOR/NEXT Loop)

Problem   Write a program that uses a FOR/NEXT loop to print a two-column table of degrees Celsius vs degrees Fahrenheit. Print CELSIUS at the top of the Celsius column and FAHRENHEIT at the top of the Fahrenheit column for your column headings.

FIGURE 5.1

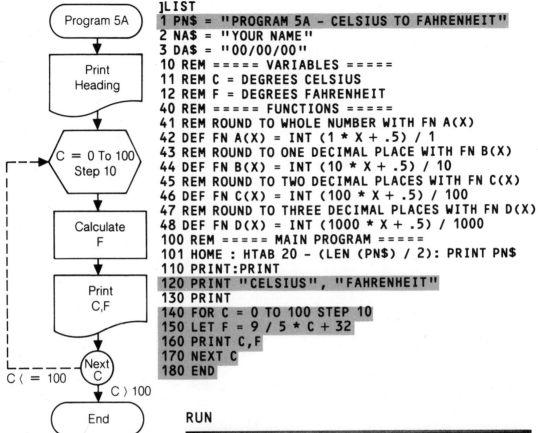

```
]LIST
1 PN$ = "PROGRAM 5A - CELSIUS TO FAHRENHEIT"
2 NA$ = "YOUR NAME"
3 DA$ = "00/00/00"
10 REM ===== VARIABLES =====
11 REM C = DEGREES CELSIUS
12 REM F = DEGREES FAHRENHEIT
40 REM ===== FUNCTIONS =====
41 REM ROUND TO WHOLE NUMBER WITH FN A(X)
42 DEF FN A(X) = INT (1 * X + .5) / 1
43 REM ROUND TO ONE DECIMAL PLACE WITH FN B(X)
44 DEF FN B(X) = INT (10 * X + .5) / 10
45 REM ROUND TO TWO DECIMAL PLACES WITH FN C(X)
46 DEF FN C(X) = INT (100 * X + .5) / 100
47 REM ROUND TO THREE DECIMAL PLACES WITH FN D(X)
48 DEF FN D(X) = INT (1000 * X + .5) / 1000
100 REM ===== MAIN PROGRAM =====
101 HOME : HTAB 20 - (LEN (PN$) / 2): PRINT PN$
110 PRINT:PRINT
120 PRINT "CELSIUS", "FAHRENHEIT"
130 PRINT
140 FOR C = 0 TO 100 STEP 10
150 LET F = 9 / 5 * C + 32
160 PRINT C,F
170 NEXT C
180 END
```

RUN

```
PROGRAM 5A-CELSIUS TO FAHRENHEIT

CELSIUS       FAHRENHEIT

0             32
10            50
20            68
30            86
40            104
50            122
60            140
70            158
80            176
90            194
100           212
```

IT ALL ADDS UP

In program 5B we have a flexible program that allows us to tell the program how many numbers we want to add, enter them at the keyboard, and then have the sum printed for us on the screen. Unlike the loop counter in program 5A, the loop counter in this program (designated by I) is not used for anything else. The letters I, J, and K are often used by programmers as loop counters in situations like this.

The program begins by printing the program name, two blank lines, and then in line 120 setting SUM to 0. Line 130 asks us how many numbers we will be entering, line 140 gets the answer, and line 150 prints another blank line.

The FOR/NEXT loop in this program begins at line 160:

FOR I = 1 TO N

Notice that this line is somewhat different than the line at the beginning of the loop in program 5A. For one thing, we have left out the STEP command which means that the loop counter will increase by only one each time through the loop. Another difference is that we have used a variable (N) as the upper limit of the loop rather than a number. This adds flexibility to the program because the loop will execute as many times as there are numbers we want to add. Just as the variables I, J, and K mentioned above are used as loop counters, N is often used as a limit variable for loops.

Notice that all three of the variables (I, X, and SUM) change their value every time through the loop. Each time through the loop, X is whatever number we enter from the keyboard, SUM is the previous SUM plus the number just entered, and the loop counter, I, is increased by one. In this particular run of the program, after three times through the loop all three numbers have been added to SUM (which was set to zero in line 120), and, when we get to the NEXT statement in line 190, I is set to 4. Since 4 is greater than N (which in this run of the program is set to 3), the program skips to line 200. In line 210 the results are printed and in line 220 the program ends.

EXAMPLE 5B   Sum of N Numbers (FOR/NEXT Loop)

Problem   Write a program that asks: "HOW MANY NUMBERS DO YOU WANT TO ADD?", inputs the answer to the question, inputs each number to be added, and prints: SUM = followed by the sum of the numbers entered.

FIGURE 5.2

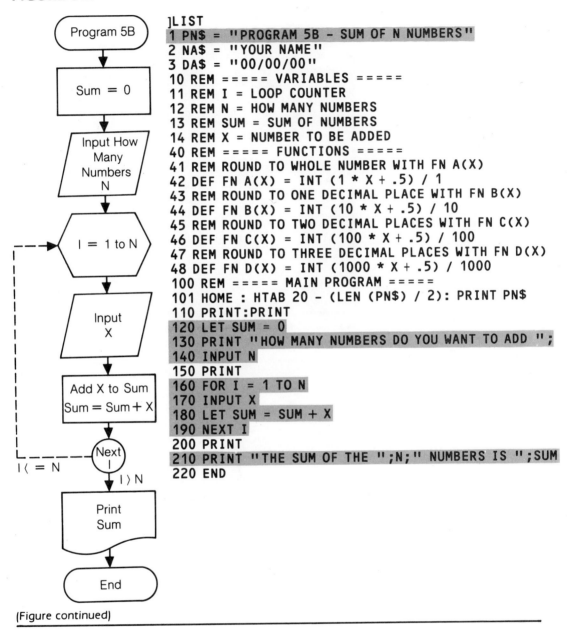

```
]LIST
1 PN$ = "PROGRAM 5B - SUM OF N NUMBERS"
2 NA$ = "YOUR NAME"
3 DA$ = "00/00/00"
10 REM = = = = = VARIABLES = = = = =
11 REM I = LOOP COUNTER
12 REM N = HOW MANY NUMBERS
13 REM SUM = SUM OF NUMBERS
14 REM X = NUMBER TO BE ADDED
40 REM = = = = = FUNCTIONS = = = = =
41 REM ROUND TO WHOLE NUMBER WITH FN A(X)
42 DEF FN A(X) = INT (1 * X + .5) / 1
43 REM ROUND TO ONE DECIMAL PLACE WITH FN B(X)
44 DEF FN B(X) = INT (10 * X + .5) / 10
45 REM ROUND TO TWO DECIMAL PLACES WITH FN C(X)
46 DEF FN C(X) = INT (100 * X + .5) / 100
47 REM ROUND TO THREE DECIMAL PLACES WITH FN D(X)
48 DEF FN D(X) = INT (1000 * X + .5) / 1000
100 REM = = = = = MAIN PROGRAM = = = = =
101 HOME : HTAB 20 - (LEN (PN$) / 2): PRINT PN$
110 PRINT:PRINT
120 LET SUM = 0
130 PRINT "HOW MANY NUMBERS DO YOU WANT TO ADD ";
140 INPUT N
150 PRINT
160 FOR I = 1 TO N
170 INPUT X
180 LET SUM = SUM + X
190 NEXT I
200 PRINT
210 PRINT "THE SUM OF THE ";N;" NUMBERS IS ";SUM
220 END
```

The flowchart for Program 5B:

- Program 5B
- Sum = 0
- Input How Many Numbers N
- I = 1 to N
- Input X
- Add X to Sum / Sum = Sum + X
- Next I (I < = N loops back; I > N continues)
- Print Sum
- End

(Figure continued)

(Figure 5.2 continued)

RUN

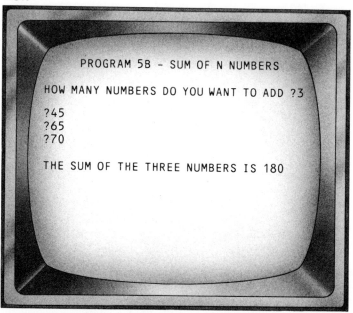

```
        PROGRAM 5B - SUM OF N NUMBERS

HOW MANY NUMBERS DO YOU WANT TO ADD ?3

?45
?65
?70

THE SUM OF THE THREE NUMBERS IS 180
```

SELF-TESTING QUESTIONS

EXAMPLE: Step through the following program and write the output produced when the program runs.

```
110 LET S = 0
120 READ N
130 IF N = 9999 THEN PRINT "SUM = ";S : END
140 LET S = S + N
150 GOTO 120
160 DATA 4, 8, 9, 6, 9999
```

Construct a step-through table as shown below. Each row represents one pass through the loop. Values of variables are printed to show the changes that occur.

Line Number:	120	120	130	140
Variables:	S	N	N = 9999?	S
Pass 1:	0	4	no	4
Pass 2:	4	8	no	12
Pass 3:	12	9	no	21
Pass 4:	21	6	no	27
Pass 5:	27	9999	yes	

ANSWER: SUM = 27

Step through the program in each problem and write the output produced when the program runs.

5.1
```
110 PRINT "YARDS","FEET"
120 FOR Y = 1 TO 5
130 LET F = 3 * Y
140 PRINT Y,F
150 NEXT Y
```

5.2
```
110 FOR Y = 1 TO 5
120 PRINT "YARDS","FEET"
130 LET F = 3 * Y
140 PRINT Y,F
150 NEXT Y
```

5.3   Assume that the following sequence of numbers is entered during a run of the program below: 7, 18, 5, 9, 6, 9999. Write the output produced by the program.

```
110 LET S = 0
120 LET C = 0
130 PRINT "ENTER NUMBERS TO BE ADDED"
140 PRINT "OR ENTER 9999 TO QUIT"
150 INPUT N
160 IF N = 9999 GOTO 200
170 LET S = S + N
180 LET C = C + 1
190 GOTO 150
200 PRINT C;" NUMBERS WERE ADDED"
210 PRINT "THE TOTAL IS ";S
220 END
```

5.4
```
110 FOR I =1 TO 5
120 PRINT I;
130 NEXT I
```

5.5
```
110 FOR I = 1 TO 8 STEP 2
120 PRINT I;
130 NEXT I
```

5.6
```
110 FOR I = 1 TO 15 STEP 3
120 PRINT I;
130 NEXT I
```

5.7
```
110 FOR I = 1 TO 4
120 READ X
130 PRINT X;
140 NEXT I
150 DATA 8, 7, 9, 4, 3
```

5.8
```
110 READ X
120 FOR I = 1 TO 8 STEP 3
130 PRINT X;
140 NEXT I
150 DATA 3, 8, 7
```

5.9
```
110 FOR I = 1 TO 5
120 READ X
130 PRINT X;
140 NEXT I
150 PRINT X
160 DATA 5, 9, 4, 7, 8, 2
```

5.10
```
110 FOR I = 1 TO 10 STEP 2
120 READ X
130 PRINT I;X;
140 NEXT I
150 DATA 5, 4, 3, 2, 1
```

EXERCISES

Choose One of the Following

5.1 Write a program that uses a FOR/NEXT loop to produce the table of miles, gallons, and miles per gallon shown below. Use INPUT statements to enter 10 sets of miles and gallon values. Round the MPG values to the nearest hundredth. Use hand calculations or a calculator to verify two of the MPG values in the table.

MILES	GALLONS	MPG
362	18.4	19.67
.	.	.
.	.	.
245	12.6	19.44

TIPS

1. Use a separate loop counter like I.
2. Use commas to format the columns on the screen.
3. Don't put the line that prints the headings inside a loop.

5.2 The state sales tax was increased from 4 percent to 5 percent. Your boss wants a sales tax table for use by the check-out person. The tax values are to be rounded to the nearest cent. Your table should go up to at least a dollar and should produce a table like the one below.

PRICE	SALES TAX
.01	0
.02	0
.	.
.	.
.20	.01
.	.
.	.
1.00	.05

TIPS

1. Use a comma to format the two columns.
2. Print the headings before entering the loop.
3. Use the variable PRICE as both the price and the loop counter.
4. Use FN C to round PRICE and TAX to the nearest cent.

5.3 An airline is preparing a booklet for passenger use on long-distance flights. They would like to include a table for converting altitude from feet to miles. Write a program that will use a FOR/NEXT loop to produce the altitude conversion table shown below. The conversion formula for feet-to-miles is:

`MILES = FEET / 5280`

Round the miles values to the nearest hundredth. Use hand calculations or a calculator to check at least two of your altitude-in-miles values.

ALTITUDE IN FEET	ALTITUDE IN MILES
0	0
1000	.19
2000	.38
3000	.57
4000	.76
.	.
.	.
.	.
50000	9.47

TIPS

1. Use a comma to print the two columns.
2. Print the headings before entering the loop.
3. Use one line to print ALTITUDE, ALTITUDE and another line to print IN FEET, IN MILES.
4. Use the variable FEET for both the altitude in feet and also the loop counter.

5.4   Write a program that will use a FOR/NEXT loop to produce the following table of X, X squared, and the square root of X for values of X from 1 to 10. Round the square-root values to the nearest hundredth. Use hand calculations or a calculator to check at least two of the values of X squared and square root of X.

X	X SQUARED	SQUARE ROOT OF X
1	1	1
2	4	1.41
3	9	1.73
.	.	.
.	.	.
.	.	.
10	100	3.16

TIPS

1. Print the headings before entering the loop.
2. Use one line to print , , SQUARE. Use a second line to print , X, ROOT and a third line to print X, SQUARED, OF X.
3. Use commas to separate the three columns.
4. Use X * X for X squared.
5. Use X ^ 0.5 for the square root of X.
6. Use X as the loop counter.

5.5 Two thousand dollars is invested at 14 percent interest compounded yearly. Write a program using a FOR/NEXT loop that will produce the table shown below. The compound interest formula is:

$$A = P * (1 + I / 100) \char`^ N$$

where: A = amount after N years
P = original amount deposited
I = yearly interest rate
N = number of years

Round the AMOUNT values to the nearest hundredth. Use hand calculations or a calculator to check at least two of the values of AMOUNT in the table.

YEAR	AMOUNT
1	2280
2	2599.2
.	.
.	.
.	.
20	27486.98

TIPS

1. Use the variable N for years and the loop counter.
2. Print the headings before entering the loop.
3. Use the variable names listed above.
4. Use commas to separate the two columns.

5.6 The Ark Manufacturing Company produces an item called Noah's Gizmo. In an effort to maximize profit, the accounting department made a cost analysis of each product. A fixed cost of $1250 per day was charged to Noah's Gizmo. Direct production costs are $120 per Gizmo, and secondary costs such as breakdowns and overtime pay are closely approximated by $0.75 * N ^ 2$ dollars per day. Profit is given by the following equation in which N is the number of Gizmos produced each day.

$$\text{PROFIT} = \underbrace{212 * N}_{\text{Revenue}} - \underbrace{(1250 + 120 * N + 0.75 * N ^ 2)}_{\text{Cost}}$$

Write a program that will use a FOR/NEXT loop to produce the profit table shown below. All profit values should be rounded to the nearest cent. Circle the maximum value of profit. Use hand calculations or a calculator to check at least two of the values of PROFIT in the table.

# OF GIZMOS	PROFIT
5	-808.75
10	-405
15	-38.75
.	.
.	.
.	.
100	450

TIPS

1. Use N as number of Gizmos produced and also as the loop counter.
2. Print the headings outside the loop.
3. Use commas to separate the columns.
4. This is a difficult program; try it at your own risk.

5.7 Write a program that will use a FOR/NEXT loop to read ten scores from a DATA statement and compute the sum and average of the 10 scores. Then print a table with two columns as shown below. Round the average value to the nearest hundredth. Use hand calculations or a calculator to check at least two of the values of SCORE and SCORE MINUS AVERAGE.

THE AVERAGE VALUE IS 14.2

SCORE	SCORE MINUS AVERAGE
18.47	4.27
11.68	-2.52
.	.
.	.
.	.
17.84	3.64

TIPS

1. Write one FOR/NEXT loop that calculates the average value and another FOR/NEXT loop that prints the table.
2. You will have to use the RESTORE command between the two parts from tip 1.
3. Use the variable I as a loop counter; don't use I for anything else.
4. Do *not* use SCORE as a variable; it contains OR which is a reserved word.
5. This program is fairly difficult; don't try it unless you're prepared for some frustration.

CHAPTER 6

WHERE DO WE GO FROM HERE?

Branching With IF Statements

NEW CONCEPTS TAUGHT

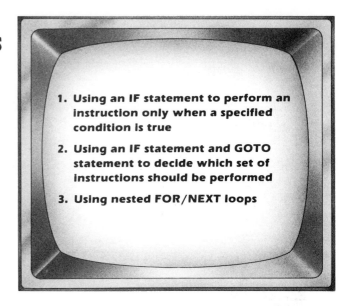

1. **Using an IF statement to perform an instruction only when a specified condition is true**

2. **Using an IF statement and GOTO statement to decide which set of instructions should be performed**

3. **Using nested FOR/NEXT loops**

IF STATEMENTS

In previous programs, all lines of the program have been executed in each run. Many times, however, we need to write sections of a program that will only be executed under certain conditions. This is accomplished with an IF statement which tells the computer that the instructions that follow it should only be performed if the conditions are right.

IF/THEN The general form of the IF/THEN statement is:

(line number) IF *(conditional)* THEN *(one or more instructions separated by colons, :)*

If the conditional is true, then the computer will execute all of the instructions that follow the word THEN. If the conditional is false, then the computer will ignore all of the instructions after the word THEN and go on to the next line.

EXAMPLE

    180 IF X < 5 THEN X = X + 1 : Y = Y + 2

The above instruction tells the computer to check the value of X to see if it is less than 5. If the value of X is less than 5, then the computer adds 1 to the value of X and adds 2 to the value of Y. If X is not less than 5, then the computer ignores both of the instructions to the right of the word THEN and goes on to the next line after line 180.

Gross Pay

Program 6A in figure 6.1 shows how to use an IF statement. We need a way of calculating overtime pay and adding it to gross pay for employees who work over 40 hours per week, but we would soon go broke if we gave everyone overtime pay regardless of the number of hours they worked. One way of handling this is to have instructions like the ones on lines 140 and 150 which are performed only if a specified condition is true (or false). In program 6A, the variable H is used for hours worked and the variable W is the wage rate per hour. If the person works 40 hours or less their pay is simply H times W with no overtime pay. This is accomplished entirely by line 140. If their hours (H) total more than 40, line 140 will not be executed and their pay (P) will be calculated by line 150.

Let's take a closer look at line 150. Since the employee has worked more than forty hours, we need to calculate the first forty of their hours at the regular rate and then add the pay they should receive for their overtime hours at the overtime rate of time and a half. We could use separate lines to do this but it is simpler and saves memory if we can do it all on one line. The equation in line 150 does all three of these at once. To the left of the + sign we see the first 40 hours are multiplied by W to give the pay for the employee's first 40 hours. To the right of the + sign we see their total hours minus the ones we have already accounted for (H – 40) are multiplied by the overtime wage rate (1.5 * W). When these two products are added together, they yield P, or gross pay.

Notice that in a single run of the program, lines 140 and 150 can't both be executed. We describe this by saying that they are mutually exclusive. If one is executed it is impossible for the other one to be executed and vice versa. When using mutually exclusive conditionals like this, it is important to make sure that the conditionals, when taken together, take care of all possibilities. If line 140 stated the condition as H < 40 instead of H < = 40, the program would fail when H was exactly equal to 40 because neither line would be executed; then line 180 would print GROSS PAY IS 0 DOLLARS. A mistake like this can lead to some very unhappy employees.

EXAMPLE 6A   Gross Pay (IF/THEN)

Problem   Write a program that will input the number of hours worked in one week and the hourly wage rate. Calculate the gross pay using time and a half for all hours over forty. Print the message "GROSS PAY IS" followed by the amount of gross pay.

FIGURE 6.1

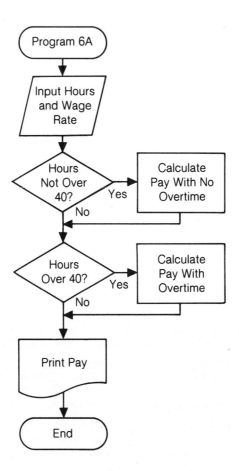

(Figure continued)

(Figure 6.1 continued)

```
]LIST
1 PN$ = "PROGRAM 6A - GROSS PAY"
2 NA$ = "YOUR NAME"
3 DA$ = "00/00/00"
10 REM ===== VARIABLES =====
11 REM H = HOURS WORKED
12 REM P = GROSS PAY
13 REM W = HOURLY WAGE RATE
40 REM ===== FUNCTIONS =====
41 REM ROUND TO WHOLE NUMBER WITH FN A(X)
42 DEF FN A(X) = INT (1 * X + .5) / 1
43 REM ROUND TO ONE DECIMAL PLACE WITH FN B(X)
44 DEF FN B(X) = INT (10 * X + .5) / 10
45 REM ROUND TO TWO DECIMAL PLACES WITH FN C(X)
46 DEF FN C(X) = INT (100 * X + .5) / 100
47 REM ROUND TO THREE DECIMAL PLACES WITH FN D(X)
48 DEF FN D(X) = INT (1000 * X + .5) / 1000
100 REM ===== MAIN PROGRAM =====
101 HOME : HTAB 20 - (LEN (PN$) / 2): PRINT PN$
110 PRINT : PRINT
120 INPUT "TYPE THE NUMBER OF HOURS WORKED: "; H
130 INPUT "TYPE THE HOURLY WAGE RATE: "; W
140 IF H < = 40 THEN P = H * W
150 IF H > 40 THEN P = 40 * W + (H - 40) * 1.5 * W
160 LET P = FN C(P)
170 PRINT
180 PRINT "GROSS PAY IS ";P;" DOLLARS."
200 END : REM ***END PROGRAM***
```

RUN 6A (to check the equation in line 140)

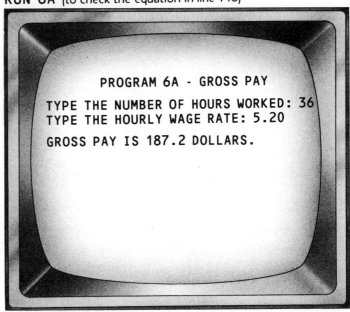

```
PROGRAM 6A - GROSS PAY

TYPE THE NUMBER OF HOURS WORKED: 36
TYPE THE HOURLY WAGE RATE: 5.20

GROSS PAY IS 187.2 DOLLARS.
```

(Figure continued)

(Figure 6.1 continued)

RUN 6A (to check the equation in line 150)

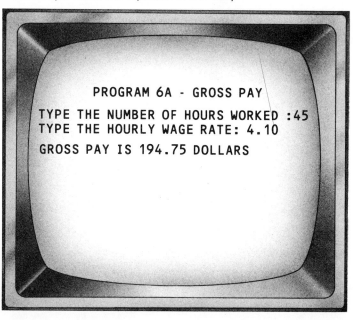

```
        PROGRAM 6A - GROSS PAY

TYPE THE NUMBER OF HOURS WORKED :45
TYPE THE HOURLY WAGE RATE: 4.10

GROSS PAY IS 194.75 DOLLARS
```

RELATIONAL SYMBOLS   A conditional consists of two expressions separated by one of the following relational symbols:

Relational Symbol	Meaning
=	equal to
>	greater than
<	less than
< > or > <	not equal to
< =	less than or equal to
> =	greater than or equal to

Example relational expressions:
$A = B + C$
$X - Y < = 27$
$2 * X - 2 > = 5 * Y + 2$

The Gas Bill

Program 6B in figure 6.2 is a little more complicated than program 6A, but it works much the same way. One difference is that it requires four mutually exclusive statements; these appear in lines 150, 160, 170, and 180. If a customer uses 3 CCF (Hundred Cubic Feet) of gas or less in one month, they are charged a flat rate of $3.50 per month. This is calculated in line 150, and if the CCF is 3 or less, the program jumps to line 190 where the output is printed. If the customer used more than 3 CCF of gas, but not more than 40, their bill is calculated in line 160 by adding the cost of the first 3 CCF to the cost of the other CCF used; again, the program jumps to line 190 to print the bill. If they used over 40 CCF but not more than 100, what they owe is calculated in line 170. If they used over 100 CCF their bill is calculated in line 180. Notice that if the conditions stated in lines 150, 160, and 170 are all false, the customer must have used more than 100 CCF of gas. Therefore no IF statement is necessary in line 180.

Since we want only one of these four statements to be executed, it is important to have the GOTO 190 at the end of each conditional; otherwise with a CCF amount of 3, for example, all of the statements would execute because 3 is less than 40, less than 100, and so forth. What this means is that the statements are not mutually exclusive in the strict sense of the phrase; however, we have made them mutually exclusive in the execution of the program by the addition of the GOTO statements. As this program is written, only one of these statements could be executed in a single run of the program.

EXAMPLE 6B   Gas Bill (IF/THEN)

Problem   The Sota Gas Company has the following rate structure for natural gas (note: CCF = hundred cubic feet).

- ☐ First 3 CCF, $ 3.50 flat fee
- ☐ Next 37 CCF, $ per CCF   0.35
- ☐ Next 60 CCF, $ per CCF   0.31
- ☐ CCF over 100, $ per CCF   0.30

The present and previous meter readings are to be entered using an INPUT statement. Write a program that prints the CCF used and the monthly gas bill.

FIGURE 6.2

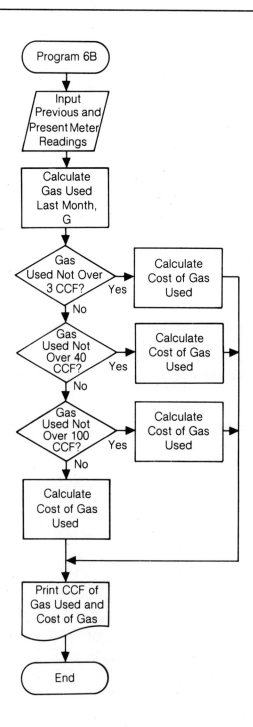

(Figure continued)

(Figure 6.2 continued)

```
]LIST
1 PN$ = "PROGRAM 6B - GAS BILL"
2 NA$ = "YOUR NAME"
3 DA$ = "00/00/00"
10 REM ===== VARIABLES =====
11 REM C = MONTHLY GAS BILL
12 REM G = CCF OF GAS USED
13 REM P1 = PREVIOUS METER READING
14 REM P2 = PRESENT METER READING
40 REM ===== FUNCTIONS =====
41 REM ROUND TO WHOLE NUMBER WITH FN A(X)
42 DEF FN A(X) = INT (1 * X + .5) / 1
43 REM ROUND TO ONE DECIMAL PLACE WITH FN B(X)
44 DEF FN B(X) = INT (10 * X + .5) / 10
45 REM ROUND TO TWO DECIMAL PLACES WITH FN C(X)
46 DEF FN C(X) = INT (100 * X + .5) / 100
47 REM ROUND TO THREE DECIMAL PLACES WITH FN D(X)
48 DEF FN D(X) = INT (1000 * X + .5) / 1000
100 REM ===== MAIN PROGRAM =====
101 HOME : HTAB 20 - (LEN (PN$) / 2): PRINT PN$
110 PRINT
120 INPUT "THE PREVIOUS READING IN CCF IS "; P1
130 INPUT "THE PRESENT READING IN CCF IS "; P2
140 G = P2 - P1
150 IF G < = 3 THEN C = 3.50 : GOTO 190
160 IF G < = 40 THEN C = 3.50 + (G-3) * 0.35 : GOTO 190
170 IF G < = 100 THEN C = 3.5 + 37 * 0.35 + (G-40) * 0.31 : GOTO 190
180 LET C = 3.5 + 37 * 0.35 + 60 * 0.31 + (G-100) * 0.30
190 PRINT "YOU USED ";G;" CCF THIS MONTH"
200 PRINT "YOUR GAS BILL THIS MONTH IS $";C
210 END : REM END OF PROGRAM
```

(Figure continued)

(Figure 6.2 continued)

RUN 6B (to check equation in line 150)

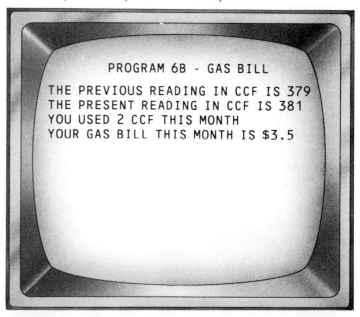

RUN 6B (to check equation in line 160)

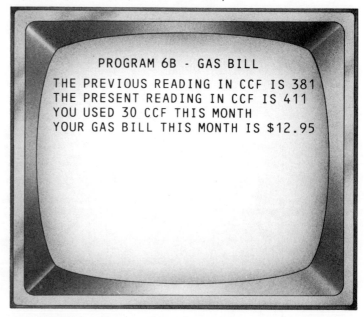

(Figure continued)

(Figure 6.2 continued)

RUN 6B (to check equation in line 170)

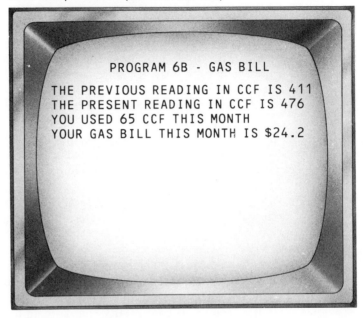

```
        PROGRAM 6B - GAS BILL

THE PREVIOUS READING IN CCF IS 411
THE PRESENT READING IN CCF IS 476
YOU USED 65 CCF THIS MONTH
YOUR GAS BILL THIS MONTH IS $24.2
```

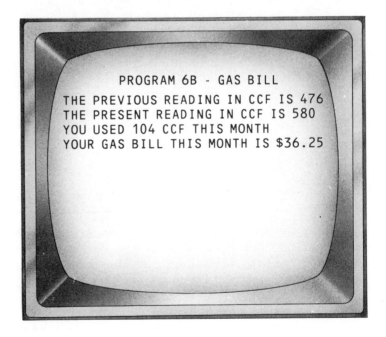

```
        PROGRAM 6B - GAS BILL
THE PREVIOUS READING IN CCF IS 476
THE PRESENT READING IN CCF IS 580
YOU USED 104 CCF THIS MONTH
YOUR GAS BILL THIS MONTH IS $36.25
```

Getting Rich

Program 6C is a more complicated program than the other two; it involves several steps and has one loop inside another loop. We call loops set up like this "nested" loops. In this program the inside loop includes lines 150 through 210 and the outside loop includes lines 140 through 230. The outer loop is performed three times because we want the results to include three years. The inner loop executes twelve times because there are twelve months in each year. It makes sense to call this inner loop the month loop and the outer loop the year loop.

In a complex program like this, it is best to try to copy the real-life process step by step. In this program, for example, we should try to follow the procedures of the bank, step by step.

In line 17 we have set the initial balance in the account and in line 18 we have set the yearly interest rate. In line 19 we set the value of the monthly deposit. These three values will not change during the program and there is no sense in setting their value each time through the loop; this would only slow down the program. Therefore we set their value before we enter the loops.

With nested loops it is often best to think about the inside loop first. Lines 160 through 200 describe the events of each month as they happen. In line 160 you deposit your hard-earned $120 on the first of the month and the bank adds it to the amount already in the account. Notice that A, the amount in the account, is continually changing. In line 170 the bank figures out the interest for this month (I) by multiplying the amount in the account by the yearly interest rate (R) divided by 12 to get monthly interest and divided by 100 to convert it to a proper decimal. In line 180 the interest calculated in line 170 is added to the amount in the account to get a new value of A. In line 190, A is rounded to the nearest cent, and in line 200 one line of the table is printed. Line 200 prints the number of the year (Y), a hyphen, and the number of the month (M); then, in the next column, the money in the account (A). The month loop executes twelve times, and then the program goes on to line 220 which prints the blank line between years. After the year loop has executed three times (each time meaning twelve executions of the month loop), the program ends and it's time to try to figure out what to do with all that money.

EXAMPLE 6C   Savings Account   (Nested FOR/NEXT Loops)

Problem   You have a savings account in the Duckburg City Bank. The account earns 9.6% interest compounded monthly. At the end of each month, the bank computes the interest earned during the month, adds the interest to the account, and prints a statement showing the balance in the account. The December statement showed a balance of $3500. Write a program that will print your account balance each month for the next three years if you make a deposit of $120 on the first of each month.

FIGURE 6.3

```
]LIST
1 PN$ = " PROGRAM 6C - SAVINGS ACCOUNT"
2 NA$ = "YOUR NAME"
3 DA$ = "00/00/00"
10 REM ===== VARIABLES =====
11 REM A = AMOUNT IN ACCOUNT
12 REM D = MONTHLY DEPOSIT
13 REM I = MONTHLY INTEREST
14 REM M = NUMBER OF MONTHS
15 REM R = YEARLY INTEREST RATE
16 REM Y = NUMBER OF YEARS
17 LET A = 3500                              ← Assign initial amount in account
18 LET R = 9.6                               ← Assign interest rate
19 LET D = 120                               ← Assign amount of monthly deposit
40 REM ===== FUNCTIONS =====
41 REM ROUND TO WHOLE NUMBER WITH FN A(X)
42 DEF FN A(X) = INT (1 * X + .5) / 1
43 REM ROUND TO ONE DECIMAL PLACE WITH FN B(X)
44 DEF FN B(X) = INT (10 * X + .5) / 10
45 REM ROUND TO TWO DECIMAL PLACES WITH FN C(X)
46 DEF FN C(X) = INT (100 * + .5) / 100
47 REM ROUND TO THREE DECIMAL PLACES WITH FN D(X)
48 DEF FN D(X) = INT (1000 * X + .5) / 1000
100 REM ===== MAIN PROGRAM =====
101 HOME : HTAB 20 - (LEN (PN$) / 2): PRINT PN$
110 PRINT "YEAR-MONTH", "BALANCE ON LAST DAY"
120 PRINT "----------", "-------------------"
130 PRINT
140 FOR Y = 1 TO 3
150 FOR M = 1 TO 12
160 LET A = A + D              ← Make monthly deposit on first of month
170 LET I = A * R / 100 / 12   ← Calculate interest on last day of month
180 LET A = A + I              ← Add interest to account on last day
190 LET A = FN C(A)
200 PRINT Y;"-";M,A            ← Print one line in table
210 NEXT M
220 PRINT                      ← Print blank line between years
230 NEXT Y
240 PRINT
250 END
```

(Figure continued)

(Figure 6.3 continued)

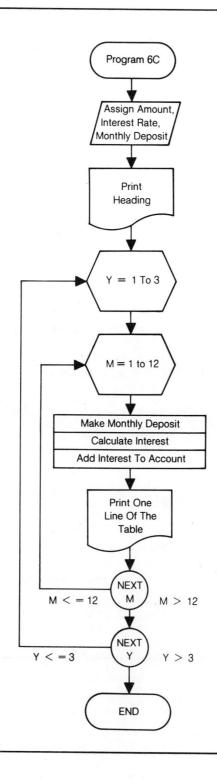

(Figure continued)

(Figure 6.3 continued)

RUN

PROGRAM 6C - SAVINGS ACCOUNT

YEAR-MONTH	BALANCE ON LAST DAY
1-1	3648.96
1-2	3799.11
1-3	3950.46
1-4	4103.02
1-5	4256.8
1-6	4411.81
1-7	4568.06
1-8	4725.56
1-9	4884.32
1-10	5044.35
1-11	5205.66
1-12	5368.27
2-1	5532.18
2-2	5697.4
2-3	5863.94
2-4	6031.81
2-5	6201.02
2-6	6371.59
2-7	6543.52
2-8	6716.83
2-9	6891.52
2-10	7067.61
2-11	7245.11
2-12	7424.03
3-1	7604.38
3-2	7786.18
3-3	7969.43
3-4	8154.15
3-5	8340.34
3-6	8528.02
3-7	8717.2
3-8	8907.9
3-9	9100.12
3-10	9293.88
3-11	9489.19
3-12	9686.06

SELF-TESTING QUESTIONS

Step through the program in each question and write the output produced when the program runs.

EXAMPLE

```
110 LET S = 0
120 IF S > 4 GOTO 160
130 PRINT "D";
140 LET S = S + 1
150 GOTO 120
160 END
```

The step-through table is shown below:

Line Number:		120	130	140
Variables:	S	S > 4?	PRINT D	S = S+1
Pass 1:	0	no	D	1
Pass 2:	1	no	D	2
Pass 3:	2	no	D	3
Pass 4:	3	no	D	4
Pass 5:	4	no	D	5
Pass 6:	5	yes		

The output is: DDDDD.

```
6.1  110 FOR I = 1 TO 4
     120 READ A,B
     130 IF A > B THEN PRINT "A IS GREATER"
     140 IF A = B THEN PRINT "EQUAL"
     150 IF A < B THEN PRINT "B IS GREATER"
     160 NEXT I
     170 DATA 4,5, 6,2, 5,5, 7,6
```

```
6.2  110 LET S = 0
     120 IF S > = 5 GOTO 160
     130 PRINT "E";
     140 LET S = S + 1
     150 GOTO 120
     160 END
```

```
6.3  110 LET S = 1
     120 PRINT "B";
     130 LET S = S + 1
     140 IF S < 3 GOTO 120
     150 END
```

6.4
```
110 LET S = 1
120 PRINT "A";
130 IF S > 3 GOTO 160
140 LET S = S + 1
150 GOTO 120
160 END
```

6.5
```
110 LET S = 0
120 LET S = S + 1
130 IF S > 4 GOTO 160
140 PRINT "K";
150 GOTO 120
160 END
```

6.6
```
110 FOR I = 1 TO 3
120 FOR J = 1 TO 3
130 PRINT I;
140 NEXT J
150 NEXT I
```

6.7
```
110 FOR I = 1 TO 3
120 FOR J = 1 TO 3
130 PRINT J;
140 NEXT J
150 NEXT I
```

6.8
```
110 FOR I = 1 TO 3
120 FOR J = 1 TO 2
130 PRINT I;J;
140 NEXT J
150 NEXT I
```

6.9
```
110 FOR I = 3 TO 1 STEP -1
120 FOR J = 1 TO 3
130 PRINT J;
140 NEXT J
150 NEXT I
```

6.10
```
110 FOR I = 3 TO 1 STEP -1
120 FOR J = 3 TO STEP -1
130 PRINT J;
140 NEXT J
150 NEXT I
```

6.11
```
110 FOR I = 3 TO 1 STEP -1
120 FOR J = 3 TO 1 STEP -1
130 PRINT I;
140 NEXT J
150 NEXT I
```

```
6.12  110 FOR I = 1 TO 3
      120 FOR J = 1 TO 3
      130 PRINT J;
      140 NEXT J
      150 PRINT
      160 NEXT I


6.13  110 FOR I = 1 TO 2
      120 FOR J = 1 TO 2
      130 FOR K = 1 TO 2
      140 PRINT K;" ";
      150 NEXT K
      160 NEXT J
      170 NEXT I


6.14  110 FOR I = 1 TO 2
      120 FOR J = 1 TO 2
      130 FOR K = 1 TO 2
      140 PRINT K; " ";
      150 NEXT K
      160 PRINT
      170 NEXT J
      180 NEXT I


6.15  110 FOR I = 1 TO 2
      120 FOR J = 1 TO 2
      130 FOR K = 1 TO 2
      140 PRINT K;" ";
      150 NEXT K
      160 PRINT
      170 NEXT J
      180 PRINT
      190 NEXT I


6.16  100 HOME
      110 FOR Y = 1 TO 3
      120 PRINT "YEAR = ";Y
      130 FOR Q = 1 TO FOUR
      140 PRINT "QUARTER = ";Q" : ";
      150 PRINT "MONTHS = ";
      160 FOR M = 1 TO 3
      170 PRINT M + 3 * (Q - 1);
      180 IF M < 3 THEN PRINT ", ";
      190 NEXT M
      200 PRINT
      210 NEXT Q
      220 PRINT
      230 NEXT Y
```

EXERCISES

Choose One of the Following

6.1 The wholesale cost of an item is to be entered using an INPUT statement. If the wholesale cost is less than $100, the markup is 20 percent. Otherwise, the markup is $20 (20 percent of the first $100), plus 30 percent of the amount over $100. Write a program that will enter the wholesale cost and print the retail price as shown below.

```
WHAT IS THE WHOLESALE COST? 450
THE RETAIL PRICE IS $575
```

Your printed output must include at least three runs of your program, one with a wholesale cost less than $100, one with a wholesale cost of $100, and one with a wholesale cost greater than $100. Your printed output should also include a written calculation verifying the selling price from each run.

TIPS

1. Be sure one of your conditionals has an equal sign in it, otherwise the program will fail when the wholesale cost is exactly $100.

6.2   A salesperson's total weekly sales are to be entered using an INPUT
statement. The commission is 8.3 percent of the first $5000 in sales and
3.5 percent of any amount over $5000 in sales. Write a program that will
enter the sales and print the commission as shown below.

```
WHAT IS THE WEEKLY SALES TOTAL? $8200
YOUR COMMISSION IS $527
```

Your printed output must include at least three runs of the program, one
with weekly sales less than $5000, one with weekly sales of $5000, and
one with weekly sales greater than $5000. Your printed output should
also include written calculations verifying the commission for each run.

TIPS

1. **One of your conditional statements must
contain an equal sign, otherwise a sales
amount of exactly $5000 will cause an error.**

6.3 A student's three exam scores are to be entered using an INPUT statement. The average score is used to determine the letter grade as follows:

95 < = AVG	GRADE = A
85 < = AVG < 95	GRADE = B
70 < = AVG < 85	GRADE = C
60 < = AVG < 70	GRADE = D
AVG < 60	GRADE = F

Write a program that will enter a student's three exam scores, calculate the average grade, and print the student's letter grade as shown below:

```
ENTER YOUR THREE EXAM SCORES.
?85,88,86
YOUR AVERAGE SCORE IS 86.3
YOUR LETTER GRADE IS B
```

Your printed output must include five runs with all five possible letter grades appearing. At least one of the average values should be on a grade borderline (e.g. 95, 85, 70 etc.). Also include a written calculation verifying two of the average values.

TIPS

1. Write double conditionals as two conditions enclosed in parentheses, separated by the word AND; for example: IF (85 < = AVG) AND (AVG < 95).
2. Remember that the variable used to print the grade will be a string variable (e.g., G$).
3. Remember also that a value assigned to a string variable must be enclosed in quotes.

6.4 On the first of each month except January of each year, a person deposits $100 into an account earning 12 percent interest compounded monthly. The account is opened February 1. How much money will be in the account on January 1 five years later. Assume that the interest is computed and added to the account on the last day of each month. Write a program that produces the following printed output, including the message that follows the table. The balance in the table is the balance on the last day of the month, after the interest for that month has been added to the account.

YEAR-MONTH	BALANCE ON LAST DAY
1–1	0
1–2	101
.	.
.	.
1–12	1168.25
2-1	1179.93
.	.
.	.
2–1	1179.93
.	.
.	.
5–12	7523.07

```
THE ACCOUNT BALANCE IS $7523.04
ON JANUARY 1 FIVE YEARS LATER.
```

TIPS

1. Look back at program 6C.
2. Try to make your program a series of steps that do what the bank does during each month.

6.5 A young woman agrees to begin working for a company at a salary of one cent per day, with the condition that her daily salary would double each week (5 work days each week). Write a program that will print a salary table as shown below. The table should end when the woman's salary exceeds $1000 per week. Your program should print the message that follows the table below using variables to print the salary and week number.

WEEK	SALARY
1	.05
2	.1
3	.2
4	.4
5	.8
6	1.6
.	.
.	.
16	1638.4

```
THE YOUNG WOMAN'S SALARY WILL BE $1638.4
DURING WEEK NUMBER 16.
```

TIPS

1. Remember that the salary is paid daily, but this daily salary doubles only once a week.
2. The salary shouldn't double until the end of the first week.
3. Use a loop to compute each week's salary and double the daily salary, use an IF/THEN statement to terminate this loop.
4. Note that the weekly salary used in the IF/THEN statement that terminates the loop will be five times the daily salary.

6.6 The Northern Lights Power Company has the following rate structure for electricity (KWHR = kilowatt-hours).

	Oct-May	June-Sept
Fixed charge each month, $	2.50	2.50
First 500 KWHR, $ per KWHR	0.0454	0.0454
Next 500 KWHR, $ per KWHR	0.0406	0.0454
Excess, per KWHR	0.0308	0.0454

Write a program that enters the number of the month (i.e. Jan = 1, etc.), the previous KWHR reading, the present KWHR reading, and prints the kilowatt-hours used and the monthly bill as shown below.

```
THE NUMBER OF THE MONTH IS? 3
THE PREVIOUS KWHR READING IS? 5973
THE PRESENT KWHR READING IS? 6623
THE KWHR USED IS 650
YOUR ELECTRICITY BILL IS $31.29
```

Your printed output should include one run for the summer months (June-Sept) and three runs for the winter months (Oct-May). The three winter runs must include one with KWHR less than 500, one with KWHR between 500 and 1000, and one with KWHR greater than 1000. Your printed output should also include a written calculation verifying each monthly bill.

TIPS

1. This is a very difficult program, if you can do it you are to be congratulated.
2. Write one part of your program that is executed only for summer months; it should be simple since there is only one rate.
3. Write another part that is executed only for winter months, with IF/THEN statements for each rate.

CHAPTER 7

GETTING ARTISTIC
Printing Patterns with Subroutines

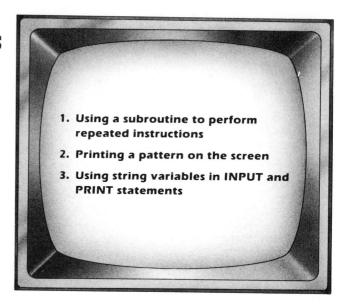

THE SUBROUTINE

The subroutine is one of the most powerful tools in programming. It speeds the execution of programs, keeps us from having to type in repeated instructions over and over again, and makes programs easier to write and understand.

The concept of the subroutine is really very simple. A subroutine is a series of normal program lines located anywhere in the program which end with the word RETURN. We use the GOSUB command to begin execution of the subroutine and the RETURN command to end the subroutine. If we have a subroutine at line 1000 in a program, any time in that program we need to have the subroutine performed we insert the command GOSUB 1000. When the computer sees this, it makes a note of where it is in the program and then jumps to line 1000. It does whatever the lines following 1000 tell it to do, and, when it comes to the RETURN statement, it returns to the first line *after* the GOSUB statement and continues with the program.

To make the program more readable, we have placed a line number followed by a single colon (:) at the end of each subroutine. Line 560, for example:

560 :

Such a line has no real effect on the execution of the program (except to slow it down by a few imperceptible microseconds). When the program is listed, these "null lines" help us to see the subroutine as a separate unit.

Complicated programs often have many subroutines, and in well-written professional programs almost all of the work is done by subroutines. This is part of what is referred to as structured programming. We will talk more about this concept later.

Pictures on the Screen

There are three basic programming techniques used to put a picture on the screen. One of these, high-resolution graphics, is beyond the scope of this book; low-resolution graphics will be covered in a later chapter. The third method, sometimes called character graphics, is the most primitive of the three. Character graphics is done by simply printing letters or symbols from the keyboard onto the screen in such a way that they make a pattern. In this chapter you will use this technique to put a pattern of your own choice on the screen.

The Christmas Tree

Program 7A is a little confusing until you understand how it works. It has two subroutines, one at line 500 which prints spaces (how many spaces is determined by the current value of the variable S), and another at line 600 to print characters (the number of characters is determined by the value of the variable C and the character printed is the value of C$). So, at any time in the program, we can print S spaces or C characters.

To understand how the program works, you must think of the Christmas tree as made up of 8 horizontal lines. Each line has a row of spaces followed by a "*****" (lines 2-5 have a row of spaces, one "*****", a row of spaces, and another "*****"). Notice that the DATA lines 301 to 308 are numbered to match the line number of the pattern and that the four lines which have the space, "*****", space, "*****" pattern (lines 2-5) have four values. By now you have probably figured out that the DATA values stand for number of spaces (S) and number of characters (C). So line 150 reads the first DATA value (19) from line 301 and then goes to the subroutine at line 500 and prints 19 spaces; the program then returns and reads the second data value (1) from line 301 and then goes to the subroutine at line 600 which prints one character. The print statement at the end of line 150 causes a carriage return, and then we're ready to print the next line. This completes line 1 of the pattern. Notice how the numbers in the DATA statements correspond to the numbers on the right side of the planning grid in figure 7.1. Lines 160 to 180 print lines 2 to 5 of the pattern by reading data values and printing the spaces and characters. Lines 190 to 210 finish the tree by printing lines 6 to 8 of the pattern. The program then drops down to line 399 (the DATA statements are ignored unless referred to by a READ statement) and ends.

EXAMPLE 7A   Christmas Tree

Problem   Write a program that will print the outline of a Christmas tree as shown on the grid below. Use subroutines to print spaces and characters. Use READ/DATA statements to specify how often each subroutine will be performed.

Figure 7.1 Planning Grid For Christmas Tree

```
#1:  19,1
#2:  18,1,1,1
#3:  17,1,3,1
#4:  16,1,5,1
#5:  15,1,7,1
#6:  14,11
#7:  19,1
#8:  17,5
```

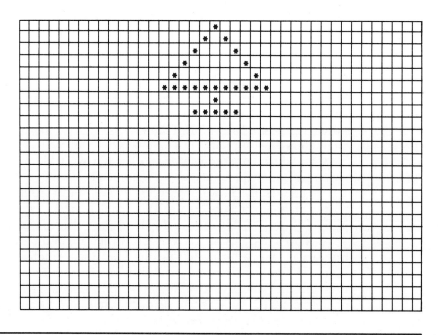

(Figure continued)

(Figure 7.1 continued)

```
]LIST
1 PN$ = "PROGRAM 7A - CHRISTMAS TREE"
2 NA$ = "YOUR NAME"
3 DA$ = "00/00/00"
10 REM ===== VARIABLES =====
11 REM C$ = CHARACTER USED IN PATTERN
12 REM C = NUMBER OF CHARACTERS PRINTED AT ONE TIME
13 REM I = LOOP COUNTER FOR NUMBER OF SPACES OR CHARACTERS
14 REM LINE = LOOP COUNTER FOR NUMBER OF LINES
15 REM S = NUMBER OF SPACES
40 REM ===== FUNCTIONS =====
41 REM ROUND TO WHOLE NUMBER WITH FN A(X)
42 DEF FN A(X) = INT (1 * X + .5) / 1
43 REM ROUND TO ONE DECIMAL PLACE WITH FN B(X)
44 DEF FN B(X) = INT (10 * X + .5) / 10
45 REM ROUND TO TWO DECIMAL PLACES WITH FN C(X)
46 DEF FN C(X) = INT (100 * X + .5) / 100
47 REM ROUND TO THREE DECIMAL PLACES WITH FN D(X)
48 DEF FN D(X) = INT (1000 * X + .5) / 1000
100 REM ===== MAIN PROGRAM =====
101 HOME : HTAB 20 - (LEN (PN$) / 2) : PRINT PN$
110 PRINT
120 INPUT "TYPE THE CHARACTER TO BE USED IN THE PATTERN: "; C$
130 REM ===== PRINT THE PATTERN =====
140 REM LINE = 1
150 GOSUB 500 : GOSUB 600 : PRINT
160 FOR LINE = 2 TO 5
170 GOSUB 500 : GOSUB 600 : GOSUB 500 : GOSUB 600 : PRINT
180 NEXT LINE
190 FOR LINE = 6 TO 8
200 GOSUB 500 : GOSUB 600 : PRINT
210 NEXT LINE
300 REM ===== DATA SECTION =====
301 DATA 19,1
302 DATA 18,1,1,1
303 DATA 17,1,3,1
304 DATA 16,1,5,1
305 DATA 15,1,7,1
306 DATA 14,11
307 DATA 19,1
308 DATA 17,5
399 END : REM == END OF MAIN PROGRAM ==
500 REM ===== SUBROUTINE TO PRINT SPACES =====
510 READ S
520 FOR I = 1 TO S
530 PRINT " ";
540 NEXT I
550 RETURN
560 :
```

(Figure continued)

(Figure 7.1 continued)

```
600 REM ===== SUBROUTINE TO PRINT CHARACTERS =====
610 READ C
620 FOR I = 1 TO C
630 PRINT C$;
640 NEXT I
650 RETURN
660 :
```

RUN

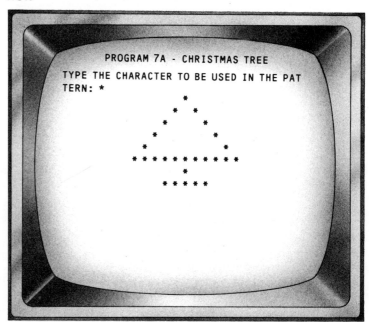

GOSUB AND RETURN   Sometimes you will find it necessary to use the same sequence of instructions in several places in your program. The GOSUB and RETURN statements allow you to write this sequence of instructions once as a subroutine. You use a GOSUB statement each time you need the subroutine, and then a RETURN statement in the subroutine transfers control back to the next statement in your main program.

EXAMPLE

```
10 FOR J = 1 TO 4
20 GOSUB 500              500 REM SUBROUTINE TO PRINT SPACES
30 PRINT "*";            510 READ S
40 GOSUB 500              520 FOR I = 1 TO S
50 PRINT "*"            530 PRINT " ";
60 NEXT J                 540 NEXT I
70 GOSUB 500              550 RETURN
80 PRINT "*"
90 STOP
100 DATA 15,7,16,5,17,3,18,1,19
```

In the above example, the GOSUB at line 20 transfers control to the subroutine at line 500 and the RETURN at line 550 transfers control back to line 30. The GOSUB at line 40 transfers control to the subroutine at line 500 and the RETURN at line 550 transfers control back to line 50. The GOSUB at line 70 transfers control to the subroutine and the RETURN transfers control back to line 80. The result is the same as it would be if the three GOSUB statements were each replaced by lines 510, 520, 530, and 540.

RUN

```
     *       *
      *     *
       *   *
        * *
         *
```

SELF-TESTING QUESTIONS

Step through the program in each question and write the output produced when the program runs. Assume the usual lines 40 through 48.

7.1
```
110 LET C$ = "*"
120 FOR I = 1 TO 5
130 PRINT C$;
140 NEXT I
```

7.2
```
110 LET C$ = "*"
120 FOR I = 1 TO 5
130 PRINT C$
140 NEXT I
```

7.3
```
110 READ C$
120 FOR I = 1 TO 5
130 READ N
140 FOR J = 1 TO N
150 PRINT " ";
160 NEXT J
170 READ M
180 FOR J = 1 TO M
190 PRINT C$;
200 NEXT J
210 PRINT
220 NEXT I
230 DATA *,7,3,8,1,7,3,6,5,6,5
```

7.4 Same program as question 7.3 except change line 230 to the following:

```
230 DATA *,10,4,10,1,10,3,10,1,10,4
```

7.5 Same program as question 7.3 except change line 230 to the following:

```
230 DATA *,10,6,10,6,12,2,12,2,12,2
```

7.6 Same program as question 7.3 except change line 230 to the following:

```
230 DATA *,10,5,14,1,14,1,14,1,13,2
```

EXERCISES

Choose One of the Following

7.1 Use the grid provided to design a pattern of your own choosing in the same manner as the Christmas tree in the example. Write the main program and DATA statements that will produce your pattern. Use the subroutines and line numbers as in program 7A. Put your DATA statements between lines 300 to 399 and put the two subroutines at lines 500 and 600. Use the same variables as in program 7A. Use the blank grid in figure 7.2 to plan your pattern.

Figure 7.2 Planning Grid For Your Pattern

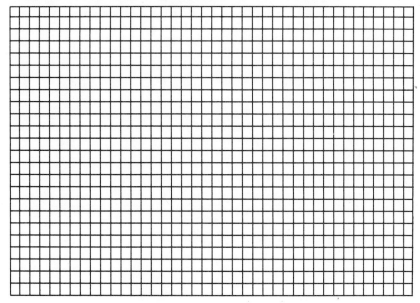

TIPS

1. As in example 7A, number your DATA lines so that their line numbers are the same as the lines of your pattern.
2. Remember to put a (;) after the PRINT statement in the subroutines.
3. Remember to put exactly one space between the quotation marks in the subroutine to print spaces.
4. Keep the variable LINE equal to the line number of the pattern.
5. Remember to finish each line of the pattern with a PRINT statement.
6. Your pattern will not look quite the same on the printer as it does on the screen. On some printers this can be corrected by using enhanced print.
7. Don't make your pattern too complicated; this exercise is hard enough as it is.

7.2   Write a program that will print a bar graph indicating the number of sales made by each member of a group of salespeople based on a set of DATA statements like the following:

```
301 DATA JONES, 21
302 DATA QUIST, 18
303 DATA SILVERMAN, 13
    .
    .
    .
```

The program should produce a graph like the following:

```
NAME          NUMBER OF SALES
- - - - - - - - - - - - - - - - - - - - - - - - - - - - - -
JONES         ! = = = = = = = = = = = = = = = = = = = =
QUIST         ! = = = = = = = = = = = = = = = = = =
SILVERMAN     ! = = = = = = = = = = = = =
    .
    .
    .
```

TIPS

1. Use a subroutine like the one in the example to print the line of characters.
2. Use a TAB statement to position the exclamation point (!). Make sure this is past the end of every name.
3. Make sure the pattern will not go off the right side of the screen. If you are ambitious, have the program check for this and make a correction.

7.3 A major design flaw of program 7A is that in order to print another
pattern, the main program must be completely rewritten. Using
subroutines to print characters and spaces, write a program that will print
any pattern. The program should be written so that when a new pattern
is to be printed *only* the DATA statements will need to be changed. This
means that all the information about the pattern will be contained in the
DATA statements.

TIPS

1. Follow the tips for exercise 7.1 (except for tip
   no. 4; the variable LINE should not be
   necessary).
2. In the DATA statements, use positive numbers
   to indicate characters, negative numbers to
   indicate spaces, zero to indicate the end of a
   line of the pattern, and 9999 to indicate the end
   of the whole pattern.
3. For example, the line

   ```
   302 DATA -18, 1, -1, 1, 0
   ```

   should print 18 spaces, 1 character, 1 space, one
   more character, and a carriage return.
4. Do not have any READ statements in the
   subroutines. There should be only one READ
   statement, and it should be in the main
   program.
5. Be sure to set the correct limit variable for each
   subroutine (C and S in the example) before
   calling it.

CHAPTER 8

FUNCTIONING
Using Functions Properly

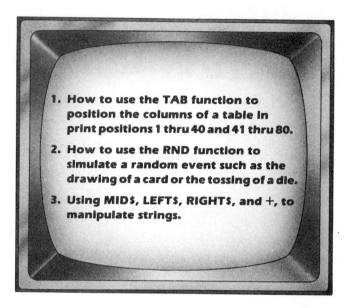

NEW CONCEPTS TAUGHT

1. **How to use the TAB function to position the columns of a table in print positions 1 thru 40 and 41 thru 80.**

2. **How to use the RND function to simulate a random event such as the drawing of a card or the tossing of a die.**

3. **Using MID$, LEFT$, RIGHT$, and +, to manipulate strings.**

WHAT IS A FUNCTION?

A function is a defined term which performs a specific job. Some functions are built into BASIC such as the INT function; others are defined by the user, like the defined functions A, B, C, and D we have used to round off. In this chapter we look at several more built-in functions.

The TAB function positions the cursor to a particular spot on the screen and is useful for making output on the screen or printer look neat and orderly. The RND function is used to generate a random number and can be used to simulate a random event such as drawing a card, tossing a coin, or throwing a pair of dice. The string functions, LEFT$, RIGHT$, MID$, LEN, and + are used for the manipulation of string variables.

Table of Squares and Square Roots

Program 8A in figure 8.1 uses the TAB function to print a table using TAB statements and a simple loop. The main program, from lines 100 to 130, is very straightforward. Line 101 prints the traditional heading centered on the screen. Line 110 calls the subroutine at line 200 that prints the headings. Line 220 calls the subroutine at line 1000 that prints the row of dashes under the headings. Line 130 calls the subroutine that does all of the hard work, printing the table.

The loop in the subroutine at line 300 is fairly short (lines 310 to 350) and each time around it prints one line of the table. Line 320 sets N2 equal to N squared and rounds it off to a whole number at the same time with FN A. Because of a quirk in some versions of BASIC (including Applesoft), some mathematical operations that should end in an integer are off by a tiny fraction and need to be rounded. Similarly, line 330 sets N3 equal to the square root of N and rounds it to three decimal places with FN D. Line 340 prints N, N2, and N3 in three columns, under the headings printed above. After the table is printed, the program returns to the main program at 130 and ends.

EXAMPLE 8A   Table of Squares and Square Roots

Problem Write a program that will print a table of squares and square roots for the numbers 1,2,3,...10. The table should have three columns; N, N ˆ 2, and N ˆ 0.5. The squared values should all be integers, and the square roots should have no more than three places to the right of the decimal point. Begin column two in the 12th print position and column three in the 24th print position.

FIGURE 8.1

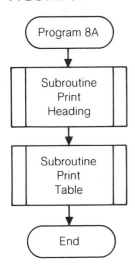

```
]LIST
1 PN$ = "PROGRAM 8A - USING THE TAB FUNCTION"
2 NA$ = "YOUR NAME"
3 DA$ = "00/00/00"
10 REM ===== VARIABLES =====
11 REM I = LOOP COUNTER
12 REM N = NUMBER AND LOOP COUNTER
13 REM N2 = N SQUARED
14 REM N3 = SQUARE ROOT OF N
40 REM ===== FUNCTIONS =====
41 REM ROUND TO WHOLE NUMBER WITH FN A(X)
42 DEF FN A(X) = INT (1 * X + .5) / 1
43 REM ROUND TO ONE DECIMAL PLACE WITH FN B(X)
44 DEF FN B(X) = INT (10 * X + .5) / 10
45 REM ROUND TO TWO DECIMAL PLACES WITH FN C(X)
46 DEF FN C(X) = INT (100 * X + .5) / 100
47 REM ROUND TO THREE DECIMAL PLACES WITH FN D(X)
48 DEF FN D(X) = INT (1000 * X + .5) / 1000
100 REM ===== MAIN PROGRAM =====
101 HOME : HTAB 20 - (LEN(PN$) / 2): PRINT PN$
110 GOSUB 200 : REM PRINT HEADING
120 GOSUB 300 : REM PRINT TABLE
130 END
140:
```

(Figure continued)

(Figure 8.1 continued)

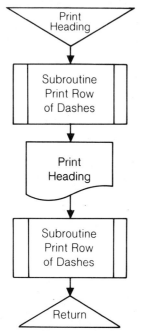

```
200 REM ===== SUBROUTINE TO PRINT HEADING =====
210 PRINT : PRINT
220 GOSUB 1000 : REM PRINT DASHES
230 PRINT "N"; TAB( 12); "N ^ 2"; TAB( 24); "N ^ 0.5"
240 GOSUB 1000 : REM PRINT DASHES
250 RETURN
299 :
```

```
300 REM ===== SUBROUTINE TO PRINT TABLE =====
310 FOR N = 1 TO 10
320 LET N2 = FN A(N ^ 2)
330 LET N3 = FN D(N ^ 0.5)
340 PRINT N; TAB( 12); N2; TAB( 24); N3
350 NEXT N
360 GOSUB 1000 : REM PRINT DASHES
370 RETURN
399 :
```

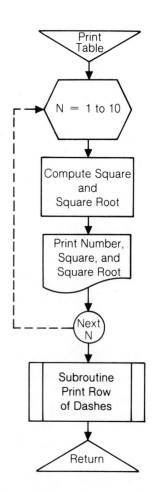

(Figure continued)

(Figure 8.1 continued)

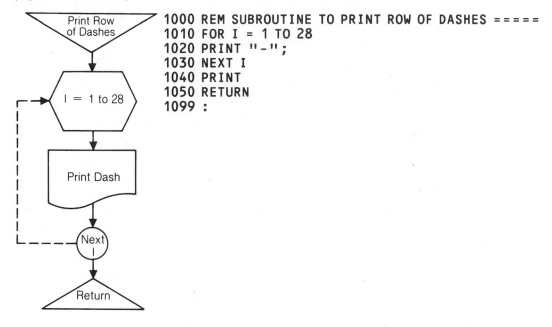

```
1000 REM SUBROUTINE TO PRINT ROW OF DASHES = = = = =
1010 FOR I = 1 TO 28
1020 PRINT "-";
1030 NEXT I
1040 PRINT
1050 RETURN
1099 :
```

RUN

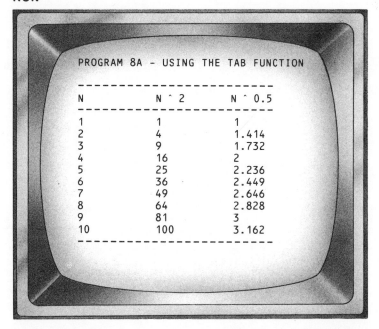

```
PROGRAM 8A - USING THE TAB FUNCTION

----------------------------
N            N ^ 2      N ^ 0.5
----------------------------
1            1          1
2            4          1.414
3            9          1.732
4            16         2
5            25         2.236
6            36         2.449
7            49         2.646
8            64         2.828
9            81         3
10           100        3.162
----------------------------
```

TAB The TAB command is used in a PRINT statement to move the cursor or the print head of the printer to any desired position on the current line. TAB must be used in a PRINT statement, and it only moves the cursor in a left to right direction. The general form of the TAB statement is:

(line number) PRINT TAB (a); (Variable Name); TAB (b); (Variable Name)...

1. The letters a, b... may be numbers, variable names, or expressions, but their value must be in the range of 0 to 255. If the value is outside of the range 0 to 255 an ILLEGAL QUANTITY ERROR message is printed.
2. The variable names that follow the TAB's in the PRINT statement may be numeric variable names, string variable names, numbers, expressions, or messages enclosed in quotes.
3. The monitor screen is 40 positions wide. The positions are numbered from 1 on the left margin to 40 on the right margin. Special note: TAB (0) should *not* be used because it is interpreted by the computer as TAB (256).

EXAMPLES

1. `110 PRINT TAB( 1);X; TAB( 10);Y; TAB( 20);Z`

   The above print statement prints the value of X starting at the left margin, the value of Y starting in position 10, and the value of Z starting in position 20.

2. `110 PRINT X TAB( 10)Y TAB( 20)Z`

   This example is equivalent to example 1 and illustrates that TAB (1) and the semicolons are optional.

3. `130 PRINT TAB( 20)X; TAB( 10)Y`

   This example prints the value of X starting in position 20 and value of Y starting immediately after the last digit of X. TAB cannot move the cursor to the left.

4. `110 PRINT TAB( 5) "NUMBER"; TAB( 20) "SQUARE"`
   `120 FOR I = 1 TO 10`
   `130 PRINT TAB( 5)I; TAB( 15)I * I`
   `140 NEXT I`

   This example shows how TAB would be used to line up the heading of at table and the numbers in the body of the table.

Pick a Card

Program 8B introduces a very handy subroutine for picking a random number. The working parts of this subroutine are all on line 210. We could substitute actual numbers for LL and UL but doing it this way makes the subroutine more general and therefore useful. Doing it this way means that in any program where we need a random number within a certain range, we can just set LL as the lower limit and UL as the upper limit and call this subroutine. We need it in this program because when picking a suit we need a number between one and four and when picking a card we need a number between one and thirteen.

In the main program we set LL and UL in line 110, and in line 120 we call the subroutine. The subroutine returns the random number N, which will be a number from 1 to 4. Here we must use another variable (S) and set it equal to N (line 130), because the next time we call the subroutine N will change.

Now that we have the suit number, we need to get a card number. The process is exactly the same, so we reset LL and UL and call the subroutine again, then in line 160 we set C equal to N. Since we now have S and C, the suit and card numbers, we go to subroutines 300 and 400 to get the suit and card names. All that's left to do is to print the results in line 190 and end.

EXAMPLE 8B   Pick a Card

Problem   Write a program that simulates the drawing of a card from a full deck. Use S$ for the suit and C$ for the name of the card. Your program should print the following message if C$ = SEVEN and S$ = SPADES:

THE CARD DRAWN IS THE SEVEN OF SPADES

FIGURE 8.2

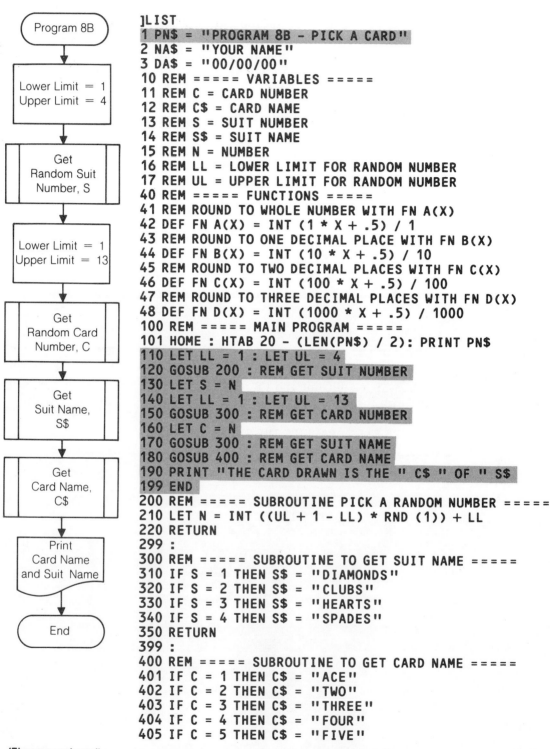

```
]LIST
1 PN$ = "PROGRAM 8B - PICK A CARD"
2 NA$ = "YOUR NAME"
3 DA$ = "00/00/00"
10 REM ===== VARIABLES =====
11 REM C = CARD NUMBER
12 REM C$ = CARD NAME
13 REM S = SUIT NUMBER
14 REM S$ = SUIT NAME
15 REM N = NUMBER
16 REM LL = LOWER LIMIT FOR RANDOM NUMBER
17 REM UL = UPPER LIMIT FOR RANDOM NUMBER
40 REM ===== FUNCTIONS =====
41 REM ROUND TO WHOLE NUMBER WITH FN A(X)
42 DEF FN A(X) = INT (1 * X + .5) / 1
43 REM ROUND TO ONE DECIMAL PLACE WITH FN B(X)
44 DEF FN B(X) = INT (10 * X + .5) / 10
45 REM ROUND TO TWO DECIMAL PLACES WITH FN C(X)
46 DEF FN C(X) = INT (100 * X + .5) / 100
47 REM ROUND TO THREE DECIMAL PLACES WITH FN D(X)
48 DEF FN D(X) = INT (1000 * X + .5) / 1000
100 REM ===== MAIN PROGRAM =====
101 HOME : HTAB 20 - (LEN(PN$) / 2): PRINT PN$
110 LET LL = 1 : LET UL = 4
120 GOSUB 200 : REM GET SUIT NUMBER
130 LET S = N
140 LET LL = 1 : LET UL = 13
150 GOSUB 300 : REM GET CARD NUMBER
160 LET C = N
170 GOSUB 300 : REM GET SUIT NAME
180 GOSUB 400 : REM GET CARD NAME
190 PRINT "THE CARD DRAWN IS THE " C$ " OF " S$
199 END
200 REM ===== SUBROUTINE PICK A RANDOM NUMBER =====
210 LET N = INT ((UL + 1 - LL) * RND (1)) + LL
220 RETURN
299 :
300 REM ===== SUBROUTINE TO GET SUIT NAME =====
310 IF S = 1 THEN S$ = "DIAMONDS"
320 IF S = 2 THEN S$ = "CLUBS"
330 IF S = 3 THEN S$ = "HEARTS"
340 IF S = 4 THEN S$ = "SPADES"
350 RETURN
399 :
400 REM ===== SUBROUTINE TO GET CARD NAME =====
401 IF C = 1 THEN C$ = "ACE"
402 IF C = 2 THEN C$ = "TWO"
403 IF C = 3 THEN C$ = "THREE"
404 IF C = 4 THEN C$ = "FOUR"
405 IF C = 5 THEN C$ = "FIVE"
```

(Figure continued)

(Figure 8.2 continued)

```
406 IF C = 6 THEN C$ = "SIX"
407 IF C = 7 THEN C$ = "SEVEN"
408 IF C = 8 THEN C$ = "EIGHT"
409 IF C = 9 THEN C$ = "NINE"
410 IF C = 10 THEN C$ = "TEN"
411 IF C = 11 THEN C$ = "JACK"
412 IF C = 12 THEN C$ = "QUEEN"
413 IF C = 13 THEN C$ = "KING"
420 RETURN
499 :
```

RUN

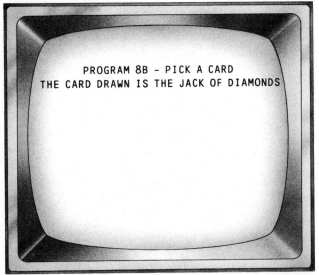

```
PROGRAM 8B - PICK A CARD
THE CARD DRAWN IS THE JACK OF DIAMONDS
```

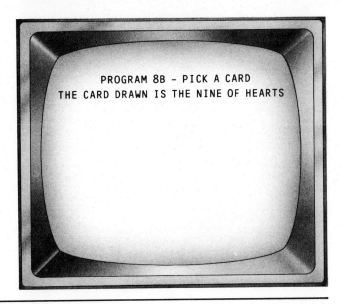

```
PROGRAM 8B - PICK A CARD
THE CARD DRAWN IS THE NINE OF HEARTS
```

RND The RND function always gives a positive number that is greater than or equal to 0 and less than 1. The general form is RND(n). The number n is a flag that tells the RND function what to do. If n is any positive number, then RND(n) produces a different random number each time it is used. If n is 0, RND(0) gives the most recent previous random number. If n is negative, then RND(n) gives the same random number each time it is used with the same value of n, but different negative values of n give different random numbers. After a random number is produced using a negative value of n, random numbers produced by a positive value of n will follow the same sequence every time. This is useful in debugging programs that use the random function.

The random function is often used to produce a random integer from a set of integers. For example, we might decide to use the random function to generate a random number between 1 and 6 to represent the outcome of the toss of a die. To see how this can be accomplished, consider the following steps. For illustration purposes, we will use 0.999999999 as the largest possible random number. While this may not be exactly correct, it is very close to the largest possible random number.

1. Use RND(1) to produce a random number between 0 and 0.999999999.
2. Multiply this random number by the number of integers in the set. There are 6 integers in the set of integers from 1 to 6 so we multiply the random number by 6. The result is a set of random numbers between 0 and 5.999999994.
3. Take the integer value of the result of step 2. In our example, this results in an integer between 0 and 5 inclusive.
4. Finally, add the value of the lowest integer in the desired set of integers. In our example, we would add 1 giving us a random integer between 1 and 6.

The four steps above are incorporated in the following formula (see line 210 of program 8B).

$$N = INT ((UL + 1 - LL) * RND(1)) + LL$$

The variable N will be a random integer between LL (lower limit) and UL (upper limit). If we let LL = 1 and UL = 6, then N will be a random integer between 1 and 6.

Multiplication Table

Program 8C is much like program 8A, but with a few twists. For one thing, it uses a nested loop to print the table. More unusual, however, is the fact that the table involves tabbing well beyond column 40. This means that when the program is running properly, it will look like garbage on the screen; but it will look proper when printed on a printer.

APPLE IIe/IIc NOTE: If you have an Apple IIe with an eighty-column card, you can get the table to look right on the screen by deleting lines 430 and 650, changing the TAB statements to "POKE 36,", and typing PR#3 before running the program. PR#3 activates the eighty-column card and POKE 36, is the eighty-column equivalent of HTAB.

In the subroutine at line 400, we print the column headings for the table. The variable P is the position on the screen where the next character will be printed. L is set equal to 16, the column where the table starts (L for left side). W is set equal to 5, the width of each column. In the loop in subroutine 400, each time through the loop, P is set to L plus the column number minus 1 (J – 1) times the width of each column (W). We use J – 1 because the first time through the loop we want P to equal L + 0.

Line 430 shows a trick we use to get around a quirk of the computer. The Apple mysteriously adds 40 to any TAB value beyond TAB 41 so we have to subtract it to keep things normal.

The subroutine at line 600 contains a typical nested loop used to print a table. Each time the inner loop (lines 630 to 670) executes, it prints one number (I * J). Each time the outer loop (lines 610 to 690) executes, it prints one row of the table. Lines 640 and 650 are the same as lines 420 and 430 and do the same thing. Notice that by setting N equal to a much larger number, you can print a table as large as your printer will handle.

EXAMPLE 8C   Multiplication Table

Problem   Write a program that generates a multiplication table from 1 to 12 and prints the table with column and row headings. Allow five spaces for each column.

FIGURE 8.3

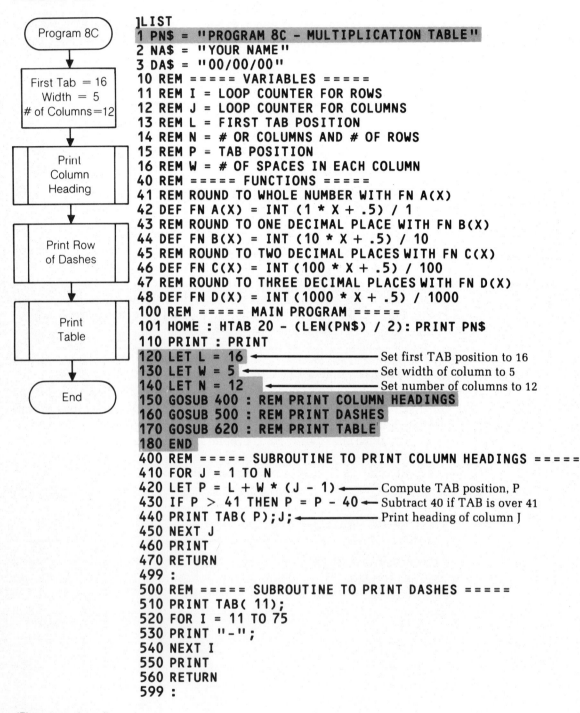

```
]LIST
1 PN$ = "PROGRAM 8C - MULTIPLICATION TABLE"
2 NA$ = "YOUR NAME"
3 DA$ = "00/00/00"
10 REM ===== VARIABLES =====
11 REM I = LOOP COUNTER FOR ROWS
12 REM J = LOOP COUNTER FOR COLUMNS
13 REM L = FIRST TAB POSITION
14 REM N = # OR COLUMNS AND # OF ROWS
15 REM P = TAB POSITION
16 REM W = # OF SPACES IN EACH COLUMN
40 REM ===== FUNCTIONS =====
41 REM ROUND TO WHOLE NUMBER WITH FN A(X)
42 DEF FN A(X) = INT (1 * X + .5) / 1
43 REM ROUND TO ONE DECIMAL PLACE WITH FN B(X)
44 DEF FN B(X) = INT (10 * X + .5) / 10
45 REM ROUND TO TWO DECIMAL PLACES WITH FN C(X)
46 DEF FN C(X) = INT (100 * X + .5) / 100
47 REM ROUND TO THREE DECIMAL PLACES WITH FN D(X)
48 DEF FN D(X) = INT (1000 * X + .5) / 1000
100 REM ===== MAIN PROGRAM =====
101 HOME : HTAB 20 - (LEN(PN$) / 2): PRINT PN$
110 PRINT : PRINT
120 LET L = 16 ──────────────────── Set first TAB position to 16
130 LET W = 5 ───────────────────── Set width of column to 5
140 LET N = 12 ──────────────────── Set number of columns to 12
150 GOSUB 400 : REM PRINT COLUMN HEADINGS
160 GOSUB 500 : REM PRINT DASHES
170 GOSUB 620 : REM PRINT TABLE
180 END
400 REM ===== SUBROUTINE TO PRINT COLUMN HEADINGS =====
410 FOR J = 1 TO N
420 LET P = L + W * (J - 1) ──────── Compute TAB position, P
430 IF P > 41 THEN P = P - 40 ◄── Subtract 40 if TAB is over 41
440 PRINT TAB( P);J; ───────────── Print heading of column J
450 NEXT J
460 PRINT
470 RETURN
499 :
500 REM ===== SUBROUTINE TO PRINT DASHES =====
510 PRINT TAB( 11);
520 FOR I = 11 TO 75
530 PRINT "-";
540 NEXT I
550 PRINT
560 RETURN
599 :
```

Program 8C

First Tab = 16
Width = 5
# of Columns=12

Print
Column
Heading

Print Row
of Dashes

Print
Table

End

(Figure continued)

(Figure 8.3 continued)

```
600 REM ===== SUBROUTINE TO PRINT ROW HEADING AND EACH  ROW OF TABLE =====
610 FOR I = 1 TO N
620 PRINT TAB( 6);I; TAB( 11);"!";
630 FOR J = 1 TO N
640 LET P = L + W * (J - 1)
650 IF P > 41 THEN P = P - 40
660 PRINT TAB( P); I * J;
670 NEXT J
680 PRINT
690 NEXT I
695 RETURN
699 :
```

Line 620 — Print Row Heading
Line 640 — Compute TAB position, P
Line 650 — Subtract 40 if TAB is over 41
Line 660 — Print number in column J

RUN

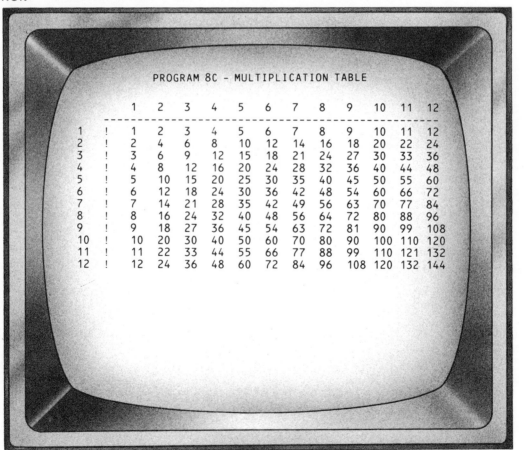

```
            PROGRAM 8C - MULTIPLICATION TABLE

            1   2   3   4   5   6   7   8   9   10  11  12
        --------------------------------------------------------
    1   !   1   2   3   4   5   6   7   8   9   10  11  12
    2   !   2   4   6   8   10  12  14  16  18  20  22  24
    3   !   3   6   9   12  15  18  21  24  27  30  33  36
    4   !   4   8   12  16  20  24  28  32  36  40  44  48
    5   !   5   10  15  20  25  30  35  40  45  50  55  60
    6   !   6   12  18  24  30  36  42  48  54  60  66  72
    7   !   7   14  21  28  35  42  49  56  63  70  77  84
    8   !   8   16  24  32  40  48  56  64  72  80  88  96
    9   !   9   18  27  36  45  54  63  72  81  90  99  108
   10   !   10  20  30  40  50  60  70  80  90  100 110 120
   11   !   11  22  33  44  55  66  77  88  99  110 121 132
   12   !   12  24  36  48  60  72  84  96  108 120 132 144
```

TAB A quirk in Applesoft BASIC causes a problem when we wish to TAB to positions 41 through 80 on the printer. When a character is printed in either space 40 or 41, the APPLE adds 40 to all TAB positions beyond 41. Thus TAB(66) becomes TAB(106), TAB(75) becomes TAB (115), and so forth. You can work around this problem by printing a space in column 41 and subtracting 40 from all TABs above 41. The space does not show, but it sets the computer so you can TAB beyond position 40 with the desired results.

An alternate solution to the TAB beyond 40 problem is presented in the TAB section of the MINI–MANUAL under the heading Rules for Printing Beyond Space 40. The rules look like something designed by the Internal Revenue Service, but the idea behind them is quite simple. The rules are designed to print a table is such a way that one of the columns begins in space 41. This assures us that a character will always be printed in space 41; and then the rule of subtracting 40 from all TABs beyond 41 will be applied. The following is an application of this procedure to the problem in example 8C.

1. The table has 12 columns so N = 12.

2. The maximum column width is INT(80/N) = INT(80/12) = 6.

3. We will select a column width of 5.

4. The first TAB value is the remainder of 41/5 which is 1. Subsequent TAB values are obtained by adding w to the previous TAB value. The TAB values are: 1, 6, 11, 16, 21, 26, 31, 36, 41, 46, 51, 56, 61, 66, 71, and 76.

5. We select TAB(6) for the row heading and a value of 16 for L, the TAB position of the first column, The last column will begin at position 71, leaving a right margin of 5.

6. The determination of TAB values by program is illustrated by the following instructions from program 8C. The TAB position, P, is computed in lines 640 and 650.

```
630 FOR J = 1 TO N
640 LET P = L + W * (J - 1)
650 IF P > 41 THEN P = P - 40
660 PRINT TAB(P); I * J;
670 NEXT J
680 PRINT
```

Name Swap

Program 8D in figure 8.4 demonstrates the use of the string functions, which allow us to do almost anything we can think of with string variables. In this program we use them to reverse a group of names and add a comma in the middle of each name. Line 120 READs a single name from the DATA section. If it is "9999" it means the program is done and we END. If not, the program continues.

How Long?   In line 140 we use the LEN function to set L to the number of characters in NAME\$. We have used this function many times before; for example, in line 101 it is used to help center the title of each program. Here we want to know how many characters are in NAME\$ because some of the subroutines need to know the length of the string they're dealing with.

Finding the Space.   Once we know the length of the name, we call the subroutine at line 400 to split the name into two parts. Since we want to split the name at the space between the first and last name, line 410 calls the subroutine at line 500 to find the space. The loop in lines 510 to 530 uses the MID\$ function to find the space. The MID\$ function in line 520 uses the three pieces of information in the parentheses (called "arguments"): the first, in this case NAME\$, is the string referred to; the second, in this case I, is the position of the beginning character; and the third, in this case 1, is the number of characters referred to. So each time through the loop this line checks to see if the Ith character of NAME\$ is a space. When the space is found, I must be the position of the space in NAME\$. For example, if NAME\$ is JANE SANCHEZ, the first time through the loop, I will be one and MID\$(NAME\$, I, 1) will be "J." When I is five (the fifth time through the loop), MID\$(NAME\$, I, 1) will be a space and the program will RETURN and continue with line 420. If the name has no space, the program falls through to line 540, prints the error message, and stops.

We should mention that the second and third arguments (items in the parentheses) of the MID\$ function can be either numbers or variables and can have any value up to 255. Instead of looking for a single character, as we do here, it is possible to search for a string of characters in a larger string.

Left and Right.   If the FIND SPACE subroutine has been successful, line 420 uses the LEFT\$ function to set LF\$ to I – 1 characters from the left side of NAME\$. To use our example of JANE JONES, since I is five, LF\$ will be the left four (5 – 1) characters of NAME\$, or "JANE."

In line 430 we do something similar using the RIGHT\$ function. Earlier, we used the LEN function to set L to the length of NAME\$. For the name JANE SANCHEZ, L is 12 (the space counts). So, RT\$ is set to 7 characters from the right side of NAME\$ or "SANCHEZ." Notice that with LEFT\$ and RIGHT\$, we have captured the first and last name (but not the space) in separate variables. When this has been accomplished, the program returns to the MAIN section.

EXAMPLE 8D   Name Swap

Problem   Write a program that takes people's names from a series of DATA statements, turns them around, inserts a comma, and prints them as a list. For example:

```
301 DATA "LORI BOSSARD"
302 DATA "ROGER STODOLA"
303 DATA "PETER RAYGOR"
```

would be printed out as follows:

```
BOSSARD, LORI
STODOLA, ROGER
RAYGOR, PETER
```

FIGURE 8.4

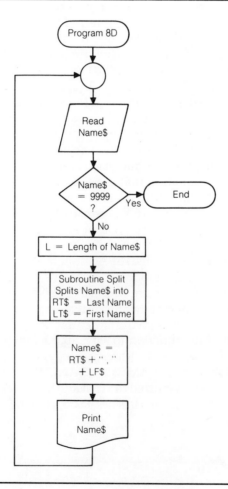

(Figure continued)

(Figure 8.4 continued)

```
]LIST
1 PN$ = "PROGRAM 8D - NAME SWAP"
2 NA$ = "YOUR NAME"
3 DA$ = "00/00/00"
10 REM ===== VARIABLES =====
11 REM I = LOOP COUNTER
12 REM L = LENGTH OF NAME
13 REM NAME$ = FULL NAME
14 REM LF$ = FIRST NAME
15 REM RT$ = LAST NAME
40 REM ===== FUNCTIONS =====
41 REM ROUND TO WHOLE NUMBER WITH FN A(X)
42 DEF FN A(X) = INT (1 * X + .5) / 1
43 REM ROUND TO ONE DECIMAL PLACE WITH FN B(X)
44 DEF FN B(X) = INT (10 * X + .5) / 10
45 REM ROUND TO TWO DECIMAL PLACES WITH FN C(X)
46 DEF FN C(X) = INT (100 * X + .5) / 100
47 REM ROUND TO THREE DECIMAL PLACES WITH FN D(X)
48 DEF FN D(X) = INT (1000 * X + .5) / 1000
100 REM ===== MAIN PROGRAM =====
101 HOME : HTAB 20 - (LEN( PN$) / 2) : PRINT PN$
110 PRINT : PRINT
120 READ NAME$
130 IF NAME$ = "9999" THEN END
140 LET L = LEN(NAME$) : REM L IS LENGTH OF NAME
150 GOSUB 400 : REM SPLIT NAME
160 LET NAME$= RT$ + ", " + LF$
170 PRINT NAME$ : PRINT
180 GOTO 120
190 REM END OF MAIN PROGRAM
195 :
300 REM ===== DATA SECTION =====
301 DATA "LON CHANEY"
302 DATA "PETER CUSHING"
303 DATA "BORIS KARLOFF"
304 DATA "CHRISTOPHER LEE"
305 DATA "PETER LORRE"
306 DATA "BELA LUGOSI"
307 DATA "9999"
390 :
400 REM ===== SUBROUTINE TO SPLIT NAMES =====
410 GOSUB 500 : REM FIND SPACE (I IS LOCATION OF SPACE)
420 LET LF$ = LEFT$ (NAME$, I - 1) : REM FIRST NAME
430 LET RT$ = RIGHT$ (NAME$, L - I) : REM LAST NAME
440 RETURN
450 :
500 REM ===== SUBROUTINE TO FIND SPACE =====
510 FOR I = 1 TO L
520 IF MID$ (NAME$, I, 1) = " " THEN RETURN
530 NEXT I
540 PRINT "NO SPACE IN THIS NAME" : STOP
550 :
```

(Figure continued)

(Figure 8.4 continued)

RUN

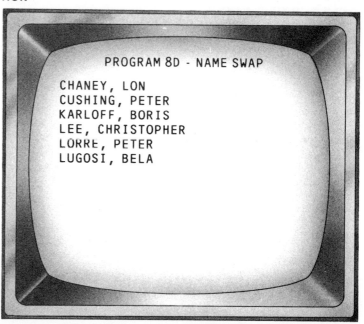

```
           PROGRAM 8D - NAME SWAP

CHANEY, LON
CUSHING, PETER
KARLOFF, BORIS
LEE, CHRISTOPHER
LORRE, PETER
LUGOSI, BELA
```

Wrapping Things Up. Back in the MAIN PROGRAM, line 160 uses the +
function to put the name back together in reverse order and add the comma
(and put the space back in). Putting strings together this way is called
"concatenation."

Since we only want to print this reversed version of the name, we use
NAME$ here. If, for some reason, we wanted to preserve the unreversed ver-
sion, we could use some other variable here (like EMAN$). Once the name
has been printed, the program loops back to line 120 to READ another name.
This process continues until all the names have been read. When NAME$ is
"9999," the program ends.

**LEFT$** The string function LEFT$ has the general form:
LEFT$ *(string variable name, n)*

This expression refers to the leftmost n characters of the string variable named.

EXAMPLE

```
10 LET C$ = "PETER PAN"
20 LET L$ = LEFT$(C$, 7)
```

The above instructions set L$ to "PETER P"

**RIGHT$** The RIGHT$ function is exactly like the LEFT$ function, except that it refers to the rightmost n characters of the variable named.

EXAMPLE

```
10 LET C$ = "PETER PAN"
20 LET R$ = RIGHT$(C$, 7)
```

The above instructions set R$ to "TER PAN"

**MID$** The MID$ function is similar to the LEFT$ and RIGHT$ functions, but, instead of two, has three arguments in the parentheses: the first is the name of the string variable referred to; the second is the starting position of the substring; and the third is the number of characters in the substring.

EXAMPLE

```
10 LET C$ = "PETER PAN"
20 LET M$ = MID$(C$, 5, 3)
```

The above instructions set M$ to "R P".

LEN The string function LEN has the general form:

LEN *(string variable name)*

This function gives the number of characters in the string variable named.

EXAMPLE

```
LET C$ = "PETER PAN"
20 LET N = LEN (C$)
```

The above instructions set N to 8.

SELF-TESTING QUESTIONS

8.1 List the set of possible numbers produced by each of the following functions:

    (a) `INT (4 * RND (1))`
    (b) `INT (4 * RND (1)) + 1`
    (c) `INT (4 * RND (1)) + 11`
    (d) `INT (13 * RND (1)) + 1`
    (e) `INT (6 * RND (1)) + 1`

Step through the program in each question and write the output produced when the program runs.

```
8.2  110 LET C$ = "*"
     120 LET N = 6
     130 FOR I = N TO 11
     140 PRINT TAB( N);C$
     150 NEXT I
     160 END
```

```
8.3  110 LET C$ = "*"
     120 LET N = 6
     130 FOR I = 13 TO 18
     140 PRINT TAB( I);C$;
     150 NEXT I
```

```
8.4  110 LET C$ = "*"
     120 LET N = 6
     130 FOR I = N TO 11
     140 PRINT TAB( I);C$
     150 NEXT I
```

```
8.5  110 LET C$= "*"
     120 LET N = 6
     130 FOR I = 1 TO N
     140 PRINT TAB( 3 * I);C$;
     150 NEXT I
```

```
8.6  110 LET C$ = "*"
     120 LET N = 6
     130 FOR I = 0 TO 5
     140 PRINT TAB( N - I);C$
     150 NEXT I
```

```
8.7  100 LET S$ = "ALL PUMA RINGS TO GO"
     110 LET L = LEN (S$)
     120 LET L$ = MID$ (S$,14,1) + MID$ (S$,16,1)
     130 LET L$ = L$ + MID$ (S$,10,4)
     140 LET R$ = MID$ (S$,7,2) + MID$ (S$,12,1)
     150 LET R$ = R$ + MID$ (S$,11,1) + MID$ (S$,5,2)
     160 LET R$ = R$ + "L" + LEFT$ (S$,1) + MID$ (S$,L-4,1)
     170 LET R$ = R$ + MID$ (S$,11,1) + RIGHT$ (S$,1)
     180 LET R$ = R$ + MID$ (S$,12,1)
     190 LET FINAL$ = L$ + " " + R$
     200 PRINT FINAL$
```

EXERCISES

Choose one of the following

8.1 Write a program that will produce the following table of X, X^2, X^3, and
X^0.5 for the values of X from 1 to 10. Use the TAB function to produce a
table with four columns. Round the numbers to the nearest thousandth.

```
X               X^2         X^3         X^0.5
---------------------------------------------
1               1           1           1
2               4           8           1.414
3               9           27          1.732
.               .           .           .
.               .           .           .
10              100         1000        3.162
```

TIPS

1. Use a single loop.
2. Use X as the counter for the loop
   (FOR X = 1 TO 10).
3. Print the four values inside the loop.

8.2   In an earlier problem, an airline was preparing a booklet which included an altitude conversion table. The booklet was popular with U.S. passengers, but foreign passengers wanted the altitude in meters. Some passengers also asked about the outside air pressure. Write a program that will produce a four column table as shown below. Use TAB statements to format the table. Round the numbers to the nearest hundredth. The relative air pressure is approximated by the following equation:

$$P = 0.0002984 * (F/1000)^2 - 0.03262 * (F/1000) + 1$$

where: P = relative air pressure in atmospheres
        (sea level pressure is one atmosphere)
     F = altitude in feet
The conversion to meters is: METERS = FEET/3.281

ALTITUDE IN FEET	ALTITUDE IN MILES	ALTITUDE IN METERS	RELATIVE PRESSURE
0	0	0	1
1000	.	.	.
.	.	.	.
.	.	.	.
50000	.	.	.

TIPS

1. Use a single loop.
2. Use FEET to stand for altitude in feet and to serve as the loop counter
   (FOR FEET = 0 TO 50000 STEP 1000).
3. Use METERS for altitude in meters, MILES for altitude in miles, and PRESSURE for relative pressure.
4. Print the four values inside the loop.

8.3 A $45000 home mortgage has a principal-plus-interest payment of $650 per month. The interest rate is 15 percent per year (1.25 percent per month). Write a program that will produce the following four-column table for the first five years. Use TAB statements to format the table. Round the numbers to the nearest cent.

```
YEAR-MONTH INTEREST PRINCIPAL BALANCE
------------------------------------------
1-1          562.5     87.5      44912.5
1-2          561.41    88.59     44823.91
.              .         .          .
.              .         .          .
5-12           .         .          .
```

TIPS

1. Use nested loops with MONTH as the counter for the inner loop and YEAR as the counter for the outer loop.
2. Inside the inner loop, try to do what the bank does—calculate the interest, calculate the principal, get the new balance, and print the four values.

8.4   Write a program that will produce the following table based on tossing three dice ten times. Use TAB statements to format the table.

DIE #1	DIE #2	DIE #3	TOTAL
4	1	3	8
1	6	5	12
.	.	.	.
.	.	.	.
4	2	6	12

TIPS

1. Use the subroutine from example 8B for picking a random number.
2. Use D1, D2, and D3 as the variables for the three dice.
3. Use a single loop to print the values and totals (FOR I = 1 TO 10).

8.5   Write a program that will produce the table below based on randomly drawing three cards. Use TAB statements to format the table. Use the subroutines from program 8B to pick and recognize the cards. Use IF statements to make sure that cards two and three have not been picked before.

CARD #	ONE	TWO	THREE
	QUEEN	SEVEN	FOUR
	OF	OF	OF
	SPADES	DIAMONDS	HEARTS

TIPS

1. Use S1, S2, S3, and S1$, S2$, S3$, as the variables for the suit numbers and suit names.
2. Use C1, C2, C3, and C1$, C2$, C3$, as the variables for the card numbers and card names.
3. Set all the variables before you try to print the table.
4. Don't use a loop to print the table, do it as five separate lines.

8.6 You are having a dinner party and would like place cards for each guest. Write a program that will take names from DATA statements like the following:

```
301 DATA "JOHNSON, SUE"
302 DATA "GREEN, BILL"
```

and produce place cards like the one below:

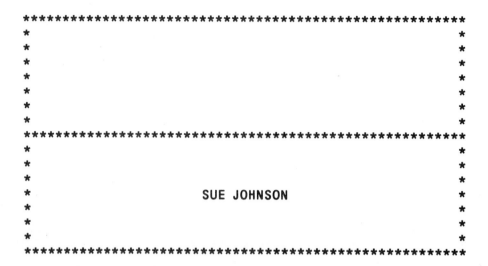

The name should be first name first, and should be centered on the card. The card should be at least 50 columns wide. Use TAB statements to position the right-hand set of stars, and the name.

TIPS

1. Write a separate subroutine to find the comma.
2. Use another subroutine to remove the comma. Then swap the two names as in example 8D.
3. Use a subroutine to print the card.
4. In the MAIN PROGRAM, call the subroutine to remove the comma, then the subroutine to split the name, and then the subroutine to print the card.

8.7 Same as 8.6 except that the names have middle initials.

> 301 DATA "JOHNSON, SUE L."

This should be printed on the card as SUE JOHNSON.

TIPS

1. See the tips for exercise 8.6.
2. Remember, you will have to find both spaces.
3. This is a very difficult program.

8.8   Same as 8.7 except that only *some* of the names should have middle initials. The program will have to detect the presence or absence of the middle initial and act accordingly.

TIPS

1. Write a subroutine that detects the middle initial by using the MID$ function to look for two separate spaces.
2. Use different loop counters for each loop to avoid side effects.
3. This is an *extremely* difficult program.

CHAPTER 9

KEEPING TRACK
Using Subscripts and Sorting

NEW CONCEPTS TAUGHT

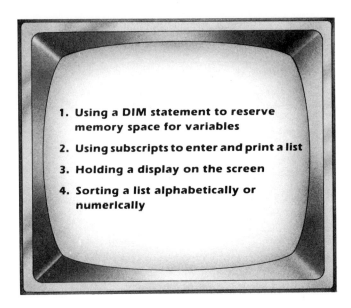

1. **Using a DIM statement to reserve memory space for variables**
2. **Using subscripts to enter and print a list**
3. **Holding a display on the screen**
4. **Sorting a list alphabetically or numerically**

SUBSCRIPTS

Subscripts are reference numbers we can give to numeric or string variables that let us use a single variable name to store a list of names or numbers. For example, in this program, instead of the variable NAME$ we use NAME$(N), where N is some number. This way we can have NAME$(1), NAME$(2), NAME$(3), and so on. In fact we can have as many as we have room for in memory.

Using NAME$, the representation in memory might be thought of as looking like this:

NAME$ | FRED |

With subscripts it might be thought of as looking like this:

NAME$(1) | SUE |

NAME$(2) | JOE |

NAME$(3) | ALICE |

If we put the subscripted variable inside a loop and use the loop counter inside the parentheses we can create a very useful list of variables.
Example

```
10 FOR I = 1 TO 10
20 LET T(I) = I
30 NEXT I
```

This way, T(1) would be 1, T(2) would be 2, and so on up to 10. Subscripts are also very handy for entering, sorting, and printing data. A list of subscripted variables is called an array and is used very often in programming.

You might think about how some of the earlier programs in this book could be written using subscripted variables. For example, the temperature conversion and miles per gallon programs could have allowed the user to enter input values as an array of subscripted variables and then looped through them to print the results.

Subscripted Variables The subscripted variable makes it more convenient for us to use a group of memory cells to store a list or table of names or numbers. By using a subscripted variable, we give the same name to every memory cell in the group and use the subscript value to distinguish between the memory cells in the group. This is a distinct advantage, because it is much easier to change the subscript value in a program than it is to change a variable name. A subscripted variable name consists of a variable name followed by a subscript enclosed in parentheses. The subscript may be a number, a variable name, or an arithmetic expression.

EXAMPLES A(1) B$(2) C2(I) SUM(J + 2 * I) F3(3 * I)

The DIM Statement

When using a subscripted variable we need to tell the computer how much memory to set aside for the variable list. This is done with a DIM statement. The DIM statement reserves memory space which cannot be used for anything but the specified list of variables.

If you will never have a subscript over 10 in the list, the DIM statement is not necessary since the computer automatically dimensions to 10 when it sees a subscripted variable for the first time. When you do use a DIM statement, it must come before any appearance of the subscripted variable in the program, otherwise a ?REDIM'D ARRAY ERROR will occur. Having the program execute a DIM statement more than once will also cause this error, so be careful not to put a DIM statement inside a loop.

In program 9A we ask how many names will be entered in line 2020 and then dimension the variables for name and score in line 2030. This way, the program does not reserve any more memory space for the variables than is necessary.

Entering Data

In lines 2040 through 2080 we see subscripts used to enter the list of names and scores. The first time through the loop, I is 1, so we are entering NAME$(1) and SC(1). Each time through the loop we enter a new name and score without losing the previous names and scores. When we're finished with the loop, we have the list of names and scores in memory and can do what we want with them.

Printing a Table

One thing we want to do with the list of names and scores is to print a table. In the loop in lines 5670 to 5690 we simply print the names and scores in two columns. Notice that the score for each bowler will be printed on the same line as his or her name.

If you look at the main section of the program at line 100, you will see that we use the subroutine to print the table three times. First, we print the names in the order they were entered; next, we sort by name and print a table that is sorted alphabetically; finally, we sort by score and print a table with the bowlers listed in rank order, the best bowlers on top. The use of well-designed subroutines, like this one, by several parts of a program is sometimes called "modular" or "structured" programming. We will talk more about this in chapter 10. For now, you might think about how much easier (and more understandable) it is to write the program in this way than to have three separate parts of the program to print the three tables.

Hold Screen

If we did not have this subroutine, the tables would flash on the screen too quickly to be read. The way we have done it here, as soon as the table is printed on the screen, the program jumps (in line 5710) to the subroutine at line 6200 which does nothing more than print the message "PRESS RETURN TO CONTINUE" and wait for an input. Since the program will not continue until the user types a return, this effectively "freezes" the table on the screen until the user is ready to have the program continue.

SORTING ALPHABETICALLY

Sorting is a very common computer procedure. It is something computers do very quickly and accurately compared to humans (the computer also enjoys it more). There are many ways to sort; the sorting technique we are using here (we call it the "simple sort") is a very slow one. We have chosen it because it is easy to understand. Since we don't have a lot of items to sort, speed is not that important.

The principle of this type of sort is really fairly simple. We have a nested loop in lines 2210 to 2250. The first time through the outer loop, I is one. In the inner loop, the first name, NAME$(1), is compared to every other name in the list as J goes from 2 to N. The computer takes " < " and " > " to mean earlier and later in the alphabet when dealing with string variables. If the first name is later in the alphabet than the Jth name, the two are swapped (in the subroutine at line 2800). After the outer loop has executed once (and the inner loop N – 1 times), the earliest name (alphabetically) is at the head of the list as NAME$(1). The second time through the outer loop, the second name is compared with all those that follow it and swapped if necessary so that at the end of this pass the second name, NAME$(2) is the second lowest in the alphabet. This continues until the whole list is in alphabetical order.

Notice that when the names are swapped in the subroutine at line 2800, the score is carried along with the name so that, no matter how many swaps occur, each bowler still has his or her own score. For example the number stored in SC(5) will always be the correct score for the bowler whose name is stored in NAME$(5).

An interesting exercise here is to put a counter, like LET SW = SW + 1, in the swap subroutine at line 2800 and see how many swaps actually occur with various numbers of names entered during the program. This is done by typing PRINT SW after the program ends. You may be surprised at this number; with a more efficient sorting routine there would be fewer swaps.

SORTING BY NUMBER

Sorting by number is exactly the same as sorting alphabetically, except that the line that checks to see if the names and scores need to be swapped (line 2630) compares scores instead of names. We have also turned the comparison sign around (> has become <) since with the names we wanted the lowest (alphabetically) at the top of the list, while here we want the bowler with the highest score at the top.

NOTE ON THE PROGRAM

The line numbers for program 9A in figure 9.1 may look a little strange to you. We used the line numbers we did so that the subroutines of this program would be compatible with the example and exercises in chapter 10. We suggest that you use these same line numbers in writing your program or programs for this chapter. That way some of your subroutines may fit easily into the program you will write for chapter 10.

EXAMPLE 9A   Bowling Team

Problem   You are the manager of a bowling team. Write a program that prompts you to enter the bowlers' names and scores and prints three tables: first, with the names and scores in the order they were entered; second, sorted alphabetically by name; and third, sorted by score with the best bowlers at the top. Each table should have a heading identifying it as unsorted, sorted by name, or sorted by number, and should stay on the screen until the user presses the RETURN key. The program should produce tables like the one below:

```
BOWLING TEAM SCORES
SORTED BY NAME
-------------------
NAME            SCORE
-------------------
ADAMS           180
 .               .
 .               .
SANCHEZ         190
-------------------
```

Figure 9.1

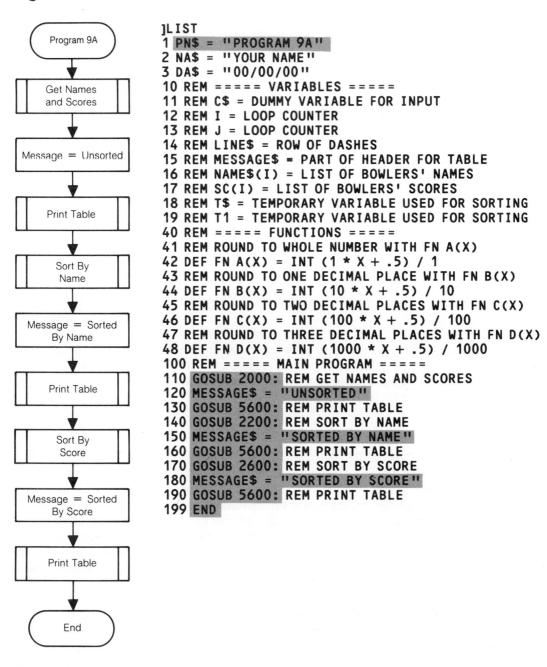

```
]LIST
1 PN$ = "PROGRAM 9A"
2 NA$ = "YOUR NAME"
3 DA$ = "00/00/00"
10 REM ===== VARIABLES =====
11 REM C$ = DUMMY VARIABLE FOR INPUT
12 REM I = LOOP COUNTER
13 REM J = LOOP COUNTER
14 REM LINE$ = ROW OF DASHES
15 REM MESSAGE$ = PART OF HEADER FOR TABLE
16 REM NAME$(I) = LIST OF BOWLERS' NAMES
17 REM SC(I) = LIST OF BOWLERS' SCORES
18 REM T$ = TEMPORARY VARIABLE USED FOR SORTING
19 REM T1 = TEMPORARY VARIABLE USED FOR SORTING
40 REM ===== FUNCTIONS =====
41 REM ROUND TO WHOLE NUMBER WITH FN A(X)
42 DEF FN A(X) = INT (1 * X + .5) / 1
43 REM ROUND TO ONE DECIMAL PLACE WITH FN B(X)
44 DEF FN B(X) = INT (10 * X + .5) / 10
45 REM ROUND TO TWO DECIMAL PLACES WITH FN C(X)
46 DEF FN C(X) = INT (100 * X + .5) / 100
47 REM ROUND TO THREE DECIMAL PLACES WITH FN D(X)
48 DEF FN D(X) = INT (1000 * X + .5) / 1000
100 REM ===== MAIN PROGRAM =====
110 GOSUB 2000: REM GET NAMES AND SCORES
120 MESSAGE$ = "UNSORTED"
130 GOSUB 5600: REM PRINT TABLE
140 GOSUB 2200: REM SORT BY NAME
150 MESSAGE$ = "SORTED BY NAME"
160 GOSUB 5600: REM PRINT TABLE
170 GOSUB 2600: REM SORT BY SCORE
180 MESSAGE$ = "SORTED BY SCORE"
190 GOSUB 5600: REM PRINT TABLE
199 END
```

Flowchart labels (top to bottom):
Program 9A
Get Names and Scores
Message = Unsorted
Print Table
Sort By Name
Message = Sorted By Name
Print Table
Sort By Score
Message = Sorted By Score
Print Table
End

(Figure continued)

(Figure 9.1 continued)

```
2000 REM ==== SUBROUTINE TO ENTER NAMES AND SCORES ====
2010 HOME
2020 INPUT "HOW MANY NAMES :";N
2030 DIM NAME$(N), SC(N)
2040 FOR I = 1 TO N
2050 PRINT
2060 PRINT I;: INPUT " ENTER NAME:";NAME$(I)
2070 INPUT "      SCORE:";SC(I)
2080 NEXT I
2090 RETURN
2099 :
```

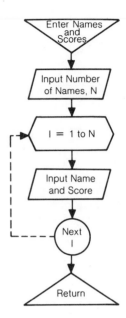

(Figure continued)

(Figure 9.1 continued)

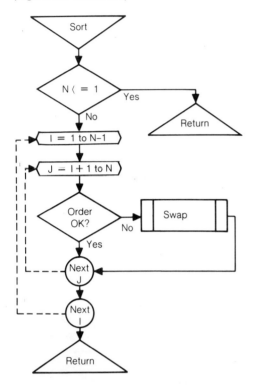

```
2200 REM === SUBROUTINE TO SORT BY NAME ===
2205 IF N < = 1 THEN RETURN : REM NO SORTING NEEDED
2210 FOR I = 1 TO N - 1
2220 FOR J = (I + 1) TO N
2230 IF NAME$(I) > NAME$(J) THEN GOSUB 2800: REM SWAP NAMES AND SCORES
2240 NEXT J
2250 NEXT I
2260 RETURN
2270 :
2600 REM === SUBROUTINE TO SORT BY SCORE ===
2605 IF N < = 1 THEN RETURN : REM NO SORTING NEEDED
2610 FOR I = 1 TO N - 1
2620 FOR J = (I + 1) TO N
2630 IF SC(I) < SC(J) THEN GOSUB 2800: REM SWAP NAMES AND SCORES
2640 NEXT J
2650 NEXT I
2660 RETURN
2670 :
2800 REM === SUBROUTINE TO SWAP NAMES AND SCORES ===
2810 LET T$ = NAME$(I): LET T1 = SC(I)
2820 LET NAME$(I) = NAME$(J) : LET SC(I) = SC(J)
2830 LET NAME$(J) = T$: LET SC(J) = T1
2840 RETURN
2850 :
```

(Figure continued)

(Figure 9.1 continued)

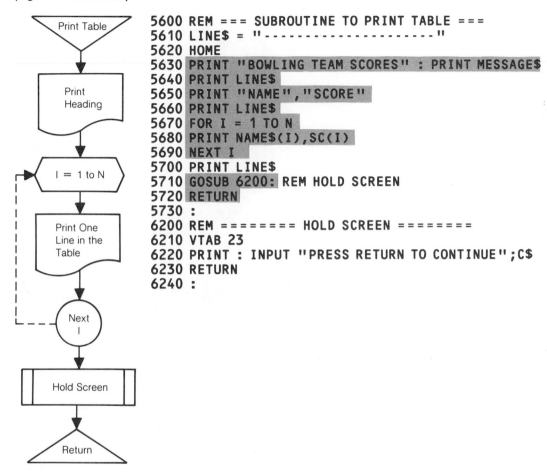

```
5600 REM === SUBROUTINE TO PRINT TABLE ===
5610 LINE$ = "--------------------"
5620 HOME
5630 PRINT "BOWLING TEAM SCORES" : PRINT MESSAGE$
5640 PRINT LINE$
5650 PRINT "NAME","SCORE"
5660 PRINT LINE$
5670 FOR I = 1 TO N
5680 PRINT NAME$(I),SC(I)
5690 NEXT I
5700 PRINT LINE$
5710 GOSUB 6200: REM HOLD SCREEN
5720 RETURN
5730 :
6200 REM ======== HOLD SCREEN ========
6210 VTAB 23
6220 PRINT : INPUT "PRESS RETURN TO CONTINUE";C$
6230 RETURN
6240 :
```

(Figure continued)

RUN (Screen #1)

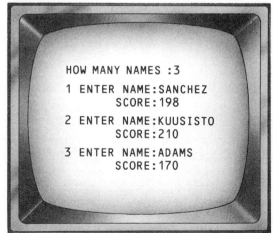

(Figure 9.1 continued)

RUN (Screen #2)

```
BOWLING TEAM SCORES
UNSORTED
- - - - - - - - - - - - - - - - - - - -
NAME                 SCORE
- - - - - - - - - - - - - - - - - - - -
SANCHEZ              198
KUUSISTO             210
ADAMS                170
- - - - - - - - - - - - - - - - - - - -


PRESS RETURN TO CONTINUE
```

RUN (Screen #3)

```
BOWLING TEAM SCORES
SORTED BY NAME
- - - - - - - - - - - - - - - - - - - -
NAME                 SCORE
- - - - - - - - - - - - - - - - - - - -
ADAMS                170
KUUSISTO             210
SANCHEZ              198
- - - - - - - - - - - - - - - - - - - -


PRESS RETURN TO CONTINUE
```

RUN (Screen #4)

```
BOWLING TEAM SCORES
SORTED BY SCORE
- - - - - - - - - - - - - - - - - - - -
NAME                 SCORE
- - - - - - - - - - - - - - - - - - - -
KUUSISTO             210
SANCHEZ              198
ADAMS                170
- - - - - - - - - - - - - - - - - - - -


PRESS RETURN TO CONTINUE
```

SELF-TESTING QUESTIONS

Step through the program in each question and write the output produced when the program runs.

9.1
```
110 FOR I = 1 TO 5
120 READ A(I)
130 NEXT I
140 DATA 8,7,5,4,3
150 FOR I = 1 TO 5
160 PRINT A(I);" ";
170 NEXT I
```

9.2
```
110 FOR I = 1 TO 5
120 READ A(I)
130 NEXT I
140 DATA 7,2,4,8,3
150 FOR I = 5 TO 1 STEP -1
160 PRINT A(I);" ";
170 NEXT I
```

9.3 Lines 110 to 140 apply to parts (a) and (b).
```
110 FOR I = 1 TO 4
120 READ N$(I), S(I)
130 NEXT I
140 DATA JANE,80, DAVE,82, CAROL,90, FRANK,88
```

(a)
```
150 FOR I = 1 TO 4
160 PRINT N$(I);TAB( 10);S(I)
170 NEXT I
```

(b)
```
150 FOR I = 1 TO 4
160 PRINT N$(I);TAB( 8 * I);
170 NEXT I
180 PRINT
190 FOR I = 1 TO 4
200 PRINT S(I);TAB( 8 * I);
210 NEXT I
```

9.4 Lines 110 to 180 apply to parts (a) through (e).
```
110 FOR I = 1 TO 3
120 FOR J = 1 TO 3
130 READ A(I,J)
140 NEXT J
150 NEXT I
160 DATA 8,14,15
170 DATA 21,3,7
180 DATA 19,2,9
```

(a)
```
190 FOR I = 1 TO 3
200 FOR J = 1 TO 3
210 PRINT A(I,J);" ";
220 NEXT J
230 PRINT
240 NEXT I
```

(b)   ```
190 FOR J = 1 TO 3
200 FOR I = 1 TO 3
210 PRINT A(I,J);" ";
220 NEXT I
230 PRINT
240 NEXT J
```

(c)    ```
190 FOR I = 1 TO 3
200 PRINT A(I,I);" ";
210 NEXT I
```

(d)   ```
190 FOR I = 1 TO 3
200 FOR J = 1 TO 3
210 PRINT A(J,I);" ";
220 NEXT J
230 PRINT
240 NEXT I
```

(e)    ```
190 FOR I = 3 TO 1 STEP -1
200 FOR J = 3 TO 1 STEP -1
210 PRINT A(I,J);" ";
220 NEXT J
230 PRINT
240 NEXT I
```

9.5   Lines 110 to 190 apply to parts (a) through (e).

```
110 FOR I = 1 TO 3
120 READ N$(I)
130 FOR J = 1 TO 3
140 READ S(I,J)
150 NEXT J
160 NEXT I
170 DATA TERRY, 82, 78, 90
180 DATA CARL, 88, 80, 85
190 DATA JUNE, 86, 90, 84
```

(a)   ```
200 FOR I = 1 TO 3
210 PRINT N$(I);
220 FOR J = 1 TO 3
230 PRINT TAB(8 * J); S(I,J);
240 NEXT J
250 PRINT
260 NEXT I
```

(b)    ```
200 FOR I = 1 TO 3
210 PRINT N$(I);TAB( 8 * I);
220 NEXT I
230 PRINT
240 FOR J = 1 TO 3
250 FOR I = 1 TO 3
260 PRINT S(I,J);TAB( 8 * I);
270 NEXT I
280 PRINT
290 NEXT J
```

(c)
```
200 FOR I = 1 TO 3
210 PRINT N$(I);TAB( 10);S(I,3)
220 NEXT I
```

(d)
```
200 FOR I = 1 TO 3
210 LET T(I) = 0
220 FOR J = 1 TO 3
230 LET T(I) = T(I) + S(I,J)
240 NEXT J
250 PRINT N$(I);TAB( 10);T(I)
260 NEXT I
```

(e)
```
200 FOR I = 1 TO 3
210 LET T(I) = 0
220 FOR J = 1 TO 3
230 LET T(I) = T(I) + S(I,J)
240 NEXT J
250 LET A(I) = INT (T(I) / 3 + 0.5)
260 PRINT N$(I); TAB( 10);A(I)
270 NEXT I
```

9.6   Lines 110 to 160 apply to parts (a) and (b).

```
110 FOR I = 1 TO 3
120 READ N$(I), S(I)
130 NEXT I
140 DATA TERRY, 78
150 DATA CARL, 64
160 DATA JUNE, 76
```

(a)
```
170 FOR I = 1 TO 2
180 FOR J = I + 1 TO 3
190 IF N$(I) < N$(J) GOTO 230
200 LET T$ = N$(I)
210 LET N$(I) = N$(J)
220 LET N$(J) = T$
230 NEXT J
240 NEXT I
250 FOR I = 1 TO 3
260 PRINT N$(I);TAB( 10);S(I)
270 NEXT I
```

(b)
```
170 FOR I = 1 TO 2
180 FOR J = I + 1 TO 3
190 IF S(I) < S(J) GOTO 230
200 LET T = S(I)
210 LET S(I) = S(J)
220 LET S(J) = T
230 NEXT J
240 NEXT I
250 FOR I = 1 TO 3
260 PRINT N$(I);TAB( 10);S(I)
270 NEXT I
```

(c) Correct the instructions in part (a) so that the scores will not be mixed up.

(d) Correct the instructions in part (b) so that the names will not be mixed up.

EXERCISES

Choose One of the Following

We *strongly* advise you to use the same line numbers for your program as those in program 9A so that you can use some of the subroutines you write for this program in chapter 10.

9.1 You manage a team of salespeople and need a program to print out their sales for the current week. Use subscripts and INPUT statements to enter the names and sales figures for the salespeople. Print three tables: one in the order the names were entered, one sorted alphabetically by name, and one sorted by sales with the best salesperson on top. Round all numbers to the nearest whole dollar. Arrange the table as shown below. Use TAB(11) for SALES. As in example 9A, each table should have a heading that tells how it is sorted.

Use the following variables:

```
N = NUMBER OF EMPLOYEES
NAME$(I) = NAME OF SALESPERSON
SALES (I) = SALES FOR THE WEEK
```

```
        WEEKLY SALES
    - - - - - - - - - - - - - - - - - - - -
    NAME          SALES
    - - - - - - - - - - - - - - - - - - - -
    SANCHEZ       416
    .             .
    .             .
    WILSON        510
    - - - - - - - - - - - - - - - - - - - -
```

9.2 You are the owner of a hardware store and would like a program to print an inventory statement. Use subscripts and INPUT statements to enter the name, price, and quantity of each item. Print three tables: one in the order the items were entered, one sorted alphabetically by item, and one sorted by price with the most expensive item on top. Use TAB(14) for PRICE, and TAB(22) for QUANTITY. Round all dollar amounts to the nearest cent. As in example 9A, each table should have a heading that tells how it was sorted. Your program should produce a table like the one shown below.

Use the following variables:

```
N = NUMBER OF ITEMS
NAME$(I) = NAME OF ITEM
PRICE(I) = PRICE OF ITEM
QUANTITY(I) = NUMBER ON HAND
```

```
            HARDWARE INVENTORY
    - - - - - - - - - - - - - - - - - - - - - - - - - - - -
    NAME        PRICE       QUANTITY
    - - - - - - - - - - - - - - - - - - - - - - - - - - - -
    HAMMER      9.5         35
    .           .           .
    .           .           .
    CHAIN SAW   285         12
    - - - - - - - - - - - - - - - - - - - - - - - - - - - -
```

9.3 You manage a baseball team and need to keep track of the players' statistics. Use subscripts and INPUT statements to enter the names, hits, and at-bats for each player and have the program calculate each player's batting average (hits/at-bats). Print three tables: one in the order the names were entered, one sorted alphabetically by name, and one sorted by batting average with the best hitter on top. Batting averages are rounded to the nearest thousandth. Arrange the table as shown below. Use TAB(14) for BATTING AVERAGE, TAB(22) for TOTAL HITS, and TAB(30) for TOTAL AT-BATS. As in example 9A, each table should have a title that tells how it was sorted.

Use the following variables:

```
N = NUMBER OF PLAYERS
NAME$(I) = NAME OF EACH PLAYER
BA(I) = CURRENT BATTING AVERAGE
HITS(I) = TOTAL HITS
AB(I) = TOTAL AT-BATS
```

```
              BASEBALL STATISTICS
- - - - - - - - - - - - - - - - - - - - - - - - - - - - -
              BATTING    TOTAL     TOTAL
NAME          AVERAGE    HITS      AT-BATS
- - - - - - - - - - - - - - - - - - - - - - - - - - - - -
BABBAGE        .308      36        120
.                .        .         .
.                .        .         .
.                .        .         .
WOZNIAK        .333      45        135
- - - - - - - - - - - - - - - - - - - - - - - - - - - - -
```

9.4 Your employees are paid by the week. Use subscripts and INPUT statements to enter the names, wage rates, and hours worked this week for each employee and have the program calculate their pay. Print three tables: one in the order the names were entered, one sorted alphabetically by name, and one sorted by pay with the highest paid employee on top. Use time and a half for overtime (Hours > 40). Round all dollar amounts to the nearest cent. Arrange the table as shown below. Use TAB(12) for WAGE RATE, and TAB(20) for PAY FOR WEEK. As in example 9A, each table should have a title that tells how it was sorted.

Use the following variables:

```
N = NUMBER OF EMPLOYEES
NAME$(I) = NAME OF EACH EMPLOYEE
WAGE(I) = WAGE RATE FOR EACH EMPLOYEE
HOURS(I) = HOURS FOR EACH EMPLOYEE
PAY(I) = PAY FOR CURRENT WEEK
```

```
                 PAYROLL
- - - - - - - - - - - - - - - - - - - - - - - - - - -
EMPLOYEE      WAGE        PAY
NAME          RATE        FOR WEEK
- - - - - - - - - - - - - - - - - - - - - - - - - - -
ARBOGAST      5.22        210.80
   .             .           .

   .             .           .
ZELNIK        7.81        312.40
- - - - - - - - - - - - - - - - - - - - - - - - - - -
```

9.5 You need a gradebook program to print out your students' grades. All your exams are worth 100 points. Use subscripts and INPUT statements to enter the names and exam scores for the students. Print three tables: one in the order the names were entered, one sorted by name, and one sorted by score (with the A's on top, of course). As in example 9A, each table should have a title that tells how it was sorted. The grades are given as follows:

$$95 \text{ and over} = A$$
$$85 \text{ to } 94 = B$$
$$70 \text{ to } 84 = C$$
$$60 \text{ to } 69 = D$$
$$\text{under } 60 = F$$

Arrange the table as follows. Use TAB(14) for WEEKLY SCORE, and TAB(22) for GRADE.

Use the following variables:

```
N = NUMBER OF STUDENTS
NAME$(I) = NAME OF EACH STUDENT
MARK(I) = THIS WEEK'S SCORE
G$(I) = CURRENT GRADE
```

```
               GRADES
- - - - - - - - - - - - - - - - - - - - - - - - -
NAME           SCORE      GRADE
- - - - - - - - - - - - - - - - - - - - - - - - -
ANTON           77          C
  .              .          .
  .              .          .
WESTON          86          B
- - - - - - - - - - - - - - - - - - - - - - - - -
```

CHAPTER 10

THE BIG ONE
Writing a Major Program

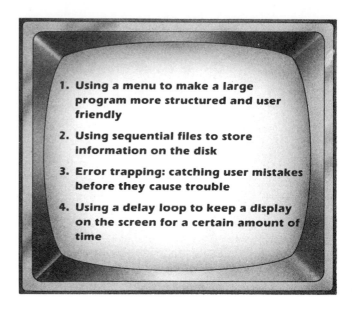

1. **Using a menu to make a large program more structured and user friendly**

2. **Using sequential files to store information on the disk**

3. **Error trapping: catching user mistakes before they cause trouble**

4. **Using a delay loop to keep a display on the screen for a certain amount of time**

WRITING A LARGE PROGRAM

Our programming standards have to become a little stricter when writing a large and complex program like program 10A in figure 10.1. The program must have a logical structure so that we can write it, debug it, and generally find our way around in it. One way of structuring a program is to use a menu. This gives the user a number of choices and makes the program more "user friendly." It also divides the program into logical units that we can work with one at a time. In program 10A, the menu divides the program into five basic parts; these are the main routines that start at line 1100.

At line 2000 and following, we have the supporting routines. These do the actual work for the main routines. If you look at the main routines, you can see that they don't actually *do* anything except call the supporting subroutines. At line 6000 are the two utility routines (to be discussed later).

By dividing the program into these sections, we not only make it easier to understand, but we also break this fairly large task into smaller jobs that are much easier to tackle. We have also made the program "modular" by planning the supporting routines so that they can be used by several of the main routines. For example, the routine that reads the file (at line 5400) is used by four of the five main routines. This kind of programming not only makes the program easier to write and understand, it also saves memory. The methods we have described here are generally called "structured-programming techniques" and are absolutely required for good programming. Although BASIC is often accused of being an "unstructured" language, programs in BASIC can be as well structured as you want to make them.

We recommend that you make a list with the name of each subroutine of the program and its line number, and that you keep this list handy at all times.

SUBSCRIPTS

The subscripts in this program are used just as they were in chapter 9. They are used to enter data, print tables, and sort. In addition, they are used in program 10A to read and write data on the disk and to set all the scores to zero.

INITIALIZATION

This is a new section of code we haven't seen before. In larger programs there are often many variables that keep the same value throughout the program. We have already seen this with PN$ for the program name. In the initialization section of program 10A in figure 10.1 (following line 50), we are dealing with file variables.

D$ as the DOS Command Character

In Applesoft, any command that deals with the operation of the disk drive such as LOAD, SAVE, DELETE, etc., must have a special character in front of it that alerts DOS (the Disk Operating System) that the following command is meant for it. This character is a CTRL-D and it would be simplest to put it into the program as a CTRL-D. The catch is that CTRL-D does not print, so that, although it might be there, you couldn't see it when listing the program. To make programs more readable, a common convention is to set D$ = CHR$(4). Whenever D$ appears in a program, most experienced programmers recognize it as another way of specifying CTRL-D.

Line 51 in this program sets up D$. This way when we want to issue a DOS command we can just use D$ in a print statement like:

```
10 PRINT D$; "DELETE PROGRAM 1"
```

Needless to say, this would cause the deletion of PROGRAM 1 from the disk.

**PRINT D$** In Applesoft, the disk control commands must all appear in a print statement in which the first character printed is a Control-D. In this manual, the Control-D character is shown as CHR$(4) and is stored in the variable D$. (The number 4 is the decimal code for Control-D in Applesoft.)

The disk unit responds only to commands that are preceded by: PRINT D$ where D$ = CHR$(4) = Control-D.

F$ as the File Name

Another new feature of this program is that it stores information on the disk in what is called a "data file" or "text file." The program will need to refer to this file by name in the DOS commands which read and write the file. We could refer to the file by name, but, to make it easier and to protect against spelling errors, we set F$ to the file name in line 52; that way we can read the file by having a line like the following:

```
10 PRINT D$; "READ" F$
```

which is the equivalent of:

```
10 PRINT D$; "READ BOWLING TEAM"
```

The DIM Statement

We have put the dimension statement here (line 53) to make sure that it is only executed once (otherwise a ?REDIM'D ARRAY ERROR would occur). Make sure when you write your program that this is the only DIM statement in it, or you will get this error. In line 53 we dimension all of the subscripted variables we will need in the program. Since we don't know for sure how many bowlers will be on the team, we dimension all the variables to 100, which should be more than enough.

THE MENU

We have put the menu at line 100 since it is the heart of the program. A menu is a list of choices the user can make to direct the operation of the program. This program always comes back to the menu and what the program does is determined by the user in making a menu choice. The section of program that prints the menu and gets the user's response is pretty straightforward, with two exceptions.

Error Trapping

At the end of the menu section, you may be able to see some of the techniques commonly used to catch user mistakes and respond to them before everything goes boom. If we had only the menu and the input statement at the end of it, what would happen if the user entered 22 as the menu choice? How about 2.2, or just hitting return without making a choice? In any good program, user input is checked *before* it is acted upon and if something is wrong, the program tries to recover gracefully. This is called "error trapping."

In line 200 we use C$ for the variable to be inputted and convert it to the numeric variable C in line 210, using the VAL function. We do this because if we input C and the user enters a letter, the program will issue a

?REENTER command. This is messy, and it also scrolls the menu off the top of the screen (one line at a time). So in line 210 the user has typed a number (C); it still may not match one of the menu choices. This is what line 240 is for. If C is between 1 and 6 (inclusive) and C is an integer, everything is fine and the program jumps to line 280, which we'll discuss in a minute. If not, the number is not a legal menu choice and in line 250 the user is informed as gently as possible that a mistake has been made. Line 260 has the job of doing nothing 1000 times so that the message of line 250 ("I respond only to integers from 1 to 6") will stay on the screen long enough for the user to read it. When the time is up, line 270 sends the program back to line 100 where the screen is cleared and the menu is started fresh. This process is repeated until the user has entered a legal menu choice.

ON/GOSUB

When the user enters a legitimate menu choice, line 280 is executed. The ON/GOSUB command is a somewhat fancy branching statement. It represents a whole string of IF THEN statements (like IF C = 1 THEN GOSUB 1100). Notice that in line 280 there are six line numbers corresponding to the five main routines and the end. The statement ON C GOSUB means that if C is one, the program should go to the first subroutine in the list (in this case the one at line 1100; if C is two, it will go to the second one on the list, and so on. Since it is a GOSUB command, after the subroutine is finished the program will return to the next line *after* the line with the ON/GOSUB command. This is line 290 which sends the user back to the menu (unless the user has picked choice 6, in which case the program goes to line 300 and ends). Applesoft also has the ON/GOTO command, but its use is usually considered to be a bad programming practice and makes programs hard to understand.

UTILITIES

Option Not Available Subroutine (Line 6000)

This subroutine is one that will not be used when the program is finished. It allows us to test the menu section without writing the whole program. If we set things up so that each of the main routines contains nothing but a call to this subroutine and a RETURN statement, then every legal menu choice (except number 6) should produce the "SORRY, THIS OPTION IS NOT AVAILABLE YET" message. Later, when each main routine is written, the GOSUB 6000 will be removed. These subroutines that don't really do anything but test other parts of a program are called "dummy subroutines," or "stubs."

Hold Screen Subroutine (Line 6200)

In chapter 9 we saw how to use this subroutine to keep a display on the screen as long as the user wants it there; we are using it the same way here.

THE MAIN ROUTINES

The following five main routines correspond to the first five menu choices. We will discuss what each one does and then talk about the supporting subroutines that they call.

Enter Names and Start New File (Line 1100)

This routine gets things started. The names are entered and sorted and the scores set to zero. Then the file is written to the disk and the table printed on the screen and held until the user is ready to return to the menu.

Read File and Print Table (Line 1200)

Now that there is a file on the disk, we can read it and print the file on the screen (sorted alphabetically by name) and hold it there. At first the file and the table will have all the scores set to zero. This will be true until the file is updated the first time.

Enter Scores and Update File (Line 1300)

Every week, new bowling scores are entered for each player, and the total scores and the new averages are written into the file on the disk. First, the current information must be read from the disk. Then the new information is entered, the new data is written to the disk, and a new table is printed and held on the screen.

Zero Scores and Write File (Line 1400)

This option is used when things get goofed up, and you need to start over. Suppose that you have successfully written the routines that read and write the file, and they work fine. Now you try to write the update part of the program, and, it not only doesn't work, it messes up the file on the disk. Now even if you fix the Update routine it won't work right (and neither will the Read routine) because the file is messed up. You need a convenient way to get the file back in shape without having to enter the names all over again. When you run it, you lose all the scores, but at least the names don't have to be reentered. Another use for this routine would be to start a new season for the team and set all scores and averages to zero.

Sort by Score and Print Table (Line 1500)

Because the Enter Names routine sorts the names alphabetically, they remain so in the file and any table will be printed that way unless re-sorted. This subroutine might be used to print a table each week sorted by total score so that whoever has the highest total score would be at the top of the list. It first reads the file, then sorts it, then prints the table (sorted by score) and holds it on the screen. This routine has no effect on the file since the newly sorted scores are not written back to the disk.

End (Line 300)

This one is pretty obvious.

SUPPORTING ROUTINES

As mentioned before, these supporting routines do the actual work of the program and are written as "modules" that can be used by various main routines (and by other programs as well).

Enter Names (Line 2000)

This subroutine does nothing but prompt the user to enter the names of the bowlers which are stored in the array NAME$(I).

Sort by Name (Line 2200)

This is like the alphabetical sorting we did in chapter 9.

Enter Scores and Update Numbers (Line 2400)

This subroutine prompts the user with the name of each bowler and gets his or her score (S) for the current week. First, WEEK is increased by one since it is a new week. Then S is entered by the user and added to T(I) to get the new total. In line 2470, the new average is computed by dividing the new total by the number of weeks and rounding the result using function B.

Sort by Score (Line 2600)

This a slightly more complicated sort than the one in chapter 9. Here we need to carry each bowler's total score and average along with their name. Otherwise we might have some pretty angry bowlers on our hands. The structure of this subroutine is exactly the same as the one to sort by name. The only difference is in which variables are compared in the decision of when to swap names and scores.

Swap Names and Scores (Line 2800)

This is the same subroutine we used in chapter 9 with the addition of another variable, since here we have a three-column table with two sets of scores.

Zero Scores (Line 5000)

This subroutine is nothing but a simple loop that sets each bowler's total score and average to zero.

Write File to Disk (Line 5200)

This subroutine does the important job of storing the information we have collected in a permanent file on the disk. Since the writing of the file to the disk is invisible to the user, we first print the message in line 5210 telling the user what is going on.

Line 5220 opens the file. Before any file can be read or written to, it must first be opened. This tells the system to set aside a buffer in memory for data going to or from the file and to find the beginning of the file. The buffer holds 256 characters (letters, digits, symbols, or spaces). When writing to a file, the information is not actually written to the disk until the buffer is full or the file is closed. This is one reason why it's important to remember to close a file after writing to it.

OPEN   The OPEN command prepares the file for a READ or WRITE operation. The command consists of PRINT D$ followed by "OPEN" and the name of the file as shown below.

```
5 D$ = CHR$(4)
10 N$ = "FILE 1"
15 PRINT D$;"OPEN";N$
```

or

```
15 PRINT D$ ;"OPEN";"FILE 1"
```

or

```
15 PRINT D$;"OPEN FILE 1"
```

CLOSE   The CLOSE command returns the file after use. The command consists of PRINT D$ followed by "CLOSE" and the file name as shown below.

```
5 D$ = CHR$(4)
10 N$ = "FILE 1"
15 PRINT D$; "CLOSE"; N$
```

(or options similar to the OPEN command)

Line 5230 tells the computer that we plan to write to the file. This means that the contents of any PRINT statements that follows will be printed on the disk rather than the screen. This condition is in effect until cancelled; thus, if you forget to close the file, the next PRINT statements in the program will print on the disk. If you're not careful, you could end up with your entire menu printed in the file; this is another good reason for remembering to close the file (closing cancels the WRITE command).

WRITE   The WRITE command sets the file up for writing names or numbers into the file. The command consists of PRINT D$ followed by "WRITE" and the file name as shown below.

```
5 D$ = CHR$(4)
10 N$ = "FILE 1"
15 PRINT D$; "WRITE"; N$
```

(or options similar to the OPEN command)

```
45 PRINT D$
```

After a WRITE file command has been executed, *all* information printed through PRINT statements will be written in the file. This continues until a PRINT D$ terminates the file's write operation. In the example above, all PRINT statements between line 15 and line 45 will write in the file.

In line 5240 we print N, the number of bowlers on the team and in line 5250 we print the week number. Then in the loop from line 5260 to line 5300 we print their name, total score, and average. If, after three weeks, we could look at the file for two bowlers, it might look like this:

```
2
3
ADAMS
300
100
SMITH
450
150
```

Actually, we *can* look at the file if we wish by using the MON command. The command MON,O will cause the computer to write on the screen everything that it writes to the file on the disk. If you use the MON,O command before entering the scores for the third week, output like that shown above will appear on the screen as the file is being written to the disk. You will have to read quickly, because as soon as the file is written to the disk, the program will clear the screen and print the table. The SPEED command is often used to slow down the screen display so you can read the output at a comfortable pace (try SPEED = 30). The command NOMON,O will turn off the file monitoring operations and SPEED = 255 will set the speed back to normal.

MON   The MON command turns on a monitoring feature that prints on the screen all information going to or coming from the file. This feature is useful while debugging programs, but may be distracting or undesirable in a perfected program. The monitor can be canceled by the NOMON command. This is often used in conjunction with the SPEED command (e.g. SPEED = 30) to slow things down and to see file operations as they happen. The MON command consists of MON followed by some combination of the letters C, I, and O separated by commas. For example:

MON, C, I, O
    C turns on monitoring of disk commands
    I turns on monitoring of input
    O turns on monitoring of output

NOMON   The NOMON command cancels the monitoring operations. The command consists of MON followed by some combination of C, I, and O, separated by commas. The C, I, and O cancel printing of disk commands, input and output respectively. NOMON, C, I, O cancels all monitoring operations.

In line 5310 we close the file. We have already mentioned the importance of closing a file after a WRITE operation. Failure to close the file will probably result in the loss of some or all of the information in the file.

Read File from Disk (Line 5400)

This subroutine is exactly the same as the one to write the file, except that instead of the WRITE command we use the READ command. This tells the computer that INPUT statements should read data from the disk instead of the keyboard. If you forget to close the file here, the next INPUT statement (probably the one at the end of the menu) will make the program try to read information from the disk. Since we are at the end of the file there is no more data and an END OF DATA ERROR results.

READ The READ command sets the file up for copying names or numbers from the file into variables in your program. The format is the same as for the WRITE command. After a READ file command has been executed, all INPUT statements will get input from the file rather than from the keyboard. The PRINT D$ command terminates a file read operation.

Print Table (Line 5600)

This is a standard subroutine that uses a FOR/NEXT loop to print a table of results, using TAB statements to divide the table into three columns.

EXAMPLE 10A   Bowling Team

Problem Write a program that keeps track of the records of a bowling team. Use INPUT statements to enter the names of the bowlers. Use a sequential file to record the names, total scores, and average scores on the disk. In the file, the bowlers should be in alphabetical order. Each week the file should be updated by having the user enter the bowler's scores for that week. Print a table showing the bowler's name, total score, and average score so far. You should have the option to print a table sorted by total score or to print a table based on the alphabetical file on the disk. The program should produce a table like the one below:

```
            BOWLING TEAM SCORES
              FOR WEEK # 3
    - - - - - - - - - - - - - - - - - - - -
    NAME           TOTAL         AVERAGE
                   SCORE         SCORE
    - - - - - - - - - - - - - - - - - - - -
    ADAMS          300           100
    .              .             .
    .              .             .
    SMITH          450           150
    - - - - - - - - - - - - - - - - - - - -
```

FIGURE 10.1   Structure Chart for Program 10A

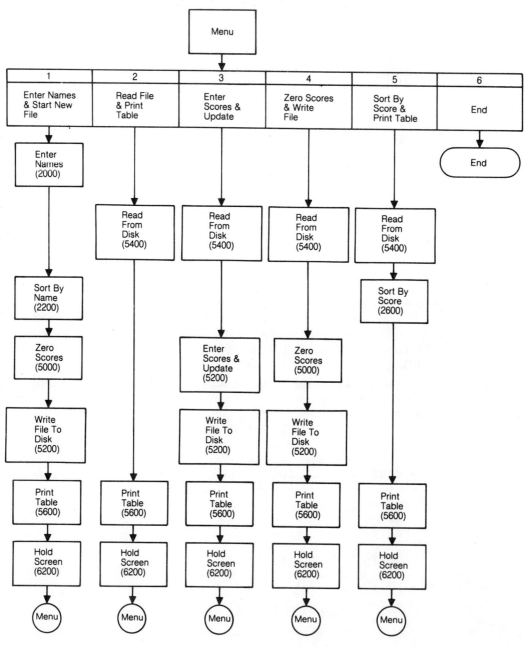

(Figure continued)

(Figure 10.1 continued)

```
]LIST
1 LET PN$ = "PROGRAM 10A - BOWLING TEAM"
2 LET NA$ = "YOUR NAME"
3 LET DA$ = "00/00/00"
4 NORMAL : HOME
10 REM =========== MENU VARIABLES ============
11 REM C$ = MENU RETURN AND INPUT CHARACTER
12 REM C = MENU CHOICE NUMBER
13 REM TIME = TIME DELAY COUNTER
20 REM =========== FILE VARIABLES ============
21 REM N = NUMBER OF NAMES IN THE FILE
22 REM WEEK = WEEK NUMBER
23 REM NAME$(I) = LIST OF NAMES
24 REM T(I) = LIST OF TOTAL SCORES
25 REM AVG(I) = LIST OF AVERAGE SCORES
30 REM ========== UTILITY VARIABLES ==========
31 REM I = LOOP COUNTER
32 REM J = LOOP COUNTER
33 REM LINE$ = A ROW OF DASHES
34 REM S = TEMPORARY VARIABLE USED FOR CURRENT WEEK'S SCORE
35 REM T$ = TEMPORARY VARIABLE USED TO SORT
36 REM T1 = TEMPORARY VARIABLE USED TO SORT
37 REM T2 = TEMPORARY VARIABLE USED TO SORT
40 REM ========== DEFINED FUNCTIONS ==========
41 REM ROUND TO WHOLE NUMBER WITH FN A(X)
42 DEF FN A(X) = INT (1 * X + 0.5) / 1
43 REM ROUND TO ONE DECIMAL PLACE WITH FN B(X)
44 DEF FN B(X) = INT (10 * X + 0.5) / 10
45 REM ROUND TO TWO DECIMAL PLACES WITH FN C(X)
46 DEF FN C(X) = INT (100 * X + 0.5) / 100
47 REM ROUND TO THREE DECIMAL PLACES WITH FN D(X)
48 DEF FN D(X) = INT (1000 * X + 0.5) / 1000
50 REM ========= INITIALIZATION ===========
51 LET D$ = CHR$ (4): REM DISK DRIVE CONTROL CHARACTER
52 LET F$ = "BOWLING TEAM": REM FILE NAME
53 DIM NAME$(100),T(100),AVG(100)
59 :
```

(Figure continued)

(Figure 10.1 continued)

```
100 REM =============== MENU ==================
101 HOME : HTAB 20 - (LEN (PN$) / 2): PRINT PN$
110 PRINT TAB( 18);"MENU"
120 PRINT : PRINT "1. ENTER NAMES & START NEW FILE"
130 PRINT : PRINT "2. READ FILE & PRINT TABLE"
140 PRINT : PRINT "3. ENTER SCORES & UPDATE FILE"
150 PRINT : PRINT "4. ZERO SCORES & WRITE FILE"
160 PRINT : PRINT "5. SORT BY SCORE & PRINT TABLE"
170 PRINT : PRINT "6. END PROGRAM"
180 PRINT : PRINT : PRINT : PRINT TAB( 3)
190 INVERSE
200 INPUT "ENTER THE NUMBER OF YOUR CHOICE";C$
210 LET C = VAL (C$)
220 NORMAL
230 PRINT : PRINT
240 IF C > 0 AND C < 7 AND INT (C) = C THEN GOTO 280
250 PRINT "I RESPOND ONLY TO INTEGERS FROM 1 TO 6"
260 FOR TIME = 1 TO 1000: NEXT TIME
270 GOTO 100
280 ON C GOSUB 1100,1200,1300,1400,1500,300
290 GOTO 100
300 PRINT "GOODBYE" : END
310 :
1100 REM ==== ENTER NAMES & START NEW FILE ====
1110 GOSUB 2000: REM ENTER NAMES
1120 GOSUB 2200: REM SORT NAMES
1130 GOSUB 5000: REM ZERO SCORES
1140 GOSUB 5200: REM WRITE FILE ON DISK
1150 GOSUB 5600: REM PRINT TABLE
1160 GOSUB 6200: REM HOLD SCREEN
1170 RETURN : REM RETURN TO MENU
1180 :
1200 REM ======= READ FILE & PRINT TABLE =======
1210 GOSUB 5400: REM READ FILE FROM DISK
1220 GOSUB 5600: REM PRINT TABLE
1230 GOSUB 6200: REM HOLD SCREEN
1240 RETURN : REM RETURN TO MENU
1250 :
1300 REM ===== ENTER SCORES & UPDATE FILE ======
1310 GOSUB 5400: REM READ FILE FROM DISK
1320 GOSUB 2400: REM ENTER SCORES & UPDATE FILE
1330 GOSUB 5200: REM WRITE UPDATED FILE ON DISK
1340 GOSUB 5600: REM PRINT TABLE
1350 GOSUB 6200: REM HOLD SCREEN
1360 RETURN : REM RETURN TO MENU
1370 :
```

(Figure continued)

(Figure 10.1 continued)

```
1400 REM === ZERO SCORES & WRITE FILE ===
1410 GOSUB 5400: REM READ FILE FROM DISK
1420 GOSUB 5000: REM ZERO SCORES
1430 GOSUB 5200: REM WRITE ZEROED FILE ON DISK
1440 GOSUB 5600: REM PRINT TABLE
1450 GOSUB 6200: REM HOLD SCREEN
1460 RETURN : REM RETURN TO MENU
1470 :
1500 REM ===== SORT BY SCORE & PRINT TABLE =====
1510 GOSUB 5400: REM READ FILE FROM DISK
1520 GOSUB 2600: REM SORT BY SCORE
1530 GOSUB 5600: REM PRINT TABLE
1540 GOSUB 6200: REM HOLD SCREEN
1550 RETURN : REM RETURN TO MENU
1560 :
2000 REM ====== SUBROUTINE TO ENTER NAMES ======
2010 TEXT : HOME
2020 PRINT "ENTER NAMES FOR NEW FILE"
2030 PRINT : PRINT
2040 INPUT "HOW MANY NAMES WILL YOU ENTER?";N
2050 LET WEEK = 0
2060 PRINT
2070 FOR I = 1 TO N
2080 PRINT I; TAB( 5);: INPUT NAME$(I)
2090 NEXT I
2100 RETURN
2110 :
2200 REM ===== SUBROUTINE TO SORT BY NAME ======
2210 FOR I = 1 TO N - 1
2220 FOR J = I + 1 TO N
2230 IF NAME$(I) > NAME$(J) THEN GOSUB 2800 : REM SWAP NAMES AND SCORES
2240 NEXT J
2250 NEXT I
2260 RETURN
2270 :
2400 REM == SUBROUTINE TO ENTER SCORES & UPDATE ==
2410 HOME
2420 LET WEEK = WEEK + 1
2430 PRINT : PRINT "ENTER THE SCORE FOR EACH PLAYER": PRINT
2440 FOR I = 1 TO N
2450 PRINT NAME$(I); TAB( 15);: INPUT S
2460 LET T(I) = T(I) + S
2470 LET AVG(I) = FN B(T(I) / WEEK)
2480 NEXT I
2490 RETURN
2500 :
```

(Figure continued)

(Figure 10.1 continued)

```
2600 REM ===== SUBROUTINE TO SORT BY SCORE =====
2610 FOR I = 1 TO N - 1
2620 FOR J = I + 1 TO N
2630 IF T(I) <  T(J) THEN GOSUB 2800 : REM SWAP NAMES AND SCORES
2640 NEXT J
2650 NEXT I
2660 RETURN
2670 :
2800 REM === SUBROUTINE TO SWAP NAMES AND SCORES ===
2810 LET T$ = NAME$(I) : LET T1 = T(I) : LET T2 = AVG(I)
2820 LET NAME$(I) = NAME$(J) : LET T(I) = T(J) : LET AVG(I) = AVG(J)
2830 LET NAME$(J) = T$ : LET T(J) = T1 : LET AVG(J) = T2
2840 RETURN
2850 :
5000 REM ====== SUBROUTINE TO ZERO SCORES ======
5010 FOR I = 1 TO N
5020 LET T(I) = 0
5030 LET AVG(I) = 0
5040 NEXT I
5050 LET WEEK = 0
5060 RETURN
5070 :
5200 REM == SUBROUTINE TO WRITE FILE ON DISK ==
5210 HOME : VTAB 10: HTAB 11: PRINT "WRITING FILE TO DISK"
5220 PRINT D$;"OPEN";F$
5230 PRINT D$;"WRITE";F$
5240 PRINT N
5250 PRINT WEEK
5260 FOR I = 1 TO N
5270 PRINT NAME$(I)
5280 PRINT T(I)
5290 PRINT AVG(I)
5300 NEXT I
5310 PRINT D$;"CLOSE";F$
5320 RETURN
5330 :
```

(Figure continued)

(Figure 10.1 continued)

```
5400 REM ======= SUBROUTINE TO READ FILE =======
5410 HOME : VTAB 10: HTAB 10: PRINT "READING FILE FROM DISK"
5420 PRINT D$;"OPEN";F$
5430 PRINT D$;"READ";F$
5440 INPUT N
5450 INPUT WEEK
5460 FOR I = 1 TO N
5470 INPUT NAME$(I)
5480 INPUT T(I)
5490 INPUT AVG(I)
5500 NEXT I
5510 PRINT D$;"CLOSE";F$
5520 RETURN
5530 :
5600 REM ====== SUBROUTINE TO PRINT TABLE ======
5610 LET LINE$ = "-----------------------------------"
5620 HOME
5630 PRINT TAB( 10);"BOWLING TEAM SCORES"
5640 PRINT TAB( 14);"FOR WEEK #";WEEK
5650 PRINT LINE$
5660 PRINT "NAME"; TAB( 15);"TOTAL"; TAB( 30);"AVERAGE"
5670 PRINT TAB( 15);"SCORE"; TAB( 30);"SCORE"
5680 PRINT LINE$
5690 FOR I = 1 TO N
5700 PRINT NAME$(I); TAB( 15);T(I); TAB( 30);AVG(I)
5710 NEXT I
5720 PRINT LINE$
5730 RETURN
5740 :
6000 REM === SUBROUTINE TO PRINT NOT AVAILABLE ===
6010 HOME : VTAB 10
6020 PRINT "SORRY, THIS OPTION IS NOT AVAILABLE YET"
6030 FOR TIME = 1 TO 1000: NEXT TIME: REM TIME DELAY
6040 RETURN
6050 :
6200 REM ======= HOLD SCREEN ========
6210 VTAB 23
6220 INPUT "PRESS RETURN TO CONTINUE";C$
6230 RETURN
6240 :
```

(Figure continued)

(Figure 10.1 continued)

RUN (Screen #1)

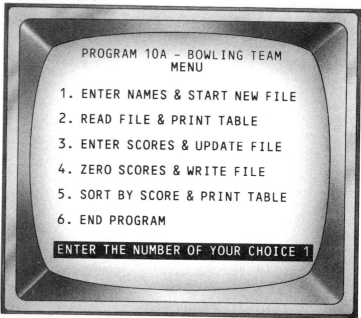

```
        PROGRAM 10A - BOWLING TEAM
                   MENU

   1. ENTER NAMES & START NEW FILE

   2. READ FILE & PRINT TABLE

   3. ENTER SCORES & UPDATE FILE

   4. ZERO SCORES & WRITE FILE

   5. SORT BY SCORE & PRINT TABLE

   6. END PROGRAM

  ENTER THE NUMBER OF YOUR CHOICE 1
```

RUN (Screen #2)

```
   ENTER NAMES FOR NEW FILE

   HOW MANY NAMES WILL YOU ENTER? 3

   1   ?SMITH
   2   ?JONES
   3   ?ADAMS
```

(Figure continued)

(Figure 10.1 continued)

RUN (Screen #3)

RUN (Screen #4)

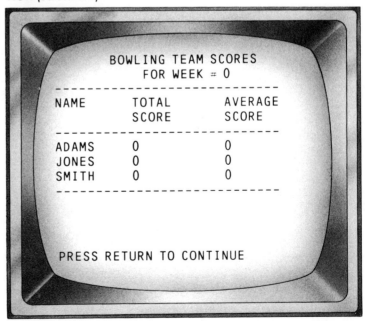

SELF-TESTING QUESTIONS

10.1 Lines 110 through 160 apply to parts (a), (b), and (c). Write the output produced by each part if the file named NUMBERS has the content shown below.

```
110 LET D$ = CHR$ (4)
120 LET F$ = "NUMBERS"
130 PRINT D$;"OPEN";F$
140 PRINT D$;"READ";F$
150 INPUT N
160 FOR I = 1 TO N
```

NUMBERS FILE

```
3
12
8
71
47
63
21
18
4
7
```

(a)
```
170 INPUT A(I)
180 INPUT B(I)
190 INPUT C(I)
200 NEXT I
210 PRINT D$;"CLOSE";F$
220 FOR I = 1 TO N
230 PRINT B(I);" ";
240 NEXT I
```

(b)
```
170 INPUT A(I)
180 INPUT B(I)
190 INPUT B(I + 3)
200 NEXT I
210 PRINT D$;"CLOSE";F$
220 FOR I = N - 1 TO N + 1
230 PRINT B(I);" ";
240 NEXT I
```

(c)
```
170 FOR J = 1 TO 3
180 INPUT A(I,J)
190 NEXT J
200 NEXT I
210 PRINT D$;"CLOSE";F$
220 FOR I = 1 TO 3
230 FOR J = 1 TO 3
240 PRINT A(J,I);" ";
250 NEXT J
260 PRINT
270 NEXT I
```

10.2   Lines 110 to 140 and line 210 apply to parts (a), (b), and (c).

```
110 LET D$ = CHR$ (4)
120 LET F$ = "STUDENT FILE"
130 PRINT D$;"OPEN";F$
140 PRINT D$;"WRITE";F$
210 PRINT D$;"CLOSE";F$
```

Assume the following values have been entered in a previous section of the program.

```
N = 3                  L = 4
N$(1) = "TERRY"    N$(2) = "CARL"    N$(3) = "JUNE"
S(1) = 92          S(2) = 88         S(3) = 84
```

Write the content of the file made by each of the three versions of a write file program given in parts (a), (b) and (c).

(a)
```
150 PRINT N
160 PRINT L
170 FOR I = 1 TO N
180 PRINT N$(I)
190 PRINT S(I)
200 NEXT I
```

(b)
```
150 PRINT N
160 FOR I = 1 TO N
170 PRINT L
180 PRINT N$(I)
190 PRINT S(I)
200 NEXT I
```

(c)
```
150 PRINT N
160 FOR I = 1 TO N
170 PRINT N$(I)
180 PRINT S(I)
190 NEXT I
200 PRINT L
```

DIRECTIONS FOR EXERCISES

Because this is a large and impressive program, the exercises for chapter 10 will take a slightly different form than earlier exercises. Although it may look extremely difficult and complex at first, we think you will find that it can be done in small, relatively easy steps. The trick is to concentrate on one step at a time; don't proceed to the next step until you are satisfied that the current version of your program is working properly.

We suggest that you keep a second "backup" copy of this program as you write it. Whenever the current version is working properly, back it up by saving it again under another name (like PROGRAM 10A. BACKUP). That way you'll have something to fall back on if you accidentally destroy your main version.

In program 10A we have presented a menu-driven program that keeps a file of scores for a bowling team on the disk. In the exercise assignments which follow, you will find that you can write programs which are, in many ways, exactly like program 10A (many parts of it you can copy line for line). Some parts will vary because of differences in the information being stored. For example, the batting average program records the name of each player, batting average, total hits, and total at-bats; this takes four columns of data rather than three. This means that the parts of the program that actually handle the data, such as the sorting, file-writing, and table-printing subroutines will be slightly different (another variable will need to be dimensioned in the DIM statement also). Another difference is that the formula for batting average is different from the one for bowling average. Once you have figured out these differences, however, we think you'll find that your program will look very much like program 10A.

Your assignment is to pick one of the exercises that follow (10.1 to 10.5) and follow the general instructions presented here. Because of the length of the program it is *essential* that you follow these directions to the letter. It is also absolutely necessary that you use the same beginning line numbers for the subroutines as those used in program 10A (it will also be a lot easier if you use the same line numbers within as many subroutines as possible). Some of the subroutines from the program you wrote for chapter 9 will be useful to you here; some may be used as they are, others may have to be modified.

Step 1:   **1.1** Load starter and change the program name in line 1.

1.2 Type in the utility subroutines at lines 6000 and 6200 from program 10A exactly as they are written.

1.3 Type in the menu section from program 10A exactly as it is written.

1.4 For all of the main routines (lines 1100, 1200, 1300, 1400, 1500), type in the remark statement with the name of the routine as it appears in program 10A. After the remark statement, add a line like the following:

```
1101 GOSUB 6000 : RETURN
```

1.5 At this point, the program should run and the menu should work without crashing (although it won't really do anything), and it should handle things when you enter an illegal number or a letter as a menu choice (try it). If it won't, correct any errors, and, when it runs properly, save it as VERSION 1 and make a backup.

Step 2:

2.1 Add the routine at line 1100 of program 10A to your program (get rid of the GOSUB 6000 : RETURN line). Put a REM at the beginning of lines 1120 and 1140 (the calls to the subroutines to sort and write the file) so that they won't execute; you will add these functions later.

2.2 Modify the subroutines to enter names (2000), zero scores (5000), and print table (5600) to fit your application and add them to the program.

2.3 Now option one of the menu should work, letting you enter the names, and should print the table (unsorted) with zero for all the amounts. Depending on which exercise you choose, you should change the word "SCORE" to whatever makes sense throughout the program (e.g. "QUANTITY" or "SALES").

2.4 When this part runs properly, save it as VERSION 2 and make a backup.

2.5 Modify the subroutines at lines 2200 and 2800 and add them to your program. Then remove the REM from line 1120 so that it calls the sort subroutine; then get the sort subroutine to work. It should print the table in alphabetical order no matter which names are entered first.

Step 3:

3.1 When the sort is working, modify and add the subroutines to read and write the file (they should be almost identical). Remove the REM from line 1140 which calls the subroutine that writes the file, and remove the GOSUB 6000 : RETURN from line 1201.

3.2 Add the initialization section at line 50. Be sure to modify the DIM statement to fit your application (it may need more variables) and change F$.

3.3 Get menu options 1 and 2 to work completely. In order to find out what is going on with the files, use the MONC,I,O command, and, if necessary, slow things down by typing SPEED = 30. These are cancelled by NOMONC,I,O and SPEED = 255.

3.4 This should make menu options 1, 2, and 4 fully functional (once you take out the GOSUB 6000 : RETURN line). If not, make the necessary corrections and save this as VERSION 3 and make a backup.

Step 4:

4.1 Modify and add the subroutine from program 10A to enter scores (or whatever) and update the file (at line 2400).

4.2 When you have the update working, modify and add the subroutine to sort the scores by number.

4.3 This should make the program fully functional. Try all the menu options. Make any corrections necessary to make them all work properly; save this as VERSION 4 and start celebrating. Congratulations!

EXERCISES
Choose One and Follow the Steps Above

10.1 You manage a team of salespeople and need a program to keep track of their sales for the current week and the total sales they have earned so far this year. Start the file by using INPUT statements to enter the names of the salespeople. Each week (in option 3, Update) you will enter their weekly sales, and calculate their total sales. The names should be alphabetical in the file, but option 5 should print a table sorted by this week's sales so that bonuses can be given to the week's top salespeople. Round all numbers to the nearest whole dollar. Arrange the table as shown below. Use TAB(12) for WEEKLY SALES, and TAB(29) for TOTAL SALES.

Use the following file variables:

```
D$ = DOS COMMAND VARIABLE: CHR$(4)
F$ = "SALES"
N = NUMBER OF EMPLOYEES
WEEK = WEEK #
NAME$(I) = NAME OF SALESPERSON
WSAL(I) = SALES FOR CURRENT WEEK
TSAL(I) = TOTAL SALES
```

```
                    SALES
                  WEEK # 11
      - - - - - - - - - - - - - - - - - - - - - - - - - - - -
      NAME          WEEKLY SALES     TOTAL SALES
      - - - - - - - - - - - - - - - - - - - - - - - - - - - -
      SMITH          416              71467
       .              .                .
       .              .                .
      WILSON         510              98275
      - - - - - - - - - - - - - - - - - - - - - - - - - - - -
```

10.2 You are the owner of a hardware store and would like a program to help you keep track of your inventory. Start the file by using INPUT statements to enter the name of each item. The items should be sorted alphabetically by name for placement in the file. Option 5 of the menu should allow you to sort the items and print the table so they are sorted by price with the most expensive at the top of the list. In your update option (option 3), you should be able to enter the quantity on hand and the current price of each item, and have the program print the table with the current price and value (quantity $*$ price) and update the file. Arrange the table as shown below. Use TAB(14) for PRICE, TAB(22) for QUANTITY, and TAB(32) for VALUE.

Use the following file variables:

```
D$ = DOS COMMAND VARIABLE: CHR$(4)
F$ ="HARDWARE INVENTORY"
N = NUMBER OF ITEMS
WEEK = WEEK #
NAME$(I) = NAME OF ITEM
PRICE(I) = PRICE OF ITEM
QUANTITY(I) = NUMBER ON HAND
V(I) = VALUE OF EACH ITEM
```

```
              HARDWARE INVENTORY
                 WEEK # 1
- - - - - - - - - - - - - - - - - - - - - - - - -
NAME          PRICE    QUANTITY VALUE
- - - - - - - - - - - - - - - - - - - - - - - - -
HAMMER        9.5      35       333
  .             .        .        .
  .             .        .        .
CHAIN SAW     285      12       3420
- - - - - - - - - - - - - - - - - - - - - - - - -
```

10.3 You manage a baseball team and need to keep track of the players' statistics. You start the file by simply entering the players' names (using INPUT statements). Each week (in option 3, Update) you enter the number of at-bats and hits for each player for that week, and the program updates their total hits and total at-bats, and calculates their current batting average (hits / at-bats). Batting averages are rounded to the nearest thousandth. The file should be alphabetical by player's name. Option 5 should allow you to print a table for the local newspaper sorted by current batting average. Arrange the table as shown below. Use TAB(14) for batting average, TAB(22) for TOTAL HITS, and TAB(30) for TOTAL AT-BATS.

Use the following file varaiables:

```
D$ = DOS COMMAND VARIABLE: CHR$(4)
F$ = "BASEBALL STATISTICS"
N = NUMBER OF PLAYERS
NAME$(I) = NAME OF EACH PLAYER
BA(I) = CURRENT BATTING AVERAGE
HITS(I) = TOTAL HITS
AB(I) = TOTAL AT-BATS
```

```
            BASEBALL STATISTICS
               WEEK # 11
- - - - - - - - - - - - - - - - - - - - - - - - - -
            BATTING   TOTAL      TOTAL
NAME        AVERAGE   HITS       AT-BATS
- - - - - - - - - - - - - - - - - - - - - - - - - -
BABBAGE     .308      37         120
  .           .        .           .
  .           .        .           .
WOZNIAK     .333      45         135
- - - - - - - - - - - - - - - - - - - - - - - - - -
```

10.4 Your employees are paid by the week. To create the file, you enter their names and wage rates (different for each employee). Each week, using option 3 (update), you will enter the number of hours each employee worked this week. You need to know how much they should be paid this week and need to keep a record of their total pay for the year. Option 5 should allow you to print the table sorted by this week's pay with this week's hardest workers on top. Use time and a half for overtime (hours > 40). Round all dollar amounts to the nearest cent. Arrange the table as shown below. Use TAB(12) for WAGE RATE, TAB(20) for PAY FOR WEEK, and TAB(31), for TOTAL PAY FOR YEAR.

Use the following variable:

```
D$ = DOS COMMAND VARIABLE: CHR$(4)
F$ ="PAYROLL"
N = NUMBER OF EMPLOYEES
WEEK = WEEK #
NAME$(I) = NAME OF EACH EMPLOYEE
WAGE(I) = WAGE RATE FOR EACH EMPLOYEE
PAY(I) = PAY FOR CURRENT WEEK
TPAY(I) = TOTAL PAY FOR YEAR
```

```
               PAYROLL
               WEEK # 7
- - - - - - - - - - - - - - - - - - - - - - - - - - - -
EMPLOYEE     WAGE      PAY        PAY
NAME         RATE      FOR WEEK   FOR YEAR
- - - - - - - - - - - - - - - - - - - - - - - - - - - -
ARBOGAST     5.22      210.8      1475.6
   .           .         .          .
   .           .         .          .
ZELNIK       7.81      312.4      2186.8
- - - - - - - - - - - - - - - - - - - - - - - - - - - -
```

10.5 You need a gradebook program to keep track of your students' grades. All your exams are worth 100 points. You start the file by entering just the names of the students. Every week you give another exam and enter each student's score (using option 3, Update). The file contains the score for the week, the total score so far, and the letter grade so far. The file should be alphabetical by student, but option 5 should print the table sorted by total score (with the A's on top, of course). The grades are given as follows:

$$95 \text{ and over} = A$$
$$85 \text{ to } 94 = B$$
$$70 \text{ to } 84 = C$$
$$60 \text{ to } 69 = D$$
$$\text{under } 60 = F$$

Arrange the table as follows. Use TAB(14) for WEEKLY SCORE, TAB(22) for AVERAGE SCORE, and TAB(30) for GRADE. Round off average scores to the nearest tenth.

Use the following file variables:

```
D$ = DOS COMMAND VARIABLE: CHR$(4)
F$ = "GRADES"
N = NUMBER OF STUDENTS
WEEK = WEEK #
NAME$(I) = NAME OF EACH STUDENT
MARK(I) = THIS WEEK'S SCORE
TS(I) = TOTAL SCORE SO FAR
G$(I) = CURRENT GRADE
```

```
                  GRADES
                 WEEK # 3
- - - - - - - - - - - - - - - - - - - - - - - - - -
              WEEKLY    AVERAGE
NAME          SCORE     SCORE      GRADE
- - - - - - - - - - - - - - - - - - - - - - - - - -
ANTON         87        83.5       C
 .             .         .          .
 .             .         .          .
WESTON        66        88.5       B
- - - - - - - - - - - - - - - - - - - - - - - - - -
```

NOTE: This program is harder than it looks.

CHAPTER 11

FLYING SAUCERS
Using Sound and Graphics

NEW
CONCEPTS
TAUGHT

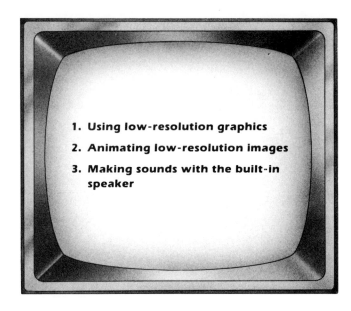

1. **Using low-resolution graphics**

2. **Animating low-resolution images**

3. **Making sounds with the built-in speaker**

GRAPHICS

No book on microcomputers would be complete without some discussion of graphics. Because of the complexity of the last few programs, we have tried to make this one a little more fun.

As we mentioned earlier, there are three ways of doing graphics on the computer: (1) character graphics, which you did in chapter 7; (2) high-resolution graphics, which is beyond the scope of this book; and (3) low-resolution graphics, which is the subject of this chapter.

The Apple has a special set of commands for low-resolution graphics. The command GR puts the computer into the graphics mode. Once in this mode, other commands can be used to change color, plot a small square, or draw a horizontal or vertical bar on the screen. The commands are simple; they tell the computer the location of the things to be drawn.

With the kind of graphics we will be using, the screen is divided into two parts. At the bottom of the screen there is a four-line text screen where messages can appear; above that is a forty-by-forty square devoted to graphics. Although the graphics grid is forty squares high and forty squares wide, the computer numbers these squares from zero to thirty-nine both ways, rather than from one to forty.

To plot a square we must first pick a color since the default color is black which is invisible on the screen. If you don't have a color monitor, you will still see some difference in the shading of the various colors.

The graphics commands will work in the immediate mode so you can try them directly even when no program is running. Try typing GR (and RE-TURN of course). This has two effects: first, it puts the computer into the low-resolution graphics mode; second, it clears the low-resolution screen. Next, type COLOR = 3.

LOW-RESOLUTION COLOR CODES

Code	Color	Code	Color
0	Black	8	Brown
1	Magenta	9	Orange
2	Dark Blue	10	Grey
3	Purple	11	Pink
4	Dark Green	12	Green
5	Grey	13	Yellow
6	Medium Blue	14	Aqua
7	Light Blue	15	White

The numbering starts in the upper left-hand corner. To plot a single square of color at the upper left of the screen you can type PLOT 0,0. If you want to plot a diagonal line from the upper left to the lower right you can type:

```
PLOT 0,0
PLOT 1,1
PLOT 2,2
   .
   .
PLOT 39,39
```

SCREEN COORDINATES

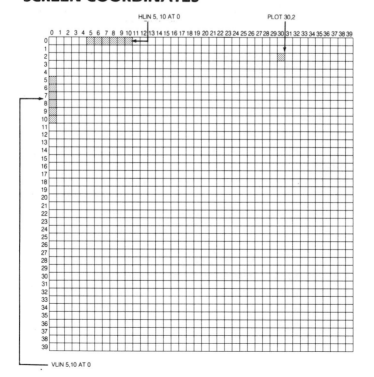

To plot a horizontal line somewhere on the screen, you can type HLIN, A,B AT C where A and B are the starting and ending columns of the line and C is the row you want the line to appear on. For example:

    HLIN 5,10 AT 0

draws a horizontal line from column 5 to column 10 on the top row of the screen (try it).

Vertical lines can be drawn using the VLIN command in the same way. For example:

    VLIN 5,10 AT 0

will print a vertical line from row 5 to row 10 at the left side of the screen (column 0). To erase the whole screen, you can use the GR command. To erase all or part of a line previously drawn, turn the color to black (COLOR = 0) and draw the part you want to erase.

To get out of the graphics mode and back to the regular text mode, type TEXT. The screen will be full of inverse garbage; this is normal. Type HOME to clear it.

PEEKS AND POKES

In the introduction to this book, we talked about how the computer stores information in specific memory locations. We were referring to the contents of memory locations devoted to particular variables. The computer automatically uses these memory locations to store and retrieve information. There is a way, however, for you to get at these memory locations directly.

There is a story that two of the originators of the Apple spent most of a night trying to decide what to call the two commands used to access memory locations directly. It was nearly sunrise when they finally settled on the names PEEK and POKE. To read a memory location, you PEEK at it. To put a value into a memory location, you simply POKE it in there. As you try these out, be very careful since indiscriminate PEEKing and POKEing can mess things up to the point that you have to re-boot and any work you have done is lost.

Some memory locations are reserved for special functions. For example, location 33 holds a number that describes the width of the screen. If you type PRINT PEEK(33) you should see this value typed on the screen. It should be a forty (unless you have an active eighty-column card, in which case it should be an 80).

Location 37 holds the vertical position of the cursor. If you check it using PRINT PEEK (37), the row number of the vertical position of the cursor should be printed on the screen. You will also find that if you change the value at this location, the cursor will move to the location you specify. *Don't use a value greater than 29.* Try POKE 37,20. This should move the cursor to the lower part of the screen. As we have said, POKEing certain values at certain memory locations can make a complete mess out of the program in memory, so be careful.

SOUND

There are two ways to make the computer sound off: one is to type or PRINT a Control-G (try it); the other is to access the speaker memory location directly using a PEEK or POKE. The speaker memory location (–16336) works in a special way. Whenever it is accessed with either a PEEK or POKE, it causes the speaker to click. Any of the following will click the speaker:

```
PRINT PEEK (-16336)
A = PEEK (-16336)
POKE (-16336),0
```

etc.

In fact, it doesn't matter what you do, as long as you access that memory location.

In the program for this chapter, we are using a loop in BASIC to make the speaker do more that just click. Since BASIC is relatively slow, the tones produced in this way are all fairly low in pitch. To produce higher tones, you would need to use faster routines that are written in assembly language rather then BASIC. To avoid this, we have cheated a little by combining the speaker sound with the higher pitched bell sound of Control-G.

NEGATIVE MEMORY LOCATIONS

It may seem odd to you that some memory locations are expressed as negative numbers. The reason for this is that although the computer has 64K of memory (actually 65,536 separate memory locations or 2^{16}), some BASICS have trouble with memory location numbers larger than 32767. As a result, we usually convert numbers larger than this by subtracting 65536 from them. As a convention, then, numbers greater than 32767 are expressed as negative numbers. Thus location –16336 mentioned above is actually location 49200.

FLYING SAUCERS

Air Attack

In program 11A in figure 11.1, we have set up a simple arcade-type game since this provides the best way to learn about graphics and animation. In this program a target moves back and forth at the top of the screen. When the space bar is pressed, a shot is fired from the cannonlike gun at the bottom of the screen. If the shell fired from the gun hits the target, some noises are made and the shooter's score goes up.

The Gun

The subroutine at line 300 draws the gun at the bottom of the graphics screen. In line 120 of the main part of the program, we entered the graphics mode and then took off (in line 130) for the subroutine at line 300. After the color is set in line 310, lines 320 and 330 draw the base of the gun and line 340 draws the barrel pointing up in the air. Line 350 prints the message in the text window and the program returns to the main section.

Shooting

The loop started at line 140 will execute five times (giving the player five shots). For each shot, the program goes to the subroutine at line 400 which moves the target back and forth at the top of the screen until the space bar is pressed and then returns (more about this later). The fact that the space bar has been pressed means that the player wants to fire, so line 150 sends the program to the subroutine at line 500 which shows the shell coming out of the gun and travelling to the top of the screen. This subroutine checks for a hit, and, if there is one, calls the HIT subroutine at line 600 which in turn calls the NOISE subroutines and increases the player's score (number of hits). Then the program returns to the main section and the loop is done five times. When the player's five shots are up, results are given by the subroutine at line 1000.

Firing a Shot

The animation of the target in this program is relatively simple. The hard part is animating the target in such a way that pressing the space bar will initiate a shot. If we used a simple loop to animate the target and a GET or INPUT statement to allow the user to press the space bar, then, when the program got to the GET or INPUT statement, the animation would stop. To solve this problem, we use two memory locations designed to contain information about the keyboard.

Locations –16384 and –16368 are special memory cells that relate to the keyboard. Location –16384 contains information about what's been happening with the keyboard. When a key has just been pressed, the value stored in this location is always greater than 128. Since we need to look for a keypress more than once, we need a way of "clearing" this location, or getting its value back down below 128 so we can tell when the next key is pressed. This is the function of memory location –16368. Whenever this location is accessed, it resets location –16384 to a value less than 128. The advantage of using these two locations is that we can "look" at the value of location –16384 without stopping execution of the program. Thus, in the subroutine at line 400, every time we move the target (lines 420 and 450), we check to see if a key has been pressed (lines 425 and 455). When we first enter this subroutine, we clear the keyboard with the POKE –16368 in line

405, otherwise the program might detect a "shot" when no key had been pressed. By now, you have probably guessed that although the player is told to press the space bar to fire the gun, any key would do it. The program could be modified so that only the space bar would work since the value in location –16384 is the ASCII value of the key pressed plus 128. Every key on the keyboard has a numeric value associated with it called its ASCII value ("American Standard Code for Information Interchange"). The ASCII value of the space bar is 32, so whenever a key has been pressed we could ignore it if the value in location –16384 was not 160 (128 + 32). As a thought exercise, you might try to devise a way to do this that would not significantly slow down the animation of the target.

Animating the Target

The subroutine at line 400 is really two different routines lumped together: one to move the target to the right (lines 420 to 440) and one to move it to the left (lines 450 to 470). We could put these in separate subroutines, but it would slow down the animation slightly.

In order to animate an object on the screen, two things have to happen. First, we need to "draw" the object (in this case the saucer) at a number of new locations on the screen. Second, we have to "erase" the object at the old locations; otherwise, in this program, we would soon have a solid line across the top of the screen.

The function of the loop in lines 420 to 440 is to move the saucer to the right across the top of the screen. First we set the color to something visible (in this case dark green). Next, we draw a horizontal line from column A to column A + W on row zero (the top line of the screen). Since A is the loop counter and W is the width of the target, each time through the loop a bar of width W will be drawn one column to the right of where it was drawn the last time through the loop. As we said above, if all we did was draw saucers, we would soon have a solid bar of dark green across the top of the screen that would stay there for the rest of the program. To avoid this, every time through the loop we not only draw the saucer, but we also erase it (in line 430). What appears on the screen seems to be a single bar of width W, moving from left to right across the screen.

Moving the target to the left is exactly the same except that the limits in the FOR statement are reversed and the STEP is negative instead of positive. By the way, we could speed up the apparent motion of the target by increasing the size of the step in lines 420 and 450.

Notice that the two FOR/NEXT loops that move the target back and forth are inside of a simple GOTO loop (lines 410 to 480). This loop is endless, so that if no shot is fired the target will move back and forth at the top of the screen forever.

Animating the Shell

Since the shell is only a single square on the screen, we use the PLOT command to draw it in the subroutine at line 500. Otherwise, the process is the same as that of animating the target. At each position along its path, we first draw the shell, and then erase it. When the loop is finished, the shell is at the top of the screen and may or may not have hit the target; the player has scored a hit if the shell location is on the target. Since the shell is always on column 19, it will be a hit if the left square of the target (A) is less than or equal to 19 and the right square of the target (A + W) is greater than or equal to 19. If the shot is a hit we go to the subroutine at line 600 to make the sound and increment the number of hits. If the shot is not a hit, we don't have to do anything.

Sounding Off

The subroutine at line 600 executes every time there is a hit. It increments the number of hits and then calls the two sound subroutines, three times each. Sound 2 just prints the Control-G character or bell. You will notice that when you list this program the bell will sound when line 810 is listed; this is normal.

Sound 1 is made by clicking the speaker 20 times in line 720. Z is a dummy variable and has no real function in the program. To click the speaker, we must make the computer "look" in memory location −16336. We don't want to PRINT the value in this location on the screen, so we tell the computer to set Z equal to whatever number is in that location. When the computer checks the location, the speaker clicks. A statement like POKE −16336,0 would work as well, but a PEEK is safer in case we mistype −16336 since it doesn't change the value at that location.

EXAMPLE 11A   Flying Saucer

Problem   Write a program that will use low-resolution graphics and sound to simulate an antiaircraft gun shooting at a flying saucer. The saucer should move back and forth at the top of the screen, and the gun should be stationary at the center of the lower part of the screen. When the space bar is pressed, a shell should come out of the gun and move up to the top of the screen. If the shell hits the saucer, sounds should be made and the player's score (number of hits) should increase by one. Each run should give the player five shots and then print the results.

FIGURE 11.1

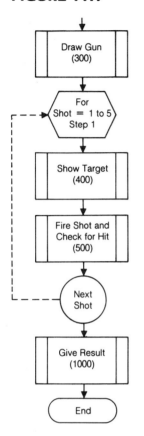

```
]LIST
1 PN$ = "PROGRAM 11A - FLYING SAUCER"
2 NA$ = "YOUR NAME"
3 DA$ = "00/00/00"
10 REM ===== VARIABLES =====
11 REM A = LEFT EDGE OF TARGET
12 REM I = LOOP COUNTER
13 REM J = LOOP COUNTER
14 REM SHOT = SHOT NUMBER
15 REM W = WIDTH OF TARGET
16 REM Z = DUMMY VARIABLE
40 REM ===== FUNCTIONS =====
41 REM ROUND TO WHOLE NUMBER WITH FN A(X)
42 DEF FN A(X) = INT ((X) * 1 + .5) / 1
43 REM ROUND TO ONE DECIMAL PLACE WITH FN B(X)
44 DEF FN B(X) = INT ((X) * 10 + .5) / 10
45 REM ROUND TO TWO DECIMAL PLACES WITH FN C(X)
46 DEF FN C(X) =INT ((X) * 100 + .5) / 100
47 REM ROUND TO THREE DECIMAL PLACES WITH FN D(X)
48 DEF FN D(X) =INT ((X) * 1000 + .5) / 1000
100 REM ===== MAIN PROGRAM =====
101 HOME : HTAB 20 - (LEN(PN$) / 2) : PRINT PN$
110 W = 2: REM WIDTH OF TARGET
120 TEXT : HOME : GR
130 GOSUB 300: REM DRAW GUN
140 FOR SHOT = 1 TO 5: GOSUB 400: REM SHOW TARGET
150 GOSUB 500: REM FIRE SHOT & CHECK FOR HIT
160 NEXT SHOT
170 GOSUB 1000: REM GIVE RESULTS
180 END
190 :
```

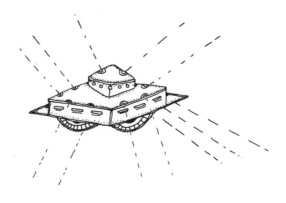

(Figure continued)

(Figure 11.1 continued)

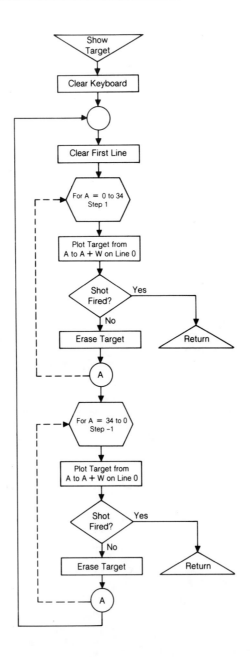

(Figure continued)

(Figure 11.1 continued)

```
300 REM = = = = = DRAW GUN = = = = =
310 COLOR= 5
320 HLIN 14,24, AT 39
330 HLIN 18,20 AT 38
340 VLIN 30,39 AT 19
350 PRINT "       PRESS SPACE BAR TO FIRE";
360 RETURN
370 :
400 REM = = = = = SHOW TARGET = = = = =
405 POKE - 16368,0: REM CLEAR KEYBOARD
410 COLOR= 0: HLIN 0,39 AT 0: REM CLEAR FIRST LINE
420 FOR A = 0 TO 34 STEP 1: COLOR= 4: HLIN A,A + W AT 0: REM TARGET, TO RIGHT
425 IF PEEK ( - 16384) > 128 THEN RETURN : REM SHOT FIRED
430 COLOR= 0: HLIN A,A + W AT 0: REM ERASE PREVIOUS TARGET
440 NEXT A
450 FOR A = 34 TO 0 STEP - 1: COLOR= 4: HLIN A,A + W AT 0: REM TARGET, TO LEFT
455 IF PEEK ( - 16384) > 128 THEN RETURN : REM SHOT FIRED
460 COLOR= 0: HLIN A,A + W AT 0: REM ERASE PREVIOUS TARGET
470 NEXT A
480 GOTO 410: REM LOOP BACK
490 STOP : REM THIS SHOULDN'T HAPPEN
495 :
```

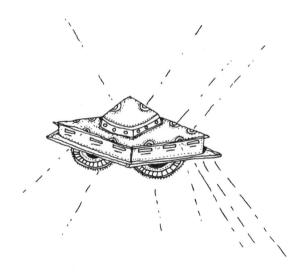

(Figure continued)

(Figure 11.1 continued)

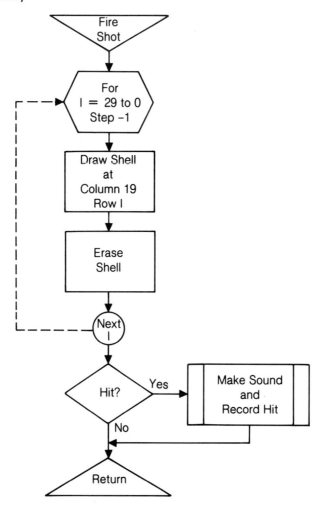

(Figure continued)

(Figure 11.1 continued)

```
500 REM ===== SHOOT =====
510 FOR I = 29 TO 0 STEP - 1
520 COLOR= 4: PLOT 19,I: REM DRAW SHELL
530 COLOR= 0: PLOT 19,I: REM ERASE SHELL
540 NEXT
550 IF A < = 19 AND A + W > = 19 THEN GOSUB 600: REM HIT
560 RETURN
570 :
600 REM ===== HIT =====
610 FOR I = 1 TO 3: GOSUB 700: GOSUB 800: NEXT I: REM SOUND
620 LET HITS = HITS + 1
630 RETURN
640 :
700 REM ===== SOUND1 =====
710 S = -16336
720 FOR J = 1 TO 20:Z = PEEK (S): NEXT
730 RETURN
740 :
800 REM ===== SOUND2 =====
810 PRINT "";: REM CTRL G
820 RETURN
830 :
1000 REM ===== GIVE RESULTS =====
1010 GR : HOME : PRINT "HITS = "HITS
1020 RETURN
```

RUN

PRESS SPACE BAR TO FIRE

EXERCISES

Choose One of the Following

11.1 Use low-resolution graphics to animate a dot of light that moves back and forth across the screen. The dot should appear to "bounce" back and forth between the edges of the screen. Have the speaker make a sound when the dot changes direction.

TIPS

1. Use one subroutine to move the dot to the right and a separate subroutine to move it to the left.
2. Don't forget to erase the dot before drawing it in each new location.
3. Be sure to set the color of the dot so it will be visible.

11.2 Write a program that will use low-resolution graphics to draw a simple figure on the screen. Then move the figure back and forth by repeatedly drawing it, then erasing it and redrawing it in a new location. Have the program make a sound each time the figure moves.

TIPS

1. Use a subroutine for drawing the figure in one location and a separate subroutine to draw it in the other location.
2 Erase the figure by setting the color to 0 and calling the same subroutine used to draw it.
3. Do not put a color statement in the subroutines that draw the figure. Set the color before calling the subroutines.

11.3 Write a program using sound and low resolution graphics to simulate program 11A, but with the following differences. Change the orientation of the gun and target to one of the following:

1. Put the gun at the left of the screen and have the target move up and down at the right.

2. Put the gun at the right of the screen and have the target move up and down at the left.

3. Put the gun at the top of the screen and have the target move back and forth at the bottom.

In addition, add a subroutine to give the player a choice of several target widths and speeds and print various messages at the end depending on the score (e.g., "Your score of 5 qualifies you as a master gunner"). Have the program make another sound when the player shoots and misses the target.

TIPS

1. **Type in the program as in program 11A and get it working before modifying it in any way.**
2. **Move the gun and target to their new locations and get the program working before adding the new features.**
3. **Replace line 110 with the GOSUB to the new subroutine that asks the player to choose the values for speed and target size.**
4. **The speed of the target may be controlled by making the step value in lines 420 and 450 a variable and changing its value (this will allow faster speeds), or by using the SPEED command which will allow slower speeds.**
5. **Remember that any operation you put inside an animation loop will slow down the animation.**

APPENDICES

APPENDIX A

The Mini–Manual Table of Contents

The Mini–Manual

1. KEYS AND COMMANDS

1.1 Keys

1.11 Cursor The cursor is a light square on the TV screen that marks the current location on the screen. When a key is pressed, the character appears on the screen where the cursor was and the cursor is moved one position to the right.

> **APPLE IIe/IIc NOTE** On the Apple IIe and IIc, the TAB key and the DELETE key are not normally used for programming.

1.12 Arrow Keys The right arrow key moves the cursor to the right and the left arrow key moves the cursor to the left. Both arrow keys can move the cursor over characters on the screen without changing them. The arrow keys are used to make changes in a program line.

> **APPLE IIe/IIc NOTE** The Apple IIe and IIc have an up and down arrow; these are normally not used in programming except for editing (described later).

1.13 Ctrl C A Ctrl C (pronounced control c) is accomplished by holding the CTRL (control) key down while pressing the C key. Ctrl C is used to stop a computer RUN or LIST. If a RUN has been stopped by Ctrl C, then you can sometimes resume the RUN by typing the letters CONT and pressing the RETURN key.

1.14 Repeat Key The repeat key is labeled REPT. If the repeat key and a character key are held down at the same time, the character will be repeated.

> **APPLE IIe/IIc NOTE** The IIe and IIc have no repeat key, but all the keys will repeat if held down.

1.15 Reset key The reset key is located in the upper right corner of the keyboard. If something is wrong, you can press reset to restart the system without destroying your program. DO NOT press reset while the red light on the drive is glowing. This can "blow" the disk.

> **APPLE IIe/IIc NOTE** On the IIe and IIc, you must press Ctrl-reset. (Some other Apples and some Apple copies are set up this way as well.)

1.16 **Return key**   You press the return key at the end of each line in your program and after typing a command such as RUN or LIST. The return key initiates the computer's response to the line you just finished typing.

1.17 **Space bar**   This is the long bar at the bottom of the keyboard. The space bar is used to produce blank spaces on the screen. It is also used with the left arrow key to remove characters from a line.

1.18 **Ctrl S**   Holding the Control key and the S key down at the same time will stop any output to the screen. Whatever is on the screen will be "frozen" there until output is restarted. On the Apple, pressing any key will restart the output. It is convenient to use Control S to both start and stop the screen display. This has no effect on the disk or memory.

1.19 **ESCAPE**   J ┿ K   If you press the ESCAPE key once, and then continue to press the I, J, K, and M keys, the cursor will move one space as follows:

- □ UP each time you press the I key
- □ LEFT each time you press the J key
- □ RIGHT each time you press the K key
- □ DOWN each time you press the M key

You can use the ESCAPE I, J, K, M to correct or change a line in a program. First LIST the line to be corrected. Then use ESCAPE I, J, K, M to move the cursor to the first digit of the line number. Now use the right arrow to move the cursor to the correction point, make the correction, move the cursor past the last character of the line and press RETURN. This is discussed in much more detail in chapter 0.

APPLE IIe/IIc NOTE   On the IIe and IIc, you can use the four arrow keys instead of I, J, K, and M if you do it right. This is discussed fully in chapter 0.

1.20 **Reading the keyboard**   Memory location –16384 contains the ASCII value of the last key pressed plus 128. It can be read by using PEEK(–16384). To get the ASCII value of the key pressed, simply subtract 128 from the value found at location –16384. To clear this location so that another key can be read, use POKE –16368,0.

1.2 Screen Commands

1.21 **FLASH**   If you type FLASH and press the return key, messages printed on the screen will alternate between white on black and black on white to produce a flashing appearance. You can turn the FLASH off by typing NORMAL and pressing the return key.

1.22 **FP** If you type FP and press the return key, the system will go into Applesoft BASIC — which is the BASIC used in this text. When the system is in Applesoft BASIC, each line begins with the prompt character shown below, ANY PROGRAM IN MEMORY WILL BE LOST!!

]10 LET X = 2

└──── prompt character for Applesoft BASIC

The system can also be in Integer BASIC or in the monitor with the following prompt characters:

>20 PRINT X

└──── prompt character for Integer BASIC

*F85E: 60 RTS

└──── prompt character for monitor

If you want to change to Applesoft BASIC from Integer BASIC, type FP and press the return key. From the monitor press CTRL-C and the return key. You should get a] prompt character. If this does not work, then turn the computer off, wait 15 seconds, insert your disk, and turn the computer on to restart the system.

1.23 **HOME** If you type HOME and press the return key, the screen will be cleared of all text, and the cursor will be in the upper left corner of the screen.

1.24 **INT** If you type INT and press the return key, the system will go into Integer BASIC. You should get a > prompt character. See section 1.22 for further details.

1.25 **INVERSE** If you type INVERSE and press the return key, messages on the screen will have black letters on a white background. You can reverse this effect by typing NORMAL and pressing the return key.

1.26 **NORMAL** If you type NORMAL and press the return key, the screen will return to a nonflashing display with white letters on a black background. See sections 1.21 and 1.25 for further details.

1.27 **SPEED** If you type SPEED = *(a number between 0 and 255)* and press the return key, you will change the speed at which characters are printed on the screen. The slowest speed is 0 and the fastest speed is 255.

EXAMPLE: SPEED = 150

1.28 **TEXT** If you type TEXT and press RETURN, the screen will be in the usual mode (24 lines of 40 characters each).

1.3 Disk Commands

1.31   **CATALOG**   If there is a disk in the disk drive and you type CATALOG and press the return key, a list of the programs stored on the disk will be displayed on the screen.

1.32   **DELETE**   If you type DELETE followed by the name of a program on the disk in the disk drive and press the return key, the named program will be removed from the disk.

1.33   **LOAD**   If you type LOAD followed by the name of a program on the disk in the disk drive and then press the return key, the named program will be copied from the disk into the computer memory.

1.34   **SAVE**   If you type SAVE followed by a name for your program and press the return key, the program in the computer memory will be saved on your disk with the given name.

1.35   **RUN**   If you type RUN followed by the name of a program on the disk in the disk drive and then press the return key, the named program will be copied from the disk into computer memory and a RUN will be executed.

1.36   **LOCK**   If you type LOCK followed by the name of a program on the disk, the file will be locked. Locked files have an asterisk (*) next to their names in the catalog. Attempts to SAVE, DELETE, RENAME, or WRITE to a locked file will fail, and the message FILE LOCKED will be printed.

1.37   **UNLOCK**   Locked files may be unlocked simply by typing UNLOCK followed by the file name.

1.38   **RENAME**   Files may be renamed by typing RENAME followed by the old name, a comma, and the new name.

1.4 Program Commands

1.41   **CONT**   When a program run has been halted by a STOP, END, or Ctrl C, you can resume the run at the next instruction after the halt by typing CONT and pressing the return key.

1.42   **DEL**   You can remove a section of a program by typing DEL followed by the beginning and ending line numbers separated by a comma. As usual, press the return key to initiate the computer action.

EXAMPLE: Type DEL 60,120 and press RETURN to remove all instructions from 60 to 120 inclusive.

1.43   **LIST**   If you type LIST and then press the return key, your entire program will be listed on the screen. Other possibilities are illustrated below (any numbers may be substituted for 60 and 120 in the examples below as long as the second number is larger than the first.

EXAMPLE 1:   LIST 60   will list only line 60 of your program.

EXAMPLE 2: LIST 60,120   will list all lines in your program from line
                     or   60 to line 120, inclusive.
                LIST 60-120

EXAMPLE 3: LIST 60,   will list all lines in your program from line
                     or   60 to the end of the program
                LIST 60–

EXAMPLE 4: LIST ,60   will list all lines in your program from the
                     or   beginning to line 60 inclusive.
                LIST –60

1.44 **NEW**   If you type NEW and press the return key, the program in your computer's memory will be removed.

1.45 **RUN**   If you type RUN and press the return key , the computer will begin to carry out the program in memory (if any) at the lowest line number.
Another possibility is: RUN 60
This will begin execution of the program at line 60.

1.5 Output Commands

1.51 **PR#0**   If you type PR#0 and press the return key, the output will appear only on the monitor screen.

1.52 **PR#1**   If you type PR#1 and press the return key, the output will appear on both the printer and the monitor screen.

1.53 **Ctrl I 85N**   If after typing PR#1 and RETURN, you hold the CTRL key down while pressing the I key and then type 85N and RETURN, the output will appear only on the printer and the full 80 positions of the printer will be used.

1.54 **PR#6**   If you type PR#6 and press the return key, the operating system will be loaded from the disk in the disk drive. Any program in memory will be lost.

1.55 **Poke 33,33**   If you type POKE 33,33 and RETURN, program lines listed on the screen will exactly fill the text window. This will eliminate the problem of getting unwanted spaces inside quotation marks when editing. When POKE 33,33 is used in conjunction with the PR#1, the full 80 columns of the printer will be used. The effect is the same as Ctrl I 85N with the added advantage that the output will appear on the screen as well as the printer.

Warning   Some programs will not look right on the screen if run following POKE 33,33. POKE 33,33 can be cancelled by typing TEXT. It is a good practice to type TEXT as soon as you no longer need the effects of POKE 33,33. It is also possible to disturb memory locations and lose your program under POKE 33,33 so it can be very important to reset the text window by typing TEXT.

2. NUMBERS, VARIABLES, AND EXPRESSIONS

2.1 Number Format

In Applesoft BASIC, numbers are printed with up to nine digits of accuracy and must be in the range from -10^{38} to 10^{38} (an error message is printed when the absolute value of a number is greater than 10^{38}). Commas are not allowed to separate the digits into groups of three.

EXAMPLES: 27.345 is printed as 27.345
$\qquad\qquad$ –1,000 is printed as –1000
$\qquad\qquad$ 1,263,457 is printed as 1263457

Numbers with absolute values less than 3×10^{-39} are converted to zero.

EXAMPLES: 1.63×10^{-50} is printed as 0
$\qquad\qquad$ -4.7×10^{-40} is printed as 0

Numbers with absolute values greater than 999,999,999 or less than 0.01 are printed in scientific notation. In place of the normal superscript notation of the exponent, the letter E is used to indicate scientific notation.

EXAMPLES: E means "times 10 to the power of"
$\qquad\qquad$ 1,000,000,000 is printed in 1E+09
$\qquad\qquad$ -24.632×10^{10} is printed as –2.4632E+11
$\qquad\qquad$ 0.00236 is printed as 2.36E–03

2.2 Variable Names

Variable names are used to identify memory cells that each contain a single number. A variable name must begin with a letter of the alphabet and may be followed by a second letter of the alphabet or a digit from 0 to 9. Applesoft allows up to 236 additional alphanumeric characters, but only the first two characters are used to distinguish one name from another. Variable names may not contain reserved words (see Appendix C).

EXAMPLES OF VARIABLE NAMES:

A $\qquad$ B $\qquad$ C2 $\qquad$ BOX $\qquad$ SUM $\qquad$ PRODUCT

NOTE: The variable names SUM and SUMMATION would identify the same memory cell because the first two letters are the same.

The ANSI standard BASIC is more limited than Applesoft BASIC in that only the digits 0 through 9 are allowed for the second character of the name, and names cannot exceed two characters in length. In this book we use Applesoft BASIC exclusively.

2.3 Names and Messages

Names and messages are enclosed between quotation marks to distinguish them from numbers. Any character except a quotation mark may be used in a message, including spaces. Names and messages are called strings because they consist of a string of characters.

EXAMPLE: The following instruction will print the message:

```
MY NAME IS JOHN
10 PRINT "MY NAME IS JOHN"
```

A message is printed exactly as it appears, including all spaces that are plac between the quotation marks. A single string may include as many as 2 characters or as few as 0 characters.

2.4 String Variable Names

When a memory cell is used to store a message, a dollar symbol, $, is append to the variable name that identifies the memory cell. Such names are called stri variable names to differentiate them from variable names which identi memory cells that store numbers. String variable names must begin with a lett of the alphabet and may be followed by one or more alphanumeric characte Only the first two characters are used to distinguish between string variat names.

EXAMPLES OF STRING VARIABLE NAMES:

A$ B$ C 1$ NAME$ ADDRESS$

2.5 Arithmetic Symbols

The following symbols are used in BASIC programs to form arithmet expressions:

Symbol	Operation	Priority	Example
( )	do what is inside the parentheses first	1	$\dfrac{1}{A+B}$ is written 1/(A+B)
^	exponentiation	3	X^2 is written X^2
/	division	4	$2 \div A$ is written 2/A
*	multiplication	4	2xA is written 2*A
−	subtraction	5	B–A is written B–A
+	addition	5	A+2 is written A+2

Priority 2 is reserved for the minus sign when it is used to indicate the negativ value of a quantity. This occurs only when there is no number or variable nam to the immediate left of the minus sign. For example, the minus sign has priorit 2 in the statement $X = -2^2$ which results in a value of 4 for the variable X However, the minus sign has priority 5 in the statement $Y = 4 - 2^2$ which set Y equal to 0. Also see section 2.8.

2.6 Arithmetic Expressions

A BASIC arithmetic expression consists of variable names and numbers separated by arithmetic operators. The computer evaluates arithmetic expressions from left to right in priority order — priority 1 is first and priority 5 is last (see section 2.5).

EXAMPLES: 4 * X ^ + 6 * X - 7
(A + B)/(A - B)

When the value of an arithmetic expression is to be put in a memory cell, an equal sign is placed between the variable name on the left and the expression on the right.

EXAMPLE: Y = 4 * X + 2

The computer calculates the value of this expression by multiplying 4 times the number stored in the memory cell named X and adding 2.

The value of the expression is stored in the memory cell named Y.

2.7 Relational Symbols and Conditionals

Conditionals are used in IF statements between the word IF and the word THEN or GOTO. A conditional has only two possible values: TRUE or FALSE. TRUE expressions have a value of 1; FALSE expressions have a value of 0.

A conditional consists of two expressions separated by one of the following relational symbols:

Relational Symbol	Meaning
=	equal to
>	greater than
<	less than
< > or > <	not equal to
< =	less than or equal to
> =	greater than or equal to

EXAMPLES OF RELATIONAL EXPRESSIONS:

A = B + C
X − Y < = 27
2 * X − 2 > = 5 * Y + 2

2.8 Logical Operators and Expressions

Applesoft BASIC allows the use of logical operators to form more complex conditionals in IF statements. The three logic operators are: AND, OR, and NOT.

A complex conditional may consist of any meaningful combination of numbers, variable names, arithmetic symbols, logical operators, and relational symbols. The combined operators and symbols are listed in priority order in the following table:

Table of Arithmetic Symbols, Logic Operators, and Relational Symbols

Symbol	Priority	Meaning
( )	1	do what is inside the parentheses first
–	2	indicates a negative quantity (only when there is nothing on the left of the minus sign)
NOT	2	logic negation operator
^	3	exponentiation
*	4	multiplication
/	4	division
+	5	addition
–	5	subtraction
=	6	equal to
>	6	greater than
<	6	less than
> = or = >	6	greater than or equal to
< = or = <	6	less than or equal to
< > or > <	6	not equal to
AND	7	logic intersection operator
OR	8	logic summation operator

Symbols of the same priority are evaluated from left to right.

EXAMPLES OF COMPLEX EXPRESSIONS:

1. A < B AND C + D

    expression 1 is TRUE only if both A < B and C = D.

2. X < = Y OR Z = 5

    expression 2 is TRUE if either X < = Y or Z = 5.

2.9 Subscripted Variables

The subscripted variable makes it more convenient for us to use a group of memory cells to store a list or table of names or numbers. By using a subscripted variable, we give the same name to every memory cell in the group and use the subscript value to distinguish between the memory cells in the group. This is a distinct advantage, because it is much easier to change the subscript value in a program than it is to change a variable name.

A subscripted variable name consists of a variable name followed by a subscript enclosed in parentheses. The subscript may be a number, a variable name, or an arithmetic expression.

EXAMPLES: A(1)   B$(2)   C2(I)   SUM(J + 2 * I)   F3$(3 * I)

See chapter 9 for a further discussion of subscripts. Also see 3.51 for a discussion of the DIMENSION statement.

3. PROGRAM STATEMENTS

3.1 Statements That Put Names or Numbers into Memory Cells

3.11 LET   The LET statement is used to assign a name to a memory cell and put a number or message into the named memory cell. The general form of the LET statement is:

(line number) LET *(variable Name)* = *(number or arithmetic expression whose value will be placed in memory)*

or

(line number) LET *(string variable)* = *("message")*

The equal sign in the LET statement has a different meaning than it does in a mathematical equation. The LET statement instructs the computer to replace the contents of the memory cell named on the left side of the equal sign by the value of the expression on the right side. For this reason the equal sign in the LET statement is sometimes referred to as the "replaced by" symbol. Computer scientists would have preferred to use a left arrow rather than an equal sign to express this operation but it wasn't available on the keyboard.

The statement LET $X = X + 1$ means replace the contents of the memory cell named X with the old contents of X plus one. If the memory cell named X contains the number three, the statement LET $X = X + 1$ will replace that three with a four.

EXAMPLE LET STATEMENTS:

```
10 LET A = 2
20 LET X = 2 * A + 4.324
30 LET B$ = "JOHN JOHNSON"
```

The use of the word LET is optional; the following statements are equivalent:

```
10 LET A = 2
10 A = 2
```

3.12   **INPUT**   The input statement is used to assign names to memory cells. When the program runs and the INPUT statement is executed, the computer waits for the user to type the data to be put in the memory cell named in the INPUT statement. The general form of the INPUT statement is:

(line number) INPUT *(variable names separated by commas)*
or

(line number) INPUT *(string variable names separated by commas)*
or

(line number) INPUT *(combination of variable names and string variable names separated by commas)*
or

(line number) INPUT "PROMPT"; *(variable name)*

NOTE: In this form the prompt is optional.

EXAMPLES OF INPUT STATEMENTS:

```
10 INPUT X
20 INPUT X,Y,Z
30 INPUT A$
40 INPUT A$,B$,C$,D$
50 INPUT N$,S1
60 INPUT "TYPE YOUR NAME"; NAME$
```

3.13   **READ, DATA, and RESTORE**   The READ and DATA statements are used together to assign names and put numbers or messages in memory cells. The READ statement gives the names for the memory cells. The DATA statement gives the numbers or messages that go into the named memory cells. The names and numbers or messages must be in exactly the same order in the READ and the DATA statements. All the DATA statements in a program are considered to be part of one overall DATA statement with the same order of occurrence of the numbers and messages. When the program run begins, the computer sets a DATA pointer above the first quantity in the overall DATA list. Each time the computer encounters a variable name in a READ statement, it puts that name on a memory cell, copies the quantity under the DATA pointer into the named memory cell, and moves the DATA pointer over the next quantity in the overall DATA list.

The computer prints the message OUT OF DATA when it encounters a name in a READ statement and the DATA pointer has moved past the last quantity in the overall DATA list.

The RESTORE statement moves the DATA pointer back to the first quantity in the overall DATA list.

The general form of the READ and DATA statements are:

(line number) READ (any combination of variable names and string variable names separated by commas)
                                    and
(line number) DATA (a corresponding combination of numbers and messages*)

EXAMPLES:
```
10 READ X
20 DATA 7.642

50 READ X,Y,Z
60 DATA 7.643,3.25,-1.43

120 READ A$
200 DATA PETER

220 READ N$,M$
230 DATA "JONES, PETER", "MACKEY, ORVILLE"

500 READ N$,S1,S2,S3
510 DATA "JONES,PETER"
511 DATA 364,34,7652
```

3.14 GET The get statement is used to get a single keypress from the keyboard. It is like the INPUT statement except that it can only get a single keypress and the user does not press RETURN.

EXAMPLE: `10 GET Q$`

Warning: Using the GET command often causes the next DOS command to be ignored. This will cause trouble in any program that uses D$ or CHR$(4) to issue DOS commands while a program is running. The only safe way to avoid this is to print a "null character" following each use of the GET command, as in the following example:

```
10 GET Q$
20 PRINT " "
```

---

* a message that includes a comma or colon must be enclosed in quotation marks.

3.2 Statements That Display Names or Numbers

3.21 PRINT   The PRINT statement is used to display the contents of memory cells or the value of an expression.

The general form of the PRINT statement is:

(line number) PRINT (any combination of variable names, string variable names, and arithmetic expressions separated by commas or semicolons)

When the comma is used as the delimiter separating the items in the PRINT statement, the monitor screen is divided into 3 zones: Zone 1 consists of positions 1 through 16. Zone 2 consists of positions 17 through 32 and is available only if nothing is printed in position 16. Zone 3 consists of positions 33 through 40 and is available only if nothing is printed in positions 24 through 32.

With the proper command, the full 80 columns of the printer can be utilized. The command is PR#1 followed by Ctrl I 85N (see sections 3.52 and 3.53 for further details). When these commands are given, the printer output is divided into 5 zones of 16 each.

Semicolons may be used as the delimiter separating the items in a PRINT statement. When a semicolon is used at the end of a PRINT statement, the usual carriage return is suppressed.

While you are programming, the question mark (?) may be used as a short-hand for the word PRINT at any time.

Examples of PRINT statements

Statement	Result
70 PRINT	Leaves a blank line on the screen or paper.
80 PRINT X	Displays the value of X in zone 1, beginning in position 1 (left adjusted)
90 PRINT A,B,C	Displays the value of A in zone 1, B in zone 2, and C in zone 3.
100 PRINT "X = "; X	Displays the message followed immediately by the value of X.
200 PRINT A, 201 PRINT B, 202 PRINT C	Result is identical to 90 PRINT A,B,C, as shown above.
300 PRINT A 301 PRINT B 302 PRINT C	Displays the value of A in zone 1 of the first line, the value of B in zone 1 of the next line, and the value of C in zone 1 of the third line.

3.22 HTAB   Used prior to a PRINT or INPUT statement to set the horizontal position of the cursor (column). Legal values 1–40.

EXAMPLE: 10 HTAB 20

positions the cursor halfway across the screen.

3.23 VTAB   Like HTAB, but sets the vertical position of the cursor (row). Legal values 1–24.

> **EXAMPLE:**   10 VTAB 12
>
> positions the cursor halfway down the screen.

3.24 TAB   The TAB command is used in a PRINT statement to cause the display to begin in a particular column. The next item will be printed in the named column (counting from the left side of the display). TAB must be used in a PRINT statement and, unlike HTAB, can only cause movement to the right of the current position.

The general form of TAB is:

(line number) PRINT TAB *(number or expression)*; *(Variable Name)*

The value of the number or expression following the word TAB, is the position on the line where the next character will be placed.

String variable names, expressions, numbers and messages may be used where the variable name appears in the general form above.

The monitor screen is 40 positions wide, numbered from 1 to 40. The printer output width is 80 positions, numbered from 1 to 80. A quirk in the Applesoft BASIC causes a problem when we wish to TAB into positions 41 through 80 on the printer. When a character is printed in either space 40 or 41, the APPLE adds 40 to all subsequent TAB positions on that line. Thus TAB(66) becomes TAB(106), TAB(75) becomes TAB(115), etc. You can work around this problem by printing a space in column 40 and subtracting 40 from all TABs above 40. The space at 40 does not show, but it sets the computer so you can TAB beyond position 40.

EXAMPLES OF THE TAB COMMAND:

```
10 READ A,B,C,D,E,F
20 DATA 1,2,3,4,5,6
30 PRINT TAB( 12);A;TAB( 24);B;TAB( 36);C;
40 PRINT TAB( 40);" ";
50 PRINT TAB( 48-40);D;TAB( 60-40);E;TAB( 72-40);F
```

The above instructions will produce the following printed output.

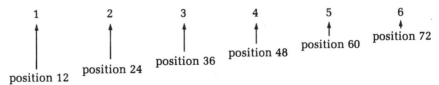

Rules for Printing Beyond Space 40

Comment: These rules are designed to print a table in such a way that one of the columns begins in print space 41. This assures us that a character will always be printed in space 41, and the TAB function will work correctly. Similar rules can be constructed based on beginning a column in print space 40 instead of 41.

1. Determine the number of columns in the table.

    N = the number of columns

2. Determine the maximum width of each column.

    a. If N is an even number

    $$W(max) = INT(80 / N)$$

    b. If N is an odd number

    $$W(max) = INT(80 / (N + 1))$$

3. Select the width you will use.

    $$W < W(max)$$

4. Determine the first TAB value necessary to make one of the columns begin in space 41.

    L = remainder of (41 / W)

5. Determine the TAB values.

    a. By Program

    ```
    10 FOR J = 1 TO N
    20 LET P = L + W * (J - 1)
    30 IF P > 41 THEN P = P - 40
    40 PRINT TAB( P); A(I, J);
    50 NEXT J
    ```

    b. By Hand calculation

    ```
    P = L, L + W, L + 2 * W, L  + 3 * W,. . . L + (N - 1) * W
    ```

EXAMPLE: N = 4, $W(max) = INT(80 / 4) = 20$
Select W = 20
L = remainder of (41 / 20) = 1
P = 1, 21, 41, 61

Results for N = 5 thru 12

```
N = 5    P = 2,15,28,41,54
N = 6    P = 2,15,28,41,54,67
N = 7    P = 1,11,21,31,41,51,61
N = 8    P = 1,11,21,31,41,51,61,71
N = 9    P = 1,9,17,25,33,41,49,57
N = 10   P = 1,9,17,25,33,41,49,57,66
N = 11   P = 5,11,17,23,29,35,41,47,53,59,65
N = 12   P = 5,11,17,23,29,35,41,47,53,59,65,71
```

3.3 Statements That Terminate a Program

3.31 END   The END statement halts the RUN of a program and no message is printed.

EXAMPLE: `200 END`

3.32 STOP   The STOP statement halts the RUN of a program and prints this message:

`BREAK IN 70`

⤷ line number of the statement that caused the halt.

EXAMPLE: `70 STOP`

3.4 Statement to Put Remarks in a Program

3.41 REM   The REM statement allows us to insert any message we wish in a program. REM statements are ignored by the program.

EXAMPLE:
```
5 REM   THIS IS AN EXAMPLE OF A REMARK.
6 REM   ALL CHARACTERS ON THE KEYBOARD
7 REM   CAN BE INCLUDED IN A REMARK.
8 REM   THE COMPUTER IGNORES ALL REM
9 REM   STATEMENTS WHEN IT RUNS A PROGRAM.
```

3.5 Statement That Reserves Memory Cells for Lists or Tables

3.51 DIM   The DIM statement reserves memory cells for subscripted variables used to store lists or tables. If a DIM statement is not used, Applesoft assigns a maximum value of 10 for each subscript in subscripted variables used in the program. If you see the message "bad subscript error" it means that you have more subscripts than your DIM statement allows for.

EXAMPLES:

`10 DIM A(20)` — assigns a maximum value of 20 for the subscript of A(I).

`20 DIM B(30,40)` — assigns a maximum value of 30 for the first subscript and 40 for the second subscript of B(I,J).

`10 DIM A(20),B(30,40)` — assigns a maximum value of 20 for the subscript of A(I), 30 for the first subscript of B(I,J), and 40 for the second subscript of B(I,J).

`5 DIM C$(15)` — assigns a maximum value of 15 for the subscript of C$(I).

3.6 Statements That Alter Program Flow

3.61 GOTO The GOTO statement causes an unconditional jump to the line number written after the word GOTO.

EXAMPLE: 120 GOTO 80

3.62 IF/GOTO This is the simpler form of the IF statement. The general form is:

(line number) IF *(conditional)* GOTO *(line number #2)*

If the conditional following the IF statement is TRUE, then the computer will jump to line number #2. If the conditional is FALSE, then the computer will go to the line immediately following the IF statement. Refer to section 2.7 for details of the conditional.

EXAMPLE:

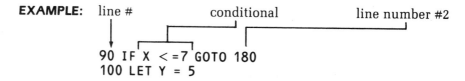

```
90 IF X < =7 GOTO 180
100 LET Y = 5
```

If X is less than or equal to 7 (i.e. conditional is TRUE), then the instruction at line 180 will be executed next. If X is greater than 7 (i.e. the conditional is FALSE), then the instruction at line 100 will be executed next.

3.63 IF/THEN A more useful form of the IF statement. The general form is:

(line number) IF *(conditional)* THEN *(one or more instructions separated by colons,:)*

If the conditional is TRUE (greater than 0), then all the instructions on the right of the word THEN will be executed in order from left to right. If the conditional is FALSE (0 or less), then *all* the instructions on the right of the word THEN will be ignored and the instruction on the next line of the program will be executed next. Refer to section 2.7 for the details of the conditional.

EXAMPLE:
```
10 INPUT H,W
20 IF H < = 40 THEN P = H * W
30 IF H > 40 THEN P = 40 * W + (H - 40) + 1.5 * W
40 PRINT H, W, P
50 END
```

3.64 FOR/TO/STEP/NEXT The FOR and NEXT statements are used together (always) to form a loop to carry out a sequence of instructions more than once.

The general form of a FOR/NEXT loop is:

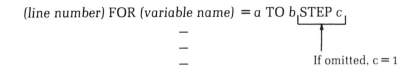

(line number) FOR *(variable name)* = *a* TO *b* STEP *c*

—
—
—
—

                                                    If omitted, c = 1

(sequence of instructions to be repeated)

—

(line number) NEXT *(variable name — same as in FOR statement)*

NOTES:

1. The letters *a*, *b*, and *c* in the FOR statement represent numbers or arithmetic expressions.

2. The variable name in the FOR and NEXT statements is called the control variable. The same control variable must be used in the FOR and the NEXT statements that form a loop.

3. The sequence of instructions located between the FOR and NEXT statements is called the body of the loop.

4. Each time the computer carries out the instructions in the body of the loop, the control variable takes on a different value. These values of the control variable are determined by the numbers represented by *a*, *b*, and *c* in the FOR statement.

☐   The value of *a* is the initial value of the control variable.

☐   The value of *b* is the final value of the control variable. The looping stops after the control variable passes the final value.

☐   The value of *c* is the amount by which the value of the control variable increases between passes through the loop.

EXAMPLE:

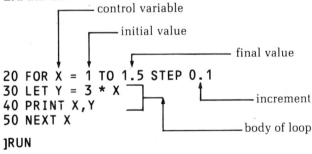

```
20 FOR X = 1 TO 1.5 STEP 0.1
30 LET Y = 3 * X
40 PRINT X,Y
50 NEXT X
```

]RUN

```
1.0    3.0
1.1    3.3
1.2    3.6
1.3    3.9
1.4    4.2
1.5    4.5
```

3.65   GOSUB and RETURN   Sometimes you will find it necessary to use the same sequence of instructions in several places in your program. The GOSUB and RETURN statements allow you to write this sequence of instructions once as a subroutine. You use a GOSUB statement each time you need the subroutine and a RETURN statement in the subroutine transfers control back to the next statement in your main program.

EXAMPLE:

```
10 FOR J = 1 TO 4
20 GOSUB 500              500 REM SUBROUTINE TO PRINT SPACES
30 PRINT "*"              510 READ S
40 GOSUB 500              520 FOR I = 1 TO S
50 PRINT "*"              530 PRINT " ";
60 NEXT J                 540 NEXT I
70 GOSUB 500              550 RETURN
80 PRINT "*"
90 STOP
100 DATA 15,7,16,5,17,3,18,1,19
```

In the above example, the GOSUB at line 20 transfers control to the subroutine at line 500 and the RETURN at line 550 transfers control back to line 30. The GOSUB at line 40 transfers control to the subroutine at line 500 and the RETURN at line 550 transfers control back to line 50. The GOSUB at line 70 transfers control to the subroutine and the RETURN transfers control back to line 80. The result is the same as it would be if the three GOSUB statements were each replaced by lines 510, 520, 530, and 540.

]RUN

3.66   ON/GOTO   The seldom used ON/GOTO statement is used to form a multiple branch in a program.

EXAMPLE:

```
10 INPUT X
20 ON X GOTO 100,200,300,400
30 GOTO 10
```

The above instructions will transfer control to

line 100 if X = 1
line 200 if X = 2
line 300 if X = 3
line 400 if X = 4
line 30 if X < > 1, 2, 3, or 4

The general form of the ON/GOTO is:

(line number) ON *(arithmetic expression)* GOTO *(a sequence of line numbers separated by commas).*

3.67 **ON/GOSUB** The ON/GOSUB statement is the preferred statement to form multiple branches in a program.

EXAMPLE:

```
10 INPUT "ENTER AN INTEGER FROM 1 TO 6 ";C
20 ON C GOSUB 1100, 1200, 1300, 1400, 1500, 300
30 ......
```

The above instructions will call the subroutine at:

```
1100 if C = 1
1200 if C = 2
1300 if C = 3
1400 if C = 4
1500 if C = 5
300 if C = 6
30  if C < > 1, 2, 3, 4, 5, or 6
```

The general form of the ON/GOSUB is as follows:

(line number) ON *(arithmetic expression)* GOSUB *(sequence of line numbers separated by commas).*

4. FUNCTIONS

4.1 Statement for Defining a Function

4.11 DEF FN The DEF statement allows you to define a function, give the function a name, and then use the name of the function each time you wish to use the function in your program.

EXAMPLE:

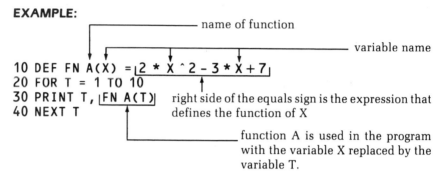

```
10 DEF FN A(X) = 2 * X ^ 2 - 3 * X + 7
20 FOR T = 1 TO 10
30 PRINT T, FN A(T)
40 NEXT T
```

— name of function

— variable name

right side of the equals sign is the expression that defines the function of X

function A is used in the program with the variable X replaced by the variable T.

The value of function A is $2 * T \char94 2 - 3 * T + 7$

4.2 Numeric Functions

4.21 ABS *(arithmetic expression)* The ABS function gives the absolute value of the expression in parentheses.

EXAMPLE: `10 LET Y = ABS(X)`

4.22 INT *(arithmetic expression)* The INT function gives the largest integer less than or equal to the value of the expression in parentheses.

EXAMPLE: `20 LET Y = INT(7.2)` (puts 7 in Y)
`30 LET X = INT(-7.2)` (puts –8 in X)

4.23 RND(1) The RND function gives a random number that is greater than or equal to 0 and less than 1.

EXAMPLE: `10 LET X = RND(1)`

4.24 SGN *(arithmetic expression)* The SGN function gives the following:

–1 if the arithmetic expression has a negative value
0 if the value of the arithmetic expression is 0
1 if the arithmetic expression has a positive value.

4.25 SQR *(arithmetic expression)* The SQR function gives the positive square root of the arithmetic expression.

4.3 Trigonometric Function

4.31 ATN *(arithmetic expression)* The ATN function gives the arc tangent in radians of the arithmetic expression.

4.32 **COS** *(arithmetic expression)*   The COS function gives the cosine of the angle in radians equal to the value of the arithmetic expression.

4.33 **SIN** *(arithmetic expression)*   The SIN function gives the sine of the angle in radians equal to the value of the arithmetic expression.

4.34 **TAN** *(arithmetic expression)*   The TAN function gives the tangent of the angle in radians equal to the value of the arithmetic expression.

4.4 Logarithmic and Exponential Expressions

4.41 **EXP** *(arithmetic expression)*   The EXP function gives the value of e = 2.718289. . . raised to a power equal to the value of the arithmetic expression.

4.42 **LOG** *(arithmetic expression)*   The LOG function gives the natural log of the arithmetic expression.

EXAMPLES: $V = 5 * EXP(5 * T)$ sets $V = 5 * e^{5 * T}$
$X = LOG(3 * A)$ sets $X = LOG_e (3 * A)$

4.5 String Functions

4.51 **LEFTS**   The string function LEFT$ has the general form:

LEFT$ *(string variable name, n)*

This expression refers to the leftmost n characters of the variable named.

```
10 LET C$ = "PETER PAN"
20 LET L$ = LEFT$ (C$, 7)
```

sets L$ to "PETER P"

4.52 **RIGHTS**   The RIGHT$ function is exactly like the LEFT$ function, except that it refers to the rightmost n characters of the variable named.

```
10 LET C$ = "PETER PAN"
20 LET R$ = RIGHT$ (C$, 7)
```

sets R$ to "TER PAN"

4.53 **MIDS**   The MID$ function is similar to the LEFT$ and RIGHT$ functions, but has three arguments in the parentheses: the first is the name of the string variable referred to; the second is the starting position of the substring; and the third is the number of characters in the substring.

```
10 LET C$ = "PETER PAN"
20 LET M$ = MID$ (C$, 5, 3)
```

sets M$ to "R P"

4.54   STR$ This function is used to convert a numeric variable to a string.

EXAMPLE: 10 LET C = 93421
                20 LET S$ = STR$ (C)

S$ is now the string "93421." It may not be used in an arithmetic expression. In fact, no mathematical operations can be performed on it at all. Since it is a string, however, you may use other string functions like LEFT$, RIGHT$, and MID$ to modify it.

4.55   LEN   The string function LEN has the general form:

   LEN (*string variable name*)

This function gives the number of characters in the string variable named.

EXAMPLE: 10 LET C$ = "PETER PAN"
                20 LET N = LEN (C$)

The above instructions set N to 9.

4.56   VAL   This is the opposite of the STR$ function. It is used to convert a string version of a number into a numeric value.

EXAMPLE: 10 LET S$ = "93421"
                20 LET N = VAL (S$)

If S$ is made up entirely of letters, N will be set to zero.

4.57   ASC   Every keyboard character has a number associated with it. The set of numbers is called the American Standard Code for Information Interchange (ASCII). This function is used to convert a string made up of a single character, to its ASCII value.

EXAMPLE: 10 LET C$ = "A"
                20 LET N = ASC (C$)

N is set to 65 which is the ASCII value of an uppercase A.

4.58 CHR$ This function is used to refer to a character by its ASCII value.

```
10 LET N = 65
20 PRINT CHR$ (N)
```

will cause an uppercase A to be printed.

```
30 LET S$ = CHR$ (65)
       or
30 LET S$ = CHR$ (N)
```

is equivalent to

```
30 LET S$ = "A"
```

4.59 Concatentation   Sometimes it is necessary to join two or more strings together to form a single string. This is called concatenation and is accomplished by using the "+" symbol.

EXAMPLE:
```
10 S1$ = "HOLD"
20 S2$ = "THE"
30 S3$ = "ONIONS"
40 LET S$ = S1$ + " " + S2$ + " " + S3$
```

is equivalent to 40 LET S$ = "HOLD THE ONIONS"

5. DATA FILES

5.1 General Information on Files

5.11 Types of Files   A file is a storage area on your floppy disk. The Apple computer has four different types of files that may be stored on a disk. All four types of files are identified by a name that must be unique (i.e., no two files can have the same name). The letter in the first column of the catalog listing identifies the type of file. The four letters are: A, B, I, and T.

LETTER   TYPE OF FILE

A   Applesoft BASIC programs

B   Binary Files

I   Integer Basic programs

T   Text files (used for all data files)

5.12 Disk Commands Used on Data Files   You may use the DELETE command to remove a data file from your disk. Just type the command DELETE, followed by the name of the file to be deleted. The command is executed when you press the RETURN key.

The SAVE, LOAD, and RUN commands are not used with data files because they are not programs. See section 5.3 for details on creating and reading sequential data files.

5.13 Field   A field is a single item of data such as a name, an ID number, a score, a wage rate, etc.

5.14 Record   A record is a group of fields that are related in some way. For example, a student's name, ID number, and exam scores could be a record. There would be a similar record for each student in the class. From a different viewpoint, the names of all the students in the class could be a record, and there would be a similar record for each class in the school.

5.15 File   A file is a group of related records. For example, a class file could consist of the records of all the students in the class. Also, the school file could consist of all class records in the school.

5.16 Sequential Access File (Sequential File)   In a sequential file, the records are stored in sequential order in much the same manner as names and numbers are stored in DATA statements in a program. Sequential files are created and read in sequential order. The entries in a sequential file may all be of different lengths, and any combination of strings and numbers is permitted.

5.17 **Random Access File (Direct File)** In a random access file, all records must be the same length. Thus each record must be as long as the longest record, with the extra space unused. The advantage of a random access file is that a single record can be read directly, regardless of its location in the file; it is not necessary to read all of the preceding records in order to get to the one you want.

5.2 Apple File Commands

5.21 **PRINT D\$** In Applesoft, the control commands must all appear in a print statement in which the first character printed is a Control-D. In this manual, the Control-D character is shown as CHR\$(4) and is stored in the variable D\$ (4 is the decimal code for Control-D in Applesoft).

The disk unit responds only to commands that are preceded by: PRINT D\$ where D\$ = CHR\$(4) = Control-D.

5.22 **OPEN** The OPEN command prepares the file for a READ or WRITE operation. This command consists of PRINT D\$ followed by "OPEN" and the name of the file as shown below.

```
5 D$ = CHR$ (4)
10 N$ = "FILE 1"
15 PRINT D$;"OPEN";N$
     or
15 PRINT D$;"OPEN";"FILE 1"
     or
15 PRINT D$;"OPEN FILE 1"
```

5.23 **WRITE** The WRITE command sets up the file for writing names or numbers into the file. The command consists of PRINT D\$ followed by "WRITE" and the file name as shown below.

```
5 D$ = CHR$ (4)
10 N$ = "FILE 1"
15 PRINT D$;"WRITE";N$
     (or options similiar to 5.22)
45 PRINT D$
```

After a WRITE file command has been executed, *all* information printed through PRINT statements will be written in the file. This continues until a PRINT D\$ terminates the file write operation. In the example above, all PRINT statements between line 15 and line 45 will write in the file.

5.24 READ The READ command sets up the file for copying names or numbers from the file into variables in your program. The format is the same as the WRITE command in section 5.23. After a READ file command has been executed, *all* input statements will get input from the file, rather than from the keyboard. A PRINT D$ terminates a file READ operation.

5.25 CLOSE The CLOSE command returns the file after use. This command consists of PRINT D$ followed by "CLOSE" and the file name as shown below.

```
5 D$ = CHR$ (4)
10 N$ = "FILE 1"
15 PRINT D$;"CLOSE";N$
```
   (or options similiar to 5.22)

5.26 MON The MON command turns on a monitoring feature that prints on the screen all information going to or coming from the file. This feature is useful while debugging programs, but may be distracting or undesirable in a perfected program. The monitor can be canceled by the NOMON command. This command is often used in conjunction with the SPEED command (e.g. SPEED = 30) in order to slow things down so that you can see file operations as they happen. The MON command consists of the word MON followed by the letters C, I, and/or O separated by commas.

   □ C turns on monitoring of disk commands

   □ I turns on monitoring of input

   □ O turns on monitoring of output

   The MON command can be typed directly from the keyboard in what is called the direct mode or it can be included in a program following the PRINT D$ command as shown below:

```
5 D$ = CHR$ (4)
10 PRINT D$;"MON C,I,O"
```

5.27 NOMON The NOMON command cancels the monitoring operations. The command consists of the word NOMON followed by C, I, and/or O. The C, I, and O cancel printing of disk commands, input and output respectively. Like the MON command, it can be typed directly from the keyboard, or included in a program as shown below:

```
5 D$ = CHR$ (4)
10 PRINT D$;"NOMON C,I,O"
```

5.3 Using Sequential Files

5.31 Creating a Sequential File The following program will create a sequential file (also called a text file) containing N numbers as data entries. The first entry in the file is the value of N, so the file actually contains N+1 entries. A file of names could be created in the same way, using a string variable such as N$(I) in place of A(I) in lines 17, 26, and 55.

```
10 LET D$ = CHR$ (4)
11 PRINT "ENTER THE FILE NAME"
12 INPUT A$
15 PRINT "HOW MANY NUMBERS";
16 INPUT N
17 DIM A(N)
20 FOR I = 1 TO N
25 PRINT I; TAB( 5);
26 INPUT A(I)
30 NEXT I
35 PRINT D$;"OPEN";A$
40 PRINT D$;"WRITE";A$
45 PRINT N
50 FOR I = 1 TO N
55 PRINT A(I)
60 NEXT I
90 PRINT D$;"CLOSE";A$
```

5.32 Reading a Sequential File The following program will copy and print the entries in a sequential file created by the program in section 5.31. Line 70 copies numbers from the file into A(I) and line 75 prints the value of A(I) on the screen. A file of names could be read in the same way, using N$(I) in place of A(I) in lines 50, 70, and 75.

```
10 LET D$ = CHR$ (4)
11 PRINT "ENTER THE FILE NAME"
12 INPUT A$
20 PRINT D$;"OPEN";A$
30 PRINT D$;"READ";A$
40 INPUT N
50 DIM A(N)
60 FOR I = 1 TO N
70 INPUT A(I)
75 PRINT A(I)
80 NEXT I
90 PRINT D$;"CLOSE";A$
```

6. LOW–RESOLUTION GRAPHICS

6.1 Graphics Commands

6.11 GR The GR command is used to put the computer in the graphics mode and clear the low-resolution graphics screen to black. This command selects low-resolution graphics screen 1, which has a four-line text screen at the bottom. This four-line screen is like a miniature version of the regular text screen. It can be cleared by using the HOME command, and characters may be printed on it by using the PRINT statement.

Once the computer is in the graphics mode, graphics can be put on the graphics screen by using the COLOR, PLOT, HLIN, and VLIN commands (see below). The GR command can be used at any time to clear the screen to black.

6.12 POKE –16392,0 When in the low-resolution graphics mode, this command allows full-screen graphics. To get to full-screen graphics when in the graphics mode, use the POKE –16392,0 command. This will eliminate the text window so that the squares generated by the graphics commands can be displayed on the full screen. To restore the text window, use the POKE –16301,0 command.

6.13 COLOR Upon entering the graphics mode, the color is automatically set to black. Anything plotted in black at this point will be invisible. To change this, a color must be selected using the COLOR command.

EXAMPLE: `10 COLOR = 3`

On a monochrome monitor (without color), the different colors will appear as different shades of the single color available.

**Low-resolution graphics colors may be selected
from the color code numbers.**

Black 0	Dark Green ...4	Brown 8	Light Green ..12
Magenta 1	Gray #1 5	Orange 9	Yellow 13
Dark Blue 2	Med. Blue 6	Gray #2 10	Aqua 14
Purple 3	Light Blue 7	Pink 11	White 15

6.14   Rows and Columns   Points on the graphics screen are described in terms of rows and columns. Rows are horizontal, and columns, like the columns that hold up buildings, are vertical.

Rows and Columns

ROW 0	C	C	*
ROW 1	O	O	
ROW 2	L	L	
ROW 3	U	U	
ROW 4	M	M	0,35
ROW 5	N	N	
ROW 6	15	25	

When plotting a point on the screen, the row is specified first and the column second. The asterisk (*) on the screen is at row 0 and column 35.

6.15   PLOT   The PLOT command causes a square of the current color to be plotted at the points specified in the command. The general form of the PLOT command is:

(line number)   PLOT *(row number)*   ,   *(column number)*

With the four-line text screen at the bottom, the text window has 40 rows and 40 columns. In both cases these are numbered 0 through 39. This means that PLOT 23,18 will plot a square of the current color at the 24th row and the 19th column. PLOT 39,39 will light up the square at the lower right of the graphics part of the screen. Of course the numbers may be replaced with variables.

6.16   HLIN   This command lights up a row of squares to make a horizontal line in the current color. The general form of the HLIN statement is:

(line number) HLIN *(left column #)* , *(right column #)* AT *(row #)*

EXAMPLE: 10 HLIN 5,10 AT 0

This statement will draw a horizontal bar from column 5 to column 10 across the top of the screen (row 0).

6.17   VLIN   The command works just like the HLIN command except that it prints a vertical line instead of a horizontal one. The general form of the VLIN statement is:

(line number) VLIN *(top row #)* , *(bottom row #)* AT *(column #)*

EXAMPLE: 10 VLIN 5,10 AT 0

This statement will light up a vertical bar from row 5 to row 10 along the left side of the screen (column 0).

7. SOUND

7.1 The Bell

The bell is a built-in sound effect in the Apple. There are several ways to ring it, but all have the same effect. If you type Ctrl G at the keyboard, you will hear the bell.

In a program, any of the following may be used:

```
10 PRINT CHR$(7) : REM RING BELL
20 PRINT "" : REM CTRL G INSIDE QUOTES DOESN'T PRINT ON SCREEN
30 PRINT PEEK(-1052) : REM RING BELL
40 LET BELL$ = CHR$(7) : REM SET UP VARIABLE
50 PRINT BELL$ : REM RING BELL
```

7.2 The Speaker

The Apple speaker is accessed by memory location -16336. Any reference to this location will click the speaker.

EXAMPLE:
```
10 PRINT PEEK(-16336)
20 POKE -16336,0
30 X = PEEK(-16336)
```

Since PEEKing is generally safer than POKEing the methods in lines 10 and 30 are more commonly used. The method in line 20 may cause serious trouble if you mistype a number. The click is barely audible; to make a useful sound, you must click the speaker a number of times.

EXAMPLE:
```
10 FOR I = 1 TO 1000
20 X = PEEK(-16336)
30 NEXT I
```

Because BASIC is not very fast, high-pitched tones can be only generated by writing a loop like the one above in assembly language, which is much faster than BASIC.

Error Messages

NOTE ABOUT ERROR MESSAGES

There are two kinds of error messages given by the Apple: (1) messages generated by the BASIC language (Applesoft) and (2) those generated by the disk operating system (DOS). Applesoft error messages are preceded by a question mark. When you see an error message that you don't understand, check to see if it has a question mark at the beginning. If it has a question mark, look it up in the Applesoft Error Messages section; if it does not have a question mark, look it up in the DOS Error Message section.

Sometimes you may hear the beep that accompanies an error message, but not be able to see the error message; for example, when in the full-screen graphics mode or when an ONERR statement is in effect. If you are in the graphics mode, try typing TEXT followed by RETURN. This may make the error message visible. If this does not work you can sometimes find out the error number by typing PRINT PEEK (222) followed by RETURN; then look up the error by number in the following sections.

APPLESOFT ERROR MESSAGES

?BAD SUBSCRIPT ERROR (107)

This message implies an error involving a subscripted variable such as A(1) or A$(1). If a subscript greater than ten is to be used, you must use a DIM statement to save space in memory for the variables [e.g., DIM A$(25)]. The most common form of this error is an attempt to print a variable like A(11) or A(N) where N is 11 without first dimensioning the variable. Another possibility is that an array has been specified with one dimension as in DIM A(25) and later in the program it is referred to with two or more dimensions as in PRINT A(22,1).

?CAN'T CONTINUE ERROR

If you try to start up a program which has halted by typing CONT, you will get this error if the program stopped due to a fatal error or if you made any changes in the program before attempting to restart it. This message will also occur if you type CONT when there is no program in memory.

?DIVISION BY ZERO ERROR (133)

This is an easy message to get. All you need to do is try PRINT X/0, or X/N where N is any expression which evaluates to zero. Dividing something by zero gives infinity as an answer, and the concept of infinity is too much for the poor computer. As a result, all divisions by zero are disallowed.

?EXTRA IGNORED

This message occurs when a response to an INPUT statement contains a comma or colon.

?FORMULA TOO COMPLEX

This one is pretty self-explanatory. It usually involves too many complex IF/THEN statements.

?ILLEGAL DIRECT ERROR

Some messages, such as INPUT, DEF FN, and GET must be in a line of the program to be legal. If you type them without a line number this message will result.

?ILLEGAL QUANTITY ERROR (53)

This means that the value of some number is too big or too small.

EXAMPLE: 10 A$ = "9999999"
20 A = VAL(A$)

or

10 A$ = " "
20 PRINT ASC(A$)

In the first case, VAL(A$) would be greater than 32767, which is not legal; in the second, A$ is set equal to the null character (nothing) and therefore can't have as ASC value.

?NEXT WITHOUT FOR ERROR (0)

Every NEXT statement in a program must be preceded by a FOR statement. As the program encounters FOR statements and NEXT statements, it counts them. If the number of NEXT statements counted ever gets to be greater than the number of FOR statements counted, you will see this message.

EXAMPLE: 10 FOR I = 1 TO 5
20 FOR J = 1 TO 7
30 NEXT J
40 NEXT I
50 NEXT I

?OUT OF DATA ERROR (42)

When you use READ and DATA statements to set the values of variables, every execution of a READ must have a data value to go with it. Every time a piece of data is "read" a pointer in memory is moved to the next position in the data list. If the pointer is at the end of the list and another "read" is called for, an out-of-data message is printed and the progam stops. One common cause of this is leaving one or two data items out of the data statement when you type it. Another common cause is to try to read the same set of data statements twice without using RESTORE to return the pointer to the beginning of the list after reading it the first time.

?OUT OF MEMORY ERROR (77)

This one is pretty obvious. It may mean your program is too large or that a DIM statement has set aside more memory than is available (e.g., 10 DIM A$ (65000). It may also be caused by too many variables or by resetting HIMEM: or LOMEM:.

?OVERFLOW ERROR (69)

You have entered or had the program calculate a positive or negative number that is too big for the computer to handle.

?REDIM'D ARRAY ERROR (120)

The program has come to a DIM statement for an array that has already been dimensioned. This usually happens in one of two ways. Either a line containing a DIM statement is executed twice, or, more often, an array is dimensioned which was previously dimensioned before, as in the following:

```
10 A(1) = 256
20 DIM A(19)
```

In this example, the variable A is dimensioned in line 10 since subscripted variables which have not been dimensioned previously are automatically dimensioned to 10. When A is dimensioned again in line 20, the program balks. A good way to avoid this is to dimension all subscripted variables at the beginning of a program.

?REENTER

When an INPUT statement specifies a number (as in INPUT NUM) and something other than a number (e.g., a letter or punctuation symbol) is entered, this message occurs.

?RETURN WITHOUT GOSUB ERROR (22)

This works very much like the NEXT WITHOUT FOR error. It means that more RETURN statements than GOSUB statements have been executed. The most common cause of this is forgetting to put an END statement in a program where the MAIN PROGRAM is followed by subroutines. At the end of the MAIN section, the program "falls through" to the following subroutine instead of ending.

EXAMPLE:
```
100 REM MAIN PROGRAM
110 PRINT "HELLO"
120 GOSUB 200
190 REM END SHOULD GO HERE
200 PRINT "GOODBYE"
210 RETURN
```

In this example, the section at line 100 should have an END statement at line 190. At line 120 the program is sent to the subroutine at line 200. When the program returns from this subroutine it should encounter the END statement at line 190; instead the program "falls through" to line 200 again, and when it hits the RETURN in line 210 the error message is generated.

?STRING TOO LONG ERROR (176)

This message occurs when you try to create a string by concatenation which would be longer than 255 characters (e.g., C$ = A$ + B$ where the total length of A$ plus B$ is greater than 255).

?SYNTAX ERROR (16)

The form of a statement is not correct. This may be the result of spelling, punctuation, or sequence error. The most common causes are missing parentheses and quotes, misplaced punctuation marks, and reserved words used in variable names. One good troubleshooting technique is to make sure that you have an even number of quotation marks and an equal number of left and right parentheses.

?TYPE MISMATCH ERROR (163)

The most common cause of this error is forgotten quotation marks. It results when you match a string with a numeric expression or variable as in the following three examples.

```
10 LET NAME$ = PETER RAYGOR
20 LET N = "43"
30 LET L$ = 255
40 LET G = "A"
```

Another common cause of this problem is an incorrect match of variable names and data when reading from DATA statements or from a file.

?UNDEF'D FUNCTION ERROR (224)

You have referred to a user-defined function which has not been defined yet.

?UNDEF'D STATEMENT ERROR (90)

The most recently executed GOTO or GOSUB statement has sent the program to a line that does not exist. One common cause of this for beginners is accidentally deleting a line while editing, or mistyping the number in a GOSUB or GOTO statement.

DOS ERROR MESSAGES

DISK FULL (9)

You have tried to store more on a disk than it will hold. Whatever you have tried to save or write has not been successfully stored on the disk. If a disk is very full you may see this message in response to any disk command.

END OF DATA (5)

This message means you have tried to read a text file or part of a text file that doesn't exist. The most common causes of this are reading beyond the end of a file, reading beyond the end of a record in a random access file, misspelling the name of a file, and trying to read from a file that has not been written properly (e.g., written to without being opened first).

FILE LOCKED (10)

Trying to SAVE, DELETE, WRITE, RENAME, or BSAVE a locked file will result in this message being printed. If you first type UNLOCK and the file name, you will be successful. Locked files are indicated in the CATALOG of a disk by a "*" at the left, next to the file type indicator.

FILE NOT FOUND (6)

A LOAD, BLOAD, DELETE, RENAME, or RUN command has referenced a file that does not exist on the disk. Usually this means that you have misspelled the file name. Remember that file names must be spelled exactly as they were when you saved the file including spaces, hyphens, etc. Be sure to explore this possibility fully before reading any further. A more frustrating (and fortunately much less common) possibility is that you accidentally typed a control character in the file name when you originally saved the file (most often a control A). The control character does not show up in the catalog but must be typed to make use of the file. If you have the program HIDDEN CHARACTERS (also called CONTROL FINDER) you can BRUN it and the control character will show up in inverse when you type CATALOG. If there is a control character, use the RENAME command with the file name (including control character) on the left side of the comma, and the file name as it should be on the right. If you don't have access to a program that shows up control characters you have two choices. One: trial and error; use the rename command as above and guess at the control character (remember that control A is by far the most common). Two: punt.

FILE TYPE MISMATCH (13)

You have directly or indirectly referenced a file with a DOS command which is wrong for that file. LOAD, RUN, and SAVE may only refer to program files. BRUN, BSAVE, and BLOAD may only refer to binary files. OPEN, READ, WRITE, APPEND, POSITION, and EXEC may only be used with text files. The most common form of this error is to try to RUN a binary file (which of course must be BRUN).

I/O ERROR (8)

An attempt to send information to a disk or retrieve information from a disk has failed. Pray for one of the following:

1. open disk drive door

2. no disk in drive or disk in sideways or upside down

3. wrong drive accessed

4. write protected disk

5. commercial disk with non standard DOS

6. disk in drive has not been initialized

7. power surge

8. faulty drive

Otherwise you may be experiencing the dreaded *disk crash*. If this is the case, try not to panic. Most crashes are not fatal.

?LANGUAGE NOT AVAILABLE (1)

Trying to change languages from Integer BASIC to Applesoft BASIC and vice versa by using the FP or INT commands when the called-for language is not available will produce this message. Another way to get this message is to try to load or run a program which was written in a language that is not now available.

NO BUFFERS AVAILABLE (12)

Certain file references set aside a buffer area for information related to that file. The maximum number of these is usually three. If all the available buffers are already in use and a DOS command is issued, this message appears. This will often prevent you from saving a file. To escape from this situation, type CLOSE. This will clear the file buffers and you can proceed. Then look at your program and try to see why so many buffers were in use. Usually it is because files are opened and then not closed.

NOT DIRECT COMMAND (15)

You have tried to use one of the following commands in immediate mode (typed directly with no line number when no program was running); OPEN, READ, WRITE, APPEND, and POSITION. These commands may only be used in PRINT statements within a program.

PROGRAM TOO LARGE (14)

This is basically an out-of-memory error resulting from a LOAD, BLOAD, RUN, or BRUN.

RANGE ERROR (2 or 3)

This is the DOS equivalent to an illegal quantity error. It means that a number used with a DOS command is not legal; for example a D (drive) number greater than 2 or a V (volume) number greater than 255.

SYNTAX ERROR (11)

This is the only DOS error message that matches an Applesoft error message. The difference is that the Applesoft message is preceded by a question mark. This message means that a DOS Command has an error in spelling, punctuation, or sequence or is missing something.

VOLUME MISMATCH (7)

You have used a V (volume) number in a DOS command which does not match the volume number of the disk being accessed.

WRITE PROTECTED(4)

Trying to SAVE, BSAVE, WRITE, or RENAME a program on a disk that is write-protected will generate this error message. Apple disks are write-protected by putting tape over the write-protect notch (more correctly called the "write-enable notch"). Some disks are produced with no notch at all, and cannot be written to unless notched.

APPENDIX C

Applesoft Reserved Words

The following words may not be used as variable names or parts of variable names in Applesoft. The line

    10 LET TOTAL = 100

would be illegal since it contains the reserved word "TO." When a program encounters a line with an improperly used reserved word, the program halts and a SYNTAX ERROR message is displayed. When listed, the line would look like this:

    10 LET TO TAL = 100

RESERVED WORDS

ABS	FRE	LET	POS	SPC(
AND	GET	LIST	PRINT	SPEED =
ASC	GOSUB	LOAD	PR#	SQR
AT	GOTO	LOG	READ	STEP
ATN	GR	LOMEM:	RECALL	STOP
CALL	HCOLOR =	MID$	REM	STORE
CHR$	HGR	NEW	RESTORE	STR$
CLEAR	HGR2	NEXT	RESUME	TAB(
COLOR =	HIMEM:	NORMAL	RETURN	TAN
CONT	HLIN	NOT	RIGHT$	TEXT
COS	HOME	NOTRACE	RND	THEN
DATA	HPLOT	ON	ROT =	TO
DEF	HTAB	ONERR	RUN	TRACE
DEL	IF	OR	SAVE	USR
DIM	IN#	PDL	SCALE =	VAL
END	INPUT	PEEK	SCRN(	VLIN
EXP	INT	PLOT	SGN	VTAB
FLASH	INVERSE	POKE	SHLOAD	WAIT
FN	LEFT$	POP	SIN	XDRAW
FOR	LEN			

APPENDIX D

Initializing a Diskette

To initialize a blank diskette you must start with another, already initialized, diskette; preferably a System Master. If you don't have access to a System Master, use any working diskette but *not* a commercial program that is protected from copying.

WARNING: The initialization process will destroy any data on the disk to be initialized so be *very sure* there is nothing valuable on the disk you intend to initialize.

Place the System Master (or other diskette) in the drive with the machine turned *off*. Close the drive door and turn on the power. If the light stays on indefinitely, try again or use another diskette. When the light goes out you should see the cursor (the little blinking square of light). If not, make sure the monitor (TV screen) is turned on. Try again if necessary. When you finally get to see the cursor, *remove the diskette in the drive* and insert the diskette you want to initialize. Many people, even experienced programmers, destroy the information on valuable diskettes by initializing them. Type NEW followed by ⟨RETURN⟩, then very carefully type:

```
10 PRINT "HELLO" <RETURN>
```

Then type:

```
RUN <RETURN>
```

you should see the word HELLO printed on the screen. If not, you have probably made a typing error and need to type line 10 again. Repeat these two steps until you see the word HELLO printed, then type:

```
INIT HELLO <RETURN>
```

The light on the drive should stay on for some time. When you see the cursor again, turn the machine off for 15 seconds and then on again. You should see "HELLO" printed on the screen. If not, something is wrong. Repeat the initialization process again from the beginning. If you are not successful after several tries, try to find someone who can help you.

NOTE: Diskettes, initialized or not, should be treated very carefully. They should not be bent, folded, or mutilated. They should not be exposed to extremes of heat or cold. Putting a diskette near a magnet will not hurt the diskette, but it will destroy the data on the diskette. The paper cover on a diskette is designed to protect the sensitive magnetic surface inside from dirt and fingerprints. Care should be taken not to get your fingers in contact with the magnetic medium where it shows through the holes in the sleeve.

Flowcharts and Programming Techniques

YOU CAN'T GET THERE FROM HERE

A person learning to program a computer is faced with an almost insurmountable problem. The problem is that you must use a programming language you have not yet learned, apply programming concepts you have not yet mastered, and run the program on a computer you are just learning to operate. This triple whammy can make the first programming experience a difficult and frustrating experience. In this section we have attempted to prevent some of this frustration with an explanation of some simple programming techniques.

A computer program is similar to a recipe for baking a cake. The recipe is a sequence of steps the baker follows to produce a cake. A computer program is a sequence of steps the computer follows to produce a desired result. We use the term *algorithm* to name the step-by-step procedure followed by the computer, just as the term recipe names the procedure used by the baker. Computer programming can be divided into two major tasks: (1) developing the algorithm that will produce the desired result and (2) translating the algorithm into a computer program. This section is concerned with the first task: developing the algorithm.

In the past 15 or 20 years, we have experienced an amazing increase in computer hardware capabilities, and an equally amazing decrease in the cost of computer hardware. We have reached the point where software (i.e. the computer programs or the labor necessary to produce them) is the most expensive part of a computer system. In the past, memory hardware was extremely expensive and it was cheaper to pay programmers to write obscure, poorly structured programs that made very efficient use of memory than to buy more memory. With the tremendous decrease in the cost of memory and computing power, the current trend is to write programs in a way that reduces the software cost. This means writing programs that are easy to understand and easy to modify when the inevitable need for change arises.

Some techniques used in this text that make a program easier to understand include the following: placing the program name on line 1; including a list of variables at the beginning of the program; using remarks to explain parts of the program; and breaking a large program into small, manageable units. These techniques sometimes use up extra memory and slow down the execution speed of the programs, but are more than worth it because of the added clarity they provide.

STEPS IN WRITING A PROGRAM

Many people, when confronted with their first programming assignments, are unsure of the steps that are necessary, or even where to begin the task. The following ten steps outline a procedure for writing, debugging, and documenting a computer program. A sample problem will be used as an example.

Sample Programming Problem

STEP 1:   Study the problem, determine the variables that will be required, and pick names for the variables.

EXAMPLE:

a.   Problem statement: Write a program that computes; the cost of gasoline for a single trip in a car.
b.   Three variables are required: the gallons of gasoline used, the price of a gallon of gasoline, and the cost of the trip.
c.   We will use G for the gallons used, P for the price of a gallon of gas, and C for the cost of the trip.

STEP 2:   Develop a method for solving the problem.

EXAMPLE: A four-step algorithm is all that is required for this simple problem.

a.   Enter values of G and P
b.   Calculate C (C = G * P)
c.   Round C to the nearest cent
d.   Print C

STEP 3:   Calculate one or more answers by hand for testing the program.

EXAMPLE:

1.   G = 10, P = 1.249
      C = 10 * 1.249 = 12.49
2.   G = 15, P = 1.249
      C = 15 * 1.249 = 18.745

STEP 4:   Write the BASIC program.

EXAMPLE:

```
110 INPUT "GALLONS USED? "; G
120 INPUT "PRICE OF A GALLON? ";P
130 LET C = G * P
140 LET C = FN C(C)
150 PRINT "COST OF THE TRIP IS $";C
160 END
```

STEP 5:   Enter the program into the computer.

STEP 6:   LIST and RUN the program.

STEP 7:   Correct syntax errors.
A syntax error is anything in your program that the computer cannot interpret as it attempts to run the program. The error message will include the line number of the problem line. LIST the line and look for errors such as a missing symbol, comma, semicolon, or quotation mark, or a spelling error.

STEP 8:   Check for logic errors.
If the answers you calculated in step 3 do not agree with the answers produced by the computer, then your program has a logic error—i.e., the program runs but the answers are incorrect.

STEP 9:   Correct the logic errors.
A logic error is any error in a program that runs but produces the wrong result. LIST the program and look for an incorrect formula. Step through the program and look for an incorrect sequence of operations.

STEP 10: Save the final version of your program and produce a LIST and RUN for the final documentation of the program.

The first two steps in the programming process are the most difficult for students to master. The remainder of this section explains in more detail techniques for accomplishing steps 1 and 2.

Problem Definition

The first step in the programming process is to study and define the problem to be solved. Start by describing the output that is to be produced by the program. Use a piece of graph paper to make a layout of the output as it will appear on the monitor screen or printed page. Four or five lines per inch is a convenient size for this purpose.

With the output firmly established, determine what input data are required to generate the output. In other words, what information will the computer need from the user to do the job (input data) and what information will the computer give to the user (output data). Prepare a list of the variables required for input and output and select a name for each variable.

Examine the input and output. Write down any equations that are required and determine the steps required to produce the output. For simple programs, a list of the required steps is sufficient. A flow diagram is a useful tool for describing complex problems with decision points and multiple branches. Large problems are often divided into smaller, more manageable modules. A structure chart is used to show the interconnections of the modules.

FLOWCHARTS

A flowchart is a useful tool for describing the sequence of steps in complex programs with multiple branches. Not all programs require a flowchart.

Large, modular programs are often best described by a structure chart. The "big one" in this text, program 10A, is an example of such a program.

Flowcharts use standard symbols to represent various programming functions. In this text, line 1 in every program assigns the name of the program to the string variable PN$. An oval-shaped symbol is used to represent the beginning of the program (line 1) and the end of the program.

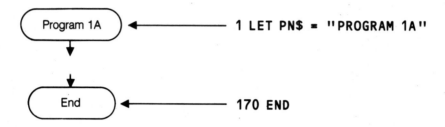

The parallelogram-shaped symbol is used for INPUT or READ statements.

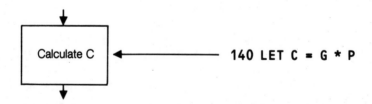

The rectangular-shaped symbol is used for assignment statements (i.e., LET statements).

The torn-sheet symbol is used for PRINT statements.

The diamond-shaped symbol is used for IF statements.

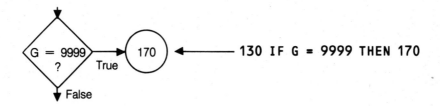

In this text, the hexagonal-shaped symbol is used for the FOR statement, and a circle is used for the NEXT statement. A dotted line indicates the return path that forms the loop.

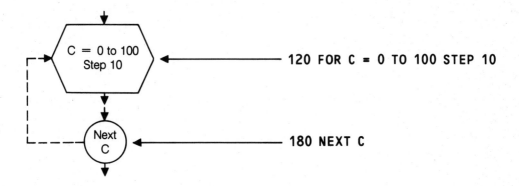

Finally, the circle is used as a connector between two parts of the flowchart where it would be too confusing or take up too much space to draw the connections.

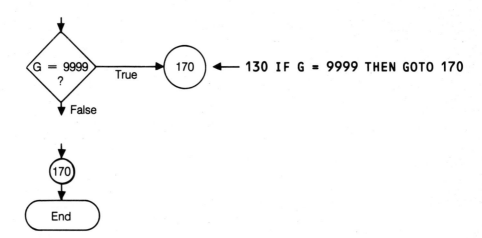

The following examples show typical flowcharts and the programs they represent.

EXAMPLE 1:   The Cost of a Trip

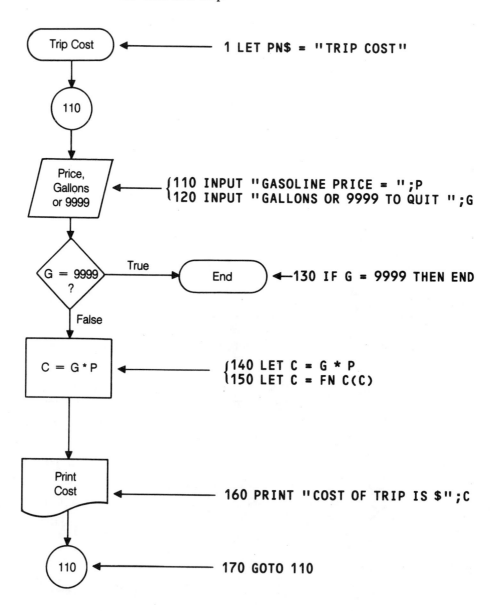

Trip Cost ◄─── **1 LET PN$ = "TRIP COST"**

110

Price, Gallons or 9999 ◄─── **{110 INPUT "GASOLINE PRICE = ";P**
{120 INPUT "GALLONS OR 9999 TO QUIT ";G

G = 9999 ? ──True──► End ◄─**130 IF G = 9999 THEN END**

False

C = G * P ◄─── **{140 LET C = G * P**
{150 LET C = FN C(C)

Print Cost ◄─── **160 PRINT "COST OF TRIP IS $";C**

110 ◄─── **170 GOTO 110**

EXAMPLE 2:   Weekly Wages

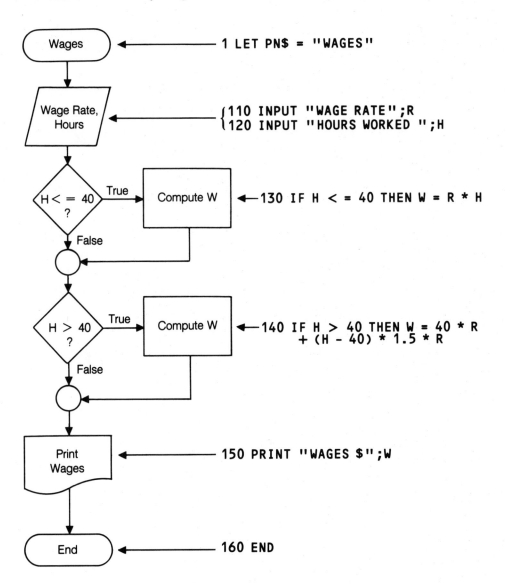

1 LET PN$ = "WAGES"

{110 INPUT "WAGE RATE";R
{120 INPUT "HOURS WORKED ";H

130 IF H < = 40 THEN W = R * H

140 IF H > 40 THEN W = 40 * R
+ (H − 40) * 1.5 * R

150 PRINT "WAGES $";W

160 END

EXAMPLE 3:   Conversion of Feet to Meters

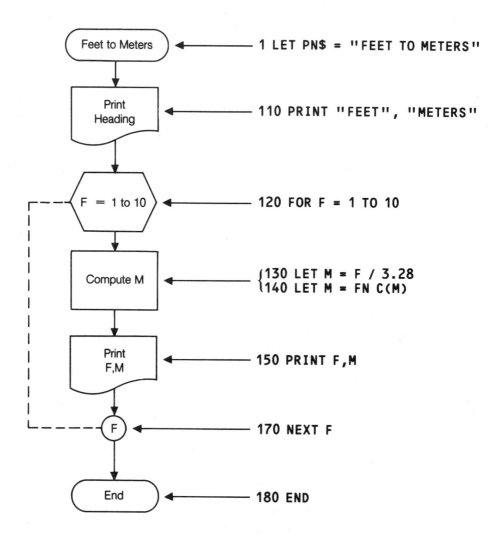

Feet to Meters	1 LET PN$ = "FEET TO METERS"
Print Heading	110 PRINT "FEET", "METERS"
F = 1 to 10	120 FOR F = 1 TO 10
Compute M	130 LET M = F / 3.28 140 LET M = FN C(M)
Print F,M	150 PRINT F,M
F	170 NEXT F
End	180 END

MODULAR PROGRAMMING AND STRUCTURE CHARTS

Large programs such as program 10A can be made more manageable by a technique known as top-down program design. The entire program is divided into several segments which are in turn divided into small modules that each perform a single function. A good rule on the size of a module is that the entire module should be shown in a single view on the screen. Modules should be small and should do only a single job. For example, if you need to sort and print a list of names, you should use two separate modules, one to sort the list, and another to print it. A point to keep in mind is that a proper module can be a programming tool that can be used in many different programs. If your module to sort a list is written properly, it can sort *any* list and can be used in many programs.

The relationship between the modules of a program is shown in a diagram called a structure chart. In programs with a menu, the menu is often the basis for the structure chart. The structure chart for program 10A is shown below.

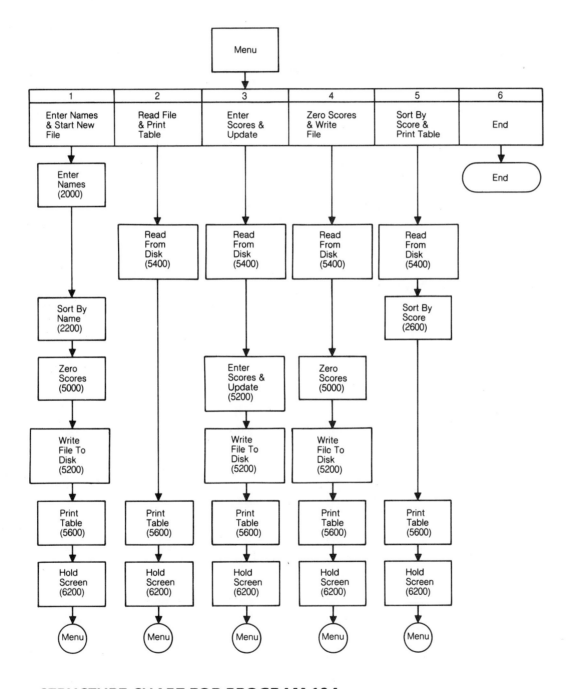

STRUCTURE CHART FOR PROGRAM 10A

Table of ASCII Character Codes

ASCII CHARACTER CODES

ASCII Code	Keystroke	ASCII Code	Keystroke	ASCII Code	Keystroke
0	Ctrl @	34	"	68	D
1	Ctrl A	35	#	69	E
2	Ctrl B	36	$	70	F
3	Ctrl C	37	%	71	G
4	Ctrl D	38	&	72	H
5	Ctrl E	39	'	73	I
6	Ctrl F	40	(	74	J
7	Ctrl G	41	)	75	K
8	Ctrl H	42	*	76	L
9	Ctrl I	43	+	77	M
10	Ctrl J	44	,	78	N
11	Ctrl K	45	–	79	O
12	Ctrl L	46	.	80	P
13	Ctrl M	47	/	81	Q
14	Ctrl N	48	0	82	R
15	Ctrl O	49	1	83	S
16	Ctrl P	50	2	84	T
17	Ctrl Q	51	3	85	U
18	Ctrl R	52	4	86	V
19	Ctrl S	53	5	87	W
20	Ctrl T	54	6	88	X
21	Ctrl U	55	7	89	Y
22	Ctrl V	56	8	90	Z
23	Ctrl W	57	9	91	*[
24	Ctrl X	58	:	92	*\
25	Ctrl Y	59	;	93	]
26	Ctrl Z	60	<	94	^
27	Esc	61	=	95	*_
28	**n.a.	62	>	96	*`
29	Ctrl Shift M	63	?	123	*{
30	Ctrl ^	64	@	124	*¦
31	**n.a.	65	A	125	*}
32	Space	66	B	126	*~
33	!	67	C		

* —not available on the Apple II keyboard
** —not available on the Apple II, IIe or IIc keyboard.

APPENDIX G

Answers to the Self-Testing Questions

CHAPTER 1

1.1	J	1.5	G	1.9	A	1.13	B
1.2	F	1.6	K	1.10	E	1.14	I
1.3	L	1.7	M	1.11	C	1.15	N
1.4	H	1.8	P	1.12	O	1.16	D

CHAPTER 2

2.1   25 MILES PER GALLON
2.2   26 MILES PER GALLON
2.3   26.3 MILES PER GALLON
2.4   26.32 MILES PER GALLON
2.5   26.316 MILES PER GALLON

CHAPTER 3

3.1   28 MILES PER GALLON
3.2   30.6 MILES PER GALLON
3.3   (a) 36.6 MILES PER GALLON
      (b) 36.2 MILES PER GALLON
3.4   THE LAST NUMBER IS 7

CHAPTER 4

4.1   7
      8
      ?OUT OF DATA ERROR IN 120

4.2   HOW MANY TRIPS? 3

      HOW MANY MILES? 412
      HOW MANY GALLONS? 11.8
      34.9 MILES PER GALLON

      HOW MANY MILES? 360
      HOW MANY GALLONS? 21.2
      17 MILES PER GALLON

```
                    HOW MANY MILES? 385
                    HOW MANY GALLONS? 14.5
                    26.6 MILES PER GALLON

    4.3     ENTER A DISTANCE OR 9999
            TO TERMINATE THE PROGRAM

                    HOW MANY MILES? 250
                    HOW MANY GALLONS? 12
                    20.8 MILES PER GALLON

                    HOW MANY MILES? 225
                    HOW MANY GALLONS? 11
                    20.5 MILES PER GALLON

                    HOW MANY MILES? 9999

    4.4     ENTER A DISTANCE OR 9999
            TO TERMINATE THE PROGRAM

                    HOW MANY MILES? 250
                    HOW MANY GALLONS? 12
                    20.8 MILES PER GALLON

                    HOW MANY MILES? 225
                    HOW MANY GALLONS? 11
                    20.5 MILES PER GALLON

                    HOW MANY MILES? 9999

                    PROGRAM TERMINATED AFTER
                    2 TRIPS. GOODBYE.
```

CHAPTER 5

```
    5.1     YARDS           FEET
            1               3
            2               6
            3               9
            4               12
            5               15

    5.2     YARDS           FEET
            1               3
            YARDS           FEET
            2               6
            YARDS           FEET
            3               9
            YARDS           FEET
            4               12
            YARDS           FEET
            5               15
```

5.3   ENTER NUMBERS TO BE ADDED
       OR ENTER 9999 TO QUIT
       ?7
       ?18
       ?5
       ?9
       ?6
       ?9999
       5 NUMBERS WERE ADDED
       THE TOTAL IS 45

5.4   12345

5.5   1357

5.6   1471013

5.7   8794

5.8   333

5.9   594788

5.10   1534537291

CHAPTER 6

6.1   B IS GREATER
       A IS GREATER
       EQUAL
       A IS GREATER

6.2   EEEEE

6.3   BB

6.4   AAAA

6.5   KKKK

6.6   111222333

6.7   123123123

6.8   111221223132

6.9   123123123

6.10   321321321

6.11   333222111

6.12   123
       123
       123

6.13   1 2 1 2 1 2 1 2

6.14   1 2
       1 2
       1 2
       1 2

6.15   1 2
       1 2

       1 2
       1 2

6.16   YEAR = 1
       QUARTER = 1 : MONTHS = 1, 2, 3
       QUARTER = 2 : MONTHS = 4, 5, 6
       QUARTER = 3 : MONTHS = 7, 8, 9
       QUARTER = 4 : MONTHS = 10, 11, 12

       YEAR = 2
       QUARTER = 1 : MONTHS = 1, 2, 3
       QUARTER = 2 : MONTHS = 4, 5, 6
       QUARTER = 3 : MONTHS = 7, 8, 9
       QUARTER = 4 : MONTHS = 10, 11, 12

       YEAR = 3
       QUARTER = 1 : MONTHS = 1, 2, 3
       QUARTER = 2 : MONTHS = 4, 5, 6
       QUARTER = 3 : MONTHS = 7, 8, 9
       QUARTER = 4 : MONTHS = 10, 11, 12

CHAPTER 7

7.1   *****

7.2   *
      *
      *
      *
      *

7.3   ***
        *
       ***
      *****
      *****

7.4   ****
      *
      ***
      *
      ****

```
7.5   ******
      ******
        **
        **
        **

7.6   *****
          *
          *
          *
        **
```

CHAPTER 8

8.1   (a)   0,1,2,3   (b)   1,2,3,4

    (c)   11,12,13,14   (d)   1,2,3,4,5,6,7,8,9,10,11,12,13

    (e)   1,2,3,4,5,6

```
8.2   *
      *
      *
      *
      *
      *

8.3   ******

8.4   *
       *
        *
         *
          *
           *

8.5   * * * * * *

8.6          *
            *
           *
          *
         *
        *
```

8.7   STRING MANIPULATION

CHAPTER 9

9.1   8 7 5 4 3

9.2   3 8 4 2 7

9.3 (a) JANE   80
          DAVE   82
          CAROL   90
          FRANK   88

     (b) JANE   DAVE   CAROL   FRANK
          80   82   90   88

9.4 (a) 8 14 15
          21 3   7
          19 2   9

     (b) 8 21 19
          14 3   2
          15 7   9

     (c) 8   3   9

     (d) 8 21 19
          14 3   2
          15 7   9

     (e) 9   2 19
          7   3 21
          15 14 8

9.5 (a) TERRY   82   78   90
          CARL   88   80   85
          JUNE   86   90   84

     (b) TERRY   CARL   JUNE
          82   88   86
          78   80   90
          90   85   84

     (c) TERRY   90
          CARL   85
          JUNE   84

     (d) TERRY   250
          CARL   253
          JUNE   260

     (e) TERRY   83
          CARL   84
          JUNE   87

9.6 (a) CARL   78
          JUNE   64
          TERRY   76

     (b) TERRY   64
          CARL   76
          JUNE   78

(c)   Add the following three lines:

```
205 LET T = S(I)
215 LET S(I) = S(J)
225 LET S(J) = T
```

(d)   Add the following three lines:

```
205 LET T$ = N$(I)
215 LET N$(I) = N$(J)
225 LET N$(J) = T$
```

CHAPTER 10

10.1   (a)   8 63 4

(b)   63 4 71

(c)   12 47 18
8 63 4
71 21 7

10.2   (a)   3
4
TERRY
92
CARL
88
JUNE
84

(b)   3
4
TERRY
92
4
CARL
88
4
JUNE
84

(c)   3
TERRY
92
CARL
88
JUNE
84
4

Index*

*Italicized page numbers that appear in this index refer to pages in the Mini-Manual (Appendix A).